Agent-Based Social Systems
Volume 5

Series Editor: Hiroshi Deguchi, Yokohama, Japan

ABSS – Agent-Based Social Systems

This series is intended to further the creation of the science of agent-based social systems, a field that is establishing itself as a transdisciplinary and cross-cultural science. The series will cover a broad spectrum of sciences, such as social systems theory, sociology, business administration, management information science, organization science, computational mathematical organization theory, economics, evolutionary economics, international political science, jurisprudence, policy science, socioinformation studies, cognitive science, artificial intelligence, complex adaptive systems theory, philosophy of science, and other related disciplines.

The series will provide a systematic study of the various new cross-cultural arenas of the human sciences. Such an approach has been successfully tried several times in the history of the modern sciences of humanities and systems and has helped to create such important conceptual frameworks and theories as cybernetics, synergetics, general systems theory, cognitive science, and complex adaptive systems.

We want to create a conceptual framework and design theory for socioeconomic systems of the twenty-first century in a cross-cultural and transdisciplinary context. For this purpose we plan to take an agent-based approach. Developed over the last decade, agent-based modeling is a new trend within the social sciences and is a child of the modern sciences of humanities and systems. In this series the term "agent-based" is used across a broad spectrum that includes not only the classical usage of the normative and rational agent but also an interpretive and subjective agent. We seek the antinomy of the macro and micro, subjective and rational, functional and structural, bottom-up and top-down, global and local, and structure and agency within the social sciences. Agent-based modeling includes both sides of these opposites. "Agent" is our grounding for modeling; simulation, theory, and real-world grounding are also required.

As an approach, agent-based simulation is an important tool for the new experimental fields of the social sciences; it can be used to provide explanations and decision support for real-world problems, and its theories include both conceptual and mathematical ones. A conceptual approach is vital for creating new frameworks of the worldview, and the mathematical approach is essential to clarify the logical structure of any new framework or model. Exploration of several different ways of real-world grounding is required for this approach. Other issues to be considered in the series include the systems design of this century's global and local socioeconomic systems.

Series Editor
Hiroshi Deguchi
Chief of Center for Agent-Based Social Systems Sciences (CABSSS)
Tokyo Institute of Technology
4259 Nagatsuta-cho, Midori-ku, Yokohama 226-8502, Japan

Editorial Board
Shu-Heng Chen, Taiwan, ROC
Claudio Cioffi-Revilla, USA
Nigel Gilbert, UK
Hajime Kita, Japan
Takao Terano, Japan

T. Imada

Self-Organization
and Society

Takatoshi Imada
Professor of Sociology
Department of Value and Decision Science
Graduate School of Decision Science and Technology
Tokyo Institute of Technology
2-12-1 Ookayama, Meguro-ku, Tokyo 152-8552, Japan

JIKO SOSHIKISEI TO SHAKAI
Copyright© 2005 by Takatoshi Imada
English translation rights arranged with University of Tokyo Press,
Tokyo through Japan UNI Agency, Inc., Tokyo

ISBN 1861-0803
ISBN 978-4-431-77919-3

Library of Congress Control Number: 2008924997

© Springer 2008, Tokyo
This work is subject to copyright. All rights are reserved, whether the whole or part of the material is concerned, specifically the rights of translation, reprinting, reuse of illustrations, recitation, broadcasting, reproduction on microfilms or in other ways, and storage in data banks.
The use of registered names, trademarks, etc. in this publication does not imply, even in the absence of a specific statement, that such names are exempt from the relevant protective laws and regulations and therefore free for general use.

Springer is a part of Springer Science+Business Media
springer.com

Printed on acid-free paper

Preface to the Original Japanese Edition

The research on self-organization is my life work, which started with my master's thesis submitted to the University of Tokyo in 1974. Since then, more than 30 years have passed. In the meantime, I discussed self-organization and society from various angles and published papers thereon. This book summarizes the results of those research activities as an interim report.

To the best of my knowledge, there were few researchers in and around 1974 who held up the theme of self-organization in the fields of social science, let alone in sociology. This situation also was true even in the natural sciences. In sociology circles, therefore, I was often referred to as a peculiar scholar and, as the object of bantering, as a distress signaler or an "SOS theorist" by making an acronym with the initial letters of "Self-Organization System."

* * *

In the Introduction to this book, I summarize two approaches to self-organization. One is cybernetic self-organization by *control schema* and the other is synergetic self-organization by *fluctuation schema*. My stance regarding the self-organization theory was cybernetic self-organization at the initial stage of my research but underwent a great change thereafter to synergetic self-organization.

Before the middle period in my thirties, my method of approaching self-organization was to rely on the control theory of cybernetics. In the 1970s, when theories of social development, social planning, and social indicators were the major concerns of sociology, I aimed at cooking these theories from the viewpoint of self-organization. Part I of this book, "Origin of the Self-Organization Theory: Control and Social Development," has been compiled based on such initial papers.

The trend of the times changed substantially in the 1980s. The postwar framework aiming at an affluent society which was worshipped in the period of high growth cracked to cause fluctuations. In parallel, postmodern theory came into fashion. In sociology, social theory that hitherto had dealt with structure and function as its central concepts gave way to the mushrooming mini-paradigms focused on meaning. As a result, the idea of planning and control was thrust away into the background, replaced with a desire to seek a society with bottom-up vitality.

In my research activities on the self-organization theory, there was a blank period for about 4 years from 1982 to 1985. During this period, I recharged my batteries in regard to self-organization theory and the new current in sociology, which bore fruit as my first book, *Jiko-Soshikisei: Shakai Riron no Fukkatsu* (Self-Organity: Revitalization of Social Theory) in 1986. Part II of the present volume, "Elaboration of the Self-Organization Theory: Metamorphosing of System and Individual," has been compiled based on the self-organization theory developed with a focus placed on self-reflexion from the viewpoint of social theory of meaning, while relying on fluctuation schema, with the publication of my first book as a momentum.

Part III, "Development of the Self-Organization Theory: Deconstruction of the Society," introduces two papers that deconstruct the existing system of social formation, which would be a sort of version of the self-organization theory concretely applied to actuality. It insists that two points are indispensable in conceptualizing society in the 21st century. One is that rhizome theory aiming at decontrol must be added, as the network admiration theory has a pitfall for rationalization that has crept in. The other is that future society should transform itself into a system of the support type and public space should be opened through practical activities based on support instead of control.

In summarizing an interim report, I reached the conclusion that the two methods approaching self-organization, control schema and fluctuation schema must be integrated from the viewpoint of reflexion, and a horizon of self-organization should be opened up to integrate the planning/control action theory and the spontaneous/performative action theory. Although this process is extremely difficult, I had already taken a step forward for this purpose in my book *Imi no Bun'mei Gaku Josetsu: Sono Saki no Kindai* (A Discourse on the Civilization of Meaning: Modernity and Beyond) in 2001. In this regard, I put the cart before the horse, therefore, as this book should have been published first.

*　*　*

I have compiled a book for the first time using already published papers. This was an extremely difficult task, contrary to my expectations. After framing the whole book with the above-mentioned interim report, I was forced to revise existing papers to accord therewith, which involved addition, modification, and deletion of descriptions in each paper to a large extent. There were also quite a few sketchy expressions or those largely affected by the conditions at the time the paper was written. As a result, 2 years were required to compile this book.

After the manuscript was brought to the publisher, however, I was able to work in a relaxed mood thanks to the precise and minute editing work by Mr. Mitsuharu Soshi. A long time passed after I promised to write this book with Mr. Osamu Sato, during which period he patiently waited for the completion of my work. I wish to express my sincere gratitude to these two editors for their cooperation.

January 2005
Takatoshi Imada

Acknowledgments for the English Edition

This book was first published in 2005 under the title of *Jiko Soshikisei to Shakai* (Self-Organization and Society) by the University of Tokyo Press. I want to thank the White Horse Press and the Future Generations Alliance Foundation that permitted the publication of the paper newly added to the English edition. Publication of the English edition was financially supported by a grant offered by the Center for Agent-Based Social Systems Sciences (CABSSS) at the Tokyo Institute of Technology. In publishing this book as part of the Springer Series on Agent-Based Social Systems, I received assistance from the series editor Professor Hiroshi Deguchi, to whom I wish to express my deep gratitude. This book, the fifth volume in this series, reports the result of the research promoted under the 21st Century Center of Excellence (COE) program formed by the Ministry of Education, Culture, Sports, Science and Technology.

December 2007
Takatoshi Imada

On the Composition of This Book

The introduction, "Scope of the Self-Organization Theory," which is the most voluminous part in this book, was newly written to correctly position each chapter and to preside over the whole of this book.

Chapter 1, "From Social Change to Self-Organization," was rewritten based on "Shisutemu Kagaku to Shakai Hendo no Ronri" (Systems Science and the Logic of Social Change) in Saburo Yasuda, Tsutomu Shiobara, Ken'ichi Tominaga, and Tamito Yoshida (eds.), 1981, *Shakai Hendo, Kiso Shakaigaku* (Social Change, Basic Sociology) Vol.5, Tokyo: Toyo Keizai Shinpo-sha, pp. 180–208.

Chapter 2, "Principles of Self-Organization and the Theory of Social Development," was rewritten based on the following two papers: "Jiko-Soshiki Kei no Genri to Shakai Hatten Ron" (The Logic of the Self-Organizing System and Theory of Social Development), *Shiso*, 647, 1978, pp. 1–25, and "Shakai Hendo no Keikaku to Seigyo" (Planning and Control of Social Change) in Kazuo Aoi and Atsushi Naoi (eds.), 1980, *Fukushi to Keikaku no Shakaigaku* (Sociology of Welfare and Planning), Tokyo: University of Tokyo Press, pp. 225–248.

Chapter 3, "Signification and Reflexive System," was rewritten based on the following three papers: "Shakai Riron no Fukkatsu wo: Jiko-Soshikisei to Shakai" (Toward Revitalization of Social Theory: Self-Organization and Society), *Gendai Shakaigaku* (Review of Contemporary Sociology), 12 (1), 1986, pp. 5–23; "Jiseiteki Kinoshugi no Kiso" (Foundations of Reflexive Functionalism), *Shakaigaku Hyoron* (Japanese Sociological Review), 37 (3), 1986, pp. 38–52; and, "Rifurekushon Shiso: Kindai no Choshutsu" (Reflexion Thought: Beyond Modernity), *Gendai Shakaigaku* (Contemporary Sociology), 14, 1989, pp. 5–22.

Chapter 4, "Self-Organization and Postmodernity," is based on the following three papers: "Jiko-Soshikisei no Shakai Riron: Posutomodanizumu no Shakaigaku wo mezashite" (Social Theory and Self-Organization: Toward a Sociology of Postmodernism), in Yosuke Koto, Takatoshi Imada, and Toshio Tomoeda (eds.), 1993, *Shakai Riron no Furontia* (Frontiers in Social Theories), Tokyo: University of Tokyo Press, pp. 1–35; "Jiko-Soshikisei to Imi: Komyunikeishonteki Koi no Chihei" (Self-Organization and Meaning: Horizon of Communicative Action),

Shakaigaku Hyoron (Japanese Sociological Review), 40 (2), 1989, pp. 21–35[1]; and "Aidentiti to Jiko-Soshikisei: Posutomodan Jidai ni okeru Jiko" (Identity and Self-Organization: Self in an Age of the Postmodern)" in Kazuo Aoi, Akira Takahashi, and Kokichi Shoji (eds.), 1998, *Gendai Shimin Shakai to Aidentiti* (Contemporary Civil Society and Identity), Chiba: Azusa Shuppan-sha, pp. 271–291.

Chapter 5, "Beyond Network Theory," is based on the following two papers: "Nettowaku Ron wo koete: Rizomikku na Sisutemu Kan" (Beyond Network Theory: Rhizomic View of Systems), *Financial Review*, 26, 1993, pp. 52–68; and "Datsu-kanri wo tsujita Jiko-Soshikika: Kobe Seiko Rugby Team wo Jirei to shite" (Self-Organization from an Anticontrol Perspective: A Case Study of the Kobe Steel Rugby Team)," *Gendai Shakaigaku Kenkyu* (Contemporary Sociological Studies), 11, 1998, pp. 27–48.

Chapter 6, "Toward a Support-based Social System," has been reprinted from "Shien-gata no Shakai Shisutemu" in Shien Kisoron Kenkyu-kai (ed.), 2000, *Shiengaku* (Supportology*)*, Osaka: Toho Shuppan, pp. 9–28.

I wish to express my sincere gratitude to the publishers and editorial boards of academic journals who kindly extended their cooperation in quoting and reprinting the above papers in this book.

---

1) The section using this paper has been deleted in the English edition, and discussion of the following paper has newly been added: "Self-identity in a Postmodern Age," in Tae-Chang Kim and Ross Harrison (eds.), 1999, *Self and Future Generations: An Intercultural Conversation*, Cambridge: The White Horse Press, pp. 235–259.

Contents

Preface to the Original Japanese Edition V

Acknowledgments for the English Edition VII

On the Composition of This Book VIII

List of Tables and Figures XII

Introduction Scope of the Self-Organization Theory **1**
  1 What is Self-Organization? 1
  2 Cybernetic Self-Organization 9
  3 Synergetic Self-Organization 14
  4 Horizon of the Self-Organization Theory 26

**Part I Origin of the Self-Organization Theory:
Control and Social Development** **31**

Chapter 1 From Social Change to Self-Organization **33**
  1 Formation of Systems Paradigm 33
  2 Social Change and Concept of Structure 37
  3 System Analysis of Social Change 42
  4 Toward the Self-Organization Theory 46

**Chapter 2 Principles of Self-Organization and the Theory of
Social Development** **53**
  1 What is Social Development? 53
  2 Basic Logic of Self-Organization 56
  3 Structure and Control of Social System 61
  4 Conditions for Social Development and Adaptive Control 66
  5 Application to the Theory of Social Planning 71

Contents

Part II Elaboration of the Self-Organization Theory: Metamorphosing of System and Individual 81

Chapter 3 Signification and Reflexive System 83
1 Linguistic and Semantic Turn in Social Theory 83
2 Reflexion and Scientific View 87
3 Theory of Reflexive System 95
4 Language Game and Self-Organization 104

Chapter 4 Self-Organization and Postmodernity 109
1 Fluctuation of Modernity 109
2 Metamorphosis of Society 116
3 Identity and Self-Organization: Transformation of Self-Image 120
4 Self in Chaos 125
5 Toward a Theory of Postmodern Identity..................... 128
6 Reflexion Thought 132

Part III Development of the Self-Organization Theory: Deconstruction of the Society 139

Chapter 5 Beyond Network Theory 141
1 Admiration of Network?................................... 141
2 Rhizome Theory and Self-Organization 145
3 Anticontrol Type of Self-Organization: A Case Study of the Kobe Steelers Rugby Team 157

Chapter 6 Toward a Support-based Social System 167
1 Decontrol and Increasing Support Activities 168
2 The Theory of Support 171
3 Some Cases of the Support................................. 177
4 Opening Publicness from Support........................... 183

End Notes 191

Bibliography 207

Author Index 215

Subject Index... 219

List of Tables and Figures

Tables

Table 0.1	Characteristic features of synergetic self-organization	23
Table 5.1	Paradigm shifts in the society	145
Table 6.1	Composition elements of support	172
Table 6.2	Conditions required for support	176

Figures

Fig. 0.1	Basic principle of control	10
Fig. 1.1	Functional multilayer and control hierarchy	47
Fig. 1.2	Internal process of social system and hierarchy of control	49
Fig. 2.1	Two levels feedback in self-organization system	60
Fig. 3.1	Triangle of menthodology and connection of cognition to existence	92
Fig. 3.2	Spiral movement of action	99
Fig. 3.3	Spiral movement of system	101
Fig. 3.4	Complex spiral movement between action and system	102
Fig. 4.1	Fluctuation from the viewpoint of function and structure	116
Fig. 4.2	Image of social change: Metamorphosis of civilization	119
Fig. 5.1	The world of hyper text	149
Fig. 5.2	The positions in the rugby football team	160
Fig. 6.1	New dimension of public space	187

Introduction
Scope of the Self-Organization Theory

1 What is Self-Organization?

Self-organization is a generic term which means the characteristics of systems to change their structure by themselves while performing interactions with the environment. The essence of self-organization is for the self to change itself by relying entirely on its own mechanisms. What is important here is the fact that the self can change itself even when it is not affected by the environment.

The action of the self to change itself is not environment-adaptive. It is not self-organizational if the self changes itself because an outsider warns it to do so, or points out problems. To be self-organizational, it is necessary to interpret the signs of a change in the self and build up a new structure or order with the change as the momentum. In other words, self-organization is a change caused by innovation within itself, or a *change through implosion*. In this sense, self-organization is not environment-determinant or environment-adaptive, but is self-determinant and self-adaptive.

Self-Organization and the Situation of the Times

It was in and after the 1980s that self-organization became an important topic in academic circles and a focus of social concern. However, it was at a conference of experts in information theory in 1954 (more than a quarter of a century before) when the term was first used.[1] After that, repeated attempts were made in the 1960s and 1970s, mainly in the field of systems science, to produce a theory of self-organization. Nevertheless, interest in self-organization did not spread across the boundaries of expert groups. All of a sudden, however, society became interested in self-organization in the 1980s. What had happened in the previous quarter of a century? The background to this phenomenon was that there had been changes in the conditions of the times and the recognition of self-organization.

In the 1960s, when the concept of self-organization was born and attempts were made to establish a theory, the viewpoint was the *logic of system and control*. In contrast, the viewpoint adopted in and after the 1980s was the *logic of creative individuals and fluctuations*. Between these two viewpoints there are antithetical differences, systemic whole versus creative individual, and control versus fluctuation. The former does not focus on "individuals" or system elements, but regards the system of aggregated individuals as the object of consideration. Thus, self-organization is formulated as the practices of a system whose functions undergo a structural change. What leads the structural change is control, or *self-control* in particular, where the viewpoint that the practices of individual components cause structural changes becomes relative, with the focus being placed on the fact that structural changes are caused by a control mechanism incorporated in systems. In the latter view of self-organization, on the other hand, the logic of the system withdraws into the background, with the principle of creative individuals surpassing that of systems. In other words, it focuses on the practices of individuals deviating from the logic of system which perform synergism to make existing systems fluctuate, and transform them to different structures. In this respect, *systems are last*, and what is important is the *amplification of fluctuations* by creative individuals.

The antithetical approaches to self-organization reflect the situation of the times. A viewpoint emphasizing the importance of the logic of system and control was required to steer society in the 1960s, when the industrial society experienced unprecedented prosperity and high economic growth. During this period, it was necessary to guide the economic process effectively, or maintain what is called *orderly prosperity*, so that society was not broken up by effervescent economic activity. If people are confused by prosperity and lose orderliness, fruitful achievement cannot be expected or does not last for long. Order is required for prosperity. The best way to acquire order is to have an idea for designing and controlling the status quo, while maintaining a definite perspective as the basis for the course to be followed by society. Thus, during "the golden 1960s," when people enjoyed great prosperity, social control of growth and development coped with the requirements of the age, and the initial theory of self-organization was born based on the logic of system and control. However, what was overwhelmingly influential during the period of high growth was the economy. Social planning, design, and control were also centered on economic aspects. Therefore, self-organization (for the self to change its structure by itself) was not able to attract widespread public attention.

With the first oil crisis as a momentum, however, the economy fluctuated on a global scale in the 1970s, and the period of high economic growth came to an end. After that, the situation rapidly changed, and the mythology of orderly prosperity quickly disappeared. As symbolized by the term "the age of uncertainties," people began to clamor for a turnabout to zero growth, or stable growth, in the fluctuating society. As the sentiment of social stagnation prevailed, the spirit of the times, *vital stability*, made its debut, reflecting the social consciousness and aiming at a vital society when a revival of the growth and development in the past could no longer be expected. What is associated with the spirit of the age of vital stability is not an image that society steadily grows, with people adapting themselves to changes while enjoying the benefits of development, but an image that individuals boldly implement various attempts to create new ideas and new systems. Society is not leading the changes; individuals change society through their own activities.

It was in the 1980s that the newly modeled theory of self-organization resonated with the conditions of the age. In an uncertain and fluctuating society, where the logic of the system had collapsed and social control did not work effectively, what was required was social vitality supported by individuals' activities. Stability requires vitality. The best way to attain vitality lies in fluctuations deviating from the logic of existing systems, and thoughts of a spontaneous order that aims at the formation of a new order through these fluctuations. In the uncertain 1980s, therefore, the formation of order through fluctuations responded to the requirements of the age. Self-organization in the hands of creative individuals and an acceptance of fluctuations rapidly gained attention.

To summarize the self-organization theory comprehensively, it is important to understand the historical development described above, since placing emphasis on one side alone tends to be unduly influenced by the circumstances of the age. Certainly, it is true that self-organization, if it centers on logic of system and control, is less attractive at this juncture when it is deemed necessary to create a society where individuals are dealt with preferentially. Whenever a large weight is placed on individuals, however, the society or organization may have elements that cannot be reduced to spontaneous activities by those individuals. If this fact is ignored, the theory will become hidebound.

What is required is to incorporate the activities of creative individuals into the logic of the system. This requires an unrestricted image of a human being which is not captured by role and status, and does not include those human beings who are absorbed in maintaining their existing status and performing their role. This is not to abandon control, but to depart from the control which crushes fluctuations and think of a control which will guide fluctuations to create a new order. It is to make conventional control by administrators and managers relative, and reform their roles into those of mentors or supporters. Placing emphasis on control opens the way to a regimented society, while placing emphasis on fluctuations reduces society to randomness. What should be done is a merger of the two approaches to overcome the problems therein. The purpose of this book is to systematize the self-organization theory toward such a merger.

Self-Control and the Amplification of Fluctuations

Based on the points explained above, there are two different methods to approach self-organization. The first is to deal with the mechanism by which systems change their structure and function through self-control. Control is normally associated with the action of a system to control the environment and effectively attain the goal. In contrast, self-control means to control the self and not the environment, or to guide the self to a desirable state by itself. We call this approach the self-organization theory based on a *control schema*. The second method is to address the mechanisms by which a new structure is created when a system leads to a state of unstable nonequilibrium through the amplification of fluctuations. Although the term fluctuation often reminds people of a deviation or perturbation that would threaten the existence of a system, since it is said that self-organization is the formation of order through fluctuations, fluctuation is not necessarily a destructive factor, and often becomes a creative factor. We call this approach the self-organization theory based on a *fluctuation schema*.

The self-organization theory based on a *control schema* has its theoretical basis in cybernetics. The etymology of cybernetics is "helmsmanship" in Greek, i.e., to steer a ship and not to deviate from the right course. When a steersman controls his ship, the ship normally responds by entering the most desirable state (to make the ship sail on the right course). In this manner, the Greek term refers to the state where an actor works upon an object (to steer the ship). What theoretically formulates this interrelation (between actor and object) is cybernetics, which has been established by Nobert Wiener as the science of control and communication. Often quoted as an example of cybernetics is the thermostat used for air conditioners to keep the room temperature constant. By reading the room temperature, it measures the deviation from the set temperature, turns off the switch when the deviation is positive (the room temperature is higher than the target value) and turns it on when the deviation is negative. The action of turning the switch on and off to maintain the room temperature at a constant level is called a control action. As referred to later, self-organization to change the self can be formulated as applying such a control action to the self and not to the environment.

In contrast, the self-organization theory based on a *fluctuation schema* has its theoretical basis in synergetics. Synergetics is a term from "syn" (cooperation) and "ergon" (work) in Greek meaning "cooperation to work" or a synergy, which expresses the interdisciplinary research field advocated by Herman Haken, a German physicist. Originally he was a laser beam researcher, and he clarified the mechanism of a number of microscopic beams which synchronize and self-organize their wavelengths as a laser beam with intense energy. Synergetics is an attempt to apply the theoretical implications of this process to different phenomena. Systems to which this theory applies are those which are large-scale, unstable, and remote from a state of equilibrium. In these systems, fluctuations occur frequently and behave cooperatively, thereby creating a new order at the macroscopic level. These fluctuations alone would result in anarchism and thrust the world toward randomness. Therefore, a mechanism is required to convert fluctuations into order. What plays the role of this mechanism is a catalyst action to self-strengthen the fluctuations, or more generally self-referentiality for the self to work upon itself.

Synergetics characterizes the science of fluctuations, in sharp contrast to the control focused on in cybernetics. As cybernetics characterizes the steering (control) of systems, so synergetics characterizes the synergy of elements. The two terms "self-organization by system control" and "self-organization by elements synergy"

1 What is Self-Organization?

characterize the two approaches to the self-organization theory simply and clearly.

The self-organization theory based on cybernetic control provides an effective means for developing policy issues to introduce social planning and development. However, society cannot exist with such a theory of planning or policies alone. A theory of performative and spontaneous order formation by the synergy of elements is also essential. What should happen in practice is self-organization in which the two versions of order formation, planned/political and performative/spontaneous, have merged into one. At the moment, however, a merger of the two has not yet been realized, as the theory from the latter viewpoint has not been sufficiently established well.

Approach to Self-Reference

Whichever theory self-organization is based on, a control schema or a fluctuation schema, a common problem is *self-reference*, i.e., for the self to work upon itself. In an extreme case, the subject of self-organization theory is how to address self-reference. Attempts have been made to deal with this problem by expanding the self-concept in the *control schema*, and by self-catalytic action in the *fluctuation schema*. As the problem of self-reference is studied from various angles throughout this book, we now provide a general introduction.

Paradigm Shifts of the System Theory

Niklas Luhmann, who tried to strengthen the social system theory through a dialog with general system theory, said that a paradigm shift of the system theory had occurred twice in the past one hundred years. The first was the shift from the part–whole schema adopted by social organic theory in the latter half of the 19th century to the system–environment schema advocated by general system theory in the middle of the 20th century. The second was the shift from the system–environment schema to the self-reference schema adopted by the autopoiesis theory developed in the field of biology in the 1970s. As Luhmann puts it, the three schemata, part–whole, system–environment, and self-reference, were changed not to deny the former schema, but to include and subsume it in a new schema for sublation. He adds that it is now necessary to reformulate the social system theory to incorporate self-reference.[2]

What is important in relation to self-organization is the second shift, or the shift from the system–environment schema to the self-reference schema, because the approach to self-organization triggered this shift. The self-reference schema is a reformulated part–whole schema which clarifies the aspect that parts are not subject to the whole to rest with wholeness, but that the interaction between parts creates the order of the whole. In other words, it provides a mechanism that the whole changes to a new phase through the interaction (synergy) between parts. We now summarize these views on the paradigm shifts of the system theory, while referring to the discussions by Luhmann.

The *part–whole schema* was a substitute for the systemic thought when people were not conscious of the systems concept itself. The central interest in this schema was the wholeness, i.e., emphasizing that the whole was not reduced to the sum of the parts. This was a presystem theory relying on an analogical inference from organic bodies, which created the insistence on naive holism. Systems science centering on general system theory has gained power as a movement to make such organic body analogism and naive holism nonmysterious. The first focus of this movement is to formulate the systems concept as an aggregation of interdependent elements. The second is to theorize open systems based on the system–environment schema.

In the *system–environment schema*, systems operate only through their input–output relation with the environment. Therefore, if the environment is not worked upon it is virtually dead. In this sense, the effects of the environment are indispensable. Thus, the system cannot help but seek the cause to change its structure in the external environment. This characteristic is called adaptation to environment, which is distinguished from self-organizing activity to change the self by endogenous working.[3] It is true that factors causing changes have been separated into two types when discussing system change. One is the exogenous factors stemming from the environment, and the other is the endogenous factors attributable to the system itself. However, this is only to distinguish the causes for change conceptually, but does not clarify the change due to endogenous factors.

The system–environment schema summarizes the objects of recognition as a system, and the rest as the environment. This method of recognition is indispensable for analytical methods. However, the character of self-organization nullifies any method of understanding by dualism. This is because, although changing the self by itself premises the fact that the self can refer to itself, or self-reference, a cumbersome problem arises here that the self plays two antipodal roles simultaneously, the subject and the object of recognition. Since self-reference means that the discourses and activities of oneself are applicable to oneself, it is not possible to guarantee that the subject of recognition is independent of, or superior to, the object of recognition. Therefore, self-reference often leads to a paradox.

As a classical anecdote, there is a well-known story of "Cretan liars." A Cretan prophet says that all Cretans are liars. Is he telling the truth or lying? If he is telling the truth, it contradicts the fact that he is a liar because he is a Cretan. If he is lying, it is contradictory to say that he is lying because Cretans are not liars.

The story of Cretan liars is a paradox in the world of language and not a paradox of logic. However, this paradox leads to a problem in logic, or to the *contradiction of self-indeterminacy*. Bertrand Russell, for example, discovered a logical version of this paradox by using the theory of sets. In the world of formal logic, Kurt Gödel proved the "incompleteness theorem," which states that it is possible to create propositions for which the truth or falsehood cannot be determined, and that formal logic cannot verify itself and falls into self-indeterminacy.[4] What is common to

1 What is Self-Organization?

these two cases is the fact that the invasion of self-referentiality generates the contradiction of self-indeterminacy. Self-organization shall intrinsically be able to construct the logic for the self to change itself. Formal logic cannot determine a self of this kind.

Modern science has coped with the paradox of self-reference by what is called the principle of "putting a lid on something that stinks." Since the problem of self-reference is an unmanageable evil spirit for modern science, it should be kept buried in a graveyard. Once the problem of self-organization has arisen, however, the evil spirit has come out of the graveyard to start haunting us. Unless we subjugate this evil spirit, self-organization will not come into our academic range.

Ross Ashby, a cyberneticist who attempted to formulate the self-organization system for the first time, came into conflict with the problem of self-reference and had a hard fight with it. As we will discuss in Chap. 2, self-organization will lead to a contradiction if it relies on analytical logic. It was after the advent of new approaches in biochemistry and thermodynamics that a new challenge to self-organization started. They deal with problems which are equivalent to self-reference, as represented by research focusing on (1) the mechanism of self-recursion that expresses the process of cyclical causation, and (2) the autocatalytic process that requires the self to reproduce itself. What is common to these theories is the *self-reference schema* represented by self-recursion or autocatalysis. This is an important innovation of science, given the fact that it has hitherto formulated theories avoiding self-reference. Thus, self-organization has become the subject matter for fully fledged discussions, and is a paradigm for the current of the times.

Self-Organization and Autopoiesis

The theory dealing with the problem of self-reference on a full-scale was that of autopoiesis (self-production) advocated by Francisco Varela and Humberto Maturana (with "auto" and "poiesis" meaning "self" and "production," respectively, in Greek).

The autopoiesis theory is an attempt to formulate the autonomy of biological organisms, or life, which does not adopt the input–output schema in conventional systems theory. An autopoietic system is an organizationally closed network without input or output, which is organized to maintain itself while reproducing the self with element-producing elements recursively related to itself through a circular network.[5]

As will be discussed in detail in Sect. 3, the autopoiesis theory does not treat self-organization, but deals with the mechanisms which keep system organizations unchanged, or the mechanisms which maintain the unchanged organic composition with each element connecting the action imposed on it with that of another element. In this theory, neither control nor fluctuations show up. The components are not controlled by others, and nor do they generate fluctuations through *differencification* (I will use this new term instead of differentiation, which usually means functional differentiation at a macro or societal level, as an expression of the activity that differs from the established order), but they repeat their action silently and steadily to produce themselves and systems recursively.

According to Hideo Kawamoto, self-organization is not autopoiesis. Autopoiesis belongs to the latest third-generation systems theory, and is a self-production system which draws a clear line of demarcation against the former second-generation theory of self-organization systems (the dynamic nonequilibrium system of Prigogine, Eigen, and Haken) and the first-generation theory of a homeostasis system (the dynamic equilibrium system by Cannon and Bertalanffy). Kawamoto states that the autopoiesis system is prescribed by the production relation, and the self-organization system is prescribed by the relation between generating processes. The autopoiesis system maintains an organization consisting of a production process network, while the self-organization system contains only the chain of generating processes for which the organizations to be maintained do not exist.[6]

It is correct to state that the self-organization system is a theory which focuses on the generating process, because it is the aim of the self-organization theory to address the becoming of systems. However, it is a misunderstanding to remark that self-organization does not have organizations to maintain. On the contrary, it maintains organizations in actuality by generating a new structure. Unlike autopoiesis, self-organization does not maintain organizations unchanged, but addresses their changes. If a living state is maintained, like that of a living organism, the organization is said to have remained unchanged in abstractive expression, even though the physical morphology (structure) has changed. It will be problematic, however, if one trivializes the changes in structure and function based only on the fact that the living organism has survived.

The metamorphosis of insects is often cited as an example of autopoiesis, in that imagos (butterflies, for example) maintain their organizational composition unchanged (autopoiesis maintained) even after a green caterpillar has developed into an imago. Although this expression is understandable as rhetoric, such an abstract and theoretical formulation is a little pointless. It should be taken that the organization has undergone a constitutional transformation (self-organizing). Otherwise, it will be difficult to differentiate autopoiesis from homeostasis, which characterizes the first-generation systems theory.

The fact that systems metamorphose is a distinctive feature of self-organization. As we will discuss in Chap. 4, the most appropriate metaphor to characterize self-organization is *metamorphosis*, not development or growth. Metamorphosis is not performed to adapt the self to the environment. It is the self-organizing which changes the structure of the self by the force of implosion under a given environment. The autopoiesis theory claims that the organizational composition is maintained unchanged between a green caterpillar and the imago, and this is also true for the characteristics of individuality and a united whole. Nevertheless, no knowledge is added other than that life is maintained.

Self-organization contains the feature of autopoiesis of creating a boundary by itself and producing the self every time it does so because, unlike the first-generation systems theory, self-organization is not boundary-maintaining but *boundary-generating*. The changes in the structure are to generate a boundary between the inside and outside of the system. In short, autopoiesis and self-organization are not antagonistic, but belong to the same family for the reason that both address the mechanism of self-reference that focuses on the behavior of elements.

Self-organization attaches importance not only to self-reference, but also to self-control and fluctuations (differencification). Autopoiesis is weak in this respect (treating these characteristics by the evolution theory of variation and selection) and narrow as a theory. As we discuss later, however, this theory is significant in that it emphasizes ontogeny while avoiding the totality concept of species or phylogeny that is the evolution of species. Since variation is not viewed as a problem from the viewpoint of fluctuation and its amplification, however, autopoiesis does not go completely outside the area of the conventional evolution theory. On the other hand, self-organization tries to overcome the limitations of evolution theory through the self-referential amplification of fluctuations.

I have briefly outlined what self-organization is. The essence is that there are two approaches to self-organization. One is the approach based on a *control schema* and the other is based on a *fluctuation schema*, each having a common problem of *self-reference*. In the following sections, I will discuss these points in more detail and give an overview of the social theory and self-organization.[7]

2 Cybernetic Self-Organization

In the early 1960s, cyberneticist Ashby tried to formulate the principles of a self-organizing system. With this as a momentum, researchers started to theorize it in the field of systems science.[8] As suggested by the fact that cybernetics is called the "science of control and communication," this was to formulate self-organization based on the modes of information feedback and control.

Principle and Typology of Control

Control is a key concept in Part I of this book. Therefore, I first want to explain its basic principle.

Let us consider a controlled system S. To maintain its behavior at a certain value (target value), a controller R changes the behavior of system S. This is the basic principle of control. In the case of a human body, it can be thought that S corresponds to the body and R corresponds to the nervous system. This control mode is called closed-loop control having a feedback action, which is schematically expressed in Fig. 0.1.

The system S converts the input X into the output Y. To simplify and schematically express this relation, let S and R represent the conversion modes as they are. Then the behavior of system S is expressed as

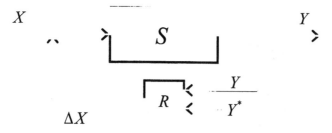

Fig. 0.1 Basic principle of control
Note: X is input, Y is output, and ΔX is an output as the parameter which carries out behavior correction of system S by controller R. Y^* shows the goal (target value) of the system.

$$Y = SX$$

The information on Y is transmitted to controller R for conversion. Then the output ΔX from R is again input to system S. After that, $X + \Delta X$ is newly input to S to reduce the deviation of the actual value (Y) from the target value (Y^*) when ΔX is expressed as $\Delta X = RY$. The format to convert the input $X + \Delta X$, which is the input to system S after circuiting the feedback loop, is expressed as

$$Y = S(X + \Delta X)$$

When $\Delta X = RY$ is substituted into this equation, the following equation is obtained after some manipulation:

$$Y = \frac{1}{1 - SR} SX$$

The action of controller R is expressed by the term $-SR$ included in the coefficient term, which indicates the effect of feedback control. This action brings the actual value (Y) close to the target value (Y^*). What develops in various ways from this basic principle of control is the theory of cybernetics.

The control is broadly divided into two categories. One is the above-mentioned *feedback control* and the other the *feedforward control*. The feedback control corrects the action of the object by considering the deviation from the target value based on its actual action but not on the expected action, which is called the posterior control. This control is further classified into the following three types.

1. Constant value control. This technique controls the state of the system to give good agreement with a constant value (e.g., a constant temperature in the case of a thermostat).
2. Program control. This technique controls the state of the system to give good agreement with a target value when it is a function of time (e.g., having a locus like a sea route).
3. Follow-up control. When the target value changes continuously, this technique adjusts the target value through observation like a guided missile reaching the target by modifying its speed and route.

2 Cybernetic Self-Organization

In contrast to feedback control, feedforward control takes measures to prevent a disturbance if it is predicted in advance, such as the vibration-preventing devices for cars, or the congestion-avoiding system used in car navigation systems. Taking measures to prevent deviant behavior by internalizing the social norms is also applicable here.

In addition to the above, there is also *adaptive control*, which is important in relation to self-organization. This control means that the system modifies its control format while it is interacting with the environment. Systems equipped with the function of adaptive control incorporate the action to modify the control format through learning and trial and error, in addition to pre-fixed formats. Adaptive control has a feedback function, other than the normal feedback action, to make the normal feedback action an object of control. Although adaptive control is often associated with passivity to change the self according to changes in the environment, in this case the term *adaptation* expresses self-adaptation by self-determination to indicate the system's activeness, as will be discussed in detail in Chap. 1. It not only changes the self according to environmental changes, but also includes the aspect of changing the environment by a self-changing action. The term adaptive control is used hereafter to include self-adaptation in addition to environment-adaptation.

As will be discussed in Chap. 2, the formulation of self-organization by Ashby means that he contrived his own adaptive control. In cybernetic system theory, however, a system–environment schema is adopted. Therefore, he encountered a problem with self-reference, and could not help but verify the impossibility of self-organization against his original intention. Self-organization leads to a contradiction in so far as it depends on the analytical (formal) logic of modern science. As a result, he concluded that self-organization could only be modeled in a limited sense.

However, cybernetics has now crossed the boundary of the framework of simple communication and control to conceive second order cybernetics, as seen in "Deviation-amplifying mutual causal processes" by Magoroh Maruyama, and "Cybernetics of cybernetics" by Von Foerster.[9] In the former case, Maruyama emphasized the importance of the amplification of the deviation from the target value by positive feedback, as against the negative feedback control to eliminate the deviation focused on in conventional cybernetics, and insisted that cybernetics should aim at morphogenesis in addition to morphostasis. In the latter case, Foerster conceived a version of cybernetics that contained observers in the system or the research object, without discriminating between observers and the system. These two cases are suggestive in that they include the growing problems of fluctuations (deviation-amplifying) and self-reference (observation of observers), but are not conscious of self-organization as a paradigm.

Furthermore, Felix Geyer advocates a field of sociocybernetics to characterize the first and second order cybernetics, as follows.[10] First order cybernetics was founded by Wiener in the 1940s and is based on information theory and engineering. This theory addresses systems that analyze the mechanism of morphostasis by negative feedback control, as represented by thermostats, and correct the deviation to attain a preset goal, with outside observers interacting with the inner variables.

The typical terms used for this method are the system boundary, subsystem, and suprasystem. A representative sociologist who advocated this theory is Talcott Parsons, who established the social system theory from the viewpoint of structural-functionalism. In contrast, second order cybernetics was founded by Foerster in the 1970s and is based on biology and the neuro-network theory. This cybernetics addresses the problem of the interaction between the observer and the observed, the mechanism of morphogenesis, and the amplification of deviation (fluctuation) by using positive feedback. Important terms used for this approach are autopoiesis, self-reference, and self-organization. A representative sociologist of this phase is Niklas Luhmann.

Although the above summary by Geyer is correct, it is hard to understand why he places the latter stage under the category of cybernetics. The origin of the term cybernetics is the technology to steer a ship to sail along a preset route to the destination. Even though we are allowed to include finding a new route or changing the course in cybernetics, it may be an excessive expansion of a theory that should attach importance to steering technology if cybernetics is thought to cover even the facts that the ship changes its own organization (self-organizing); the ship refers to itself as what the ship is (self-reference); or the ship deviates further from the preset course (amplification of fluctuation). This is because second order cybernetics fundamentally criticizes the conception of control to constitute a sort of anticontrol paradigm. I believe that this theory should be given a different name, i.e., *synergetics*.

Higher-Order Control and Feedback

The self-organization theory based on cybernetics adopts not the ordinary feedback control, but the one applied with the original contrivances. Ordinary control measures the deviation from the target value and takes a series of actions to minimize it (negative feedback). On the other hand, when cybernetic control deals with self-organization, it features the implementation of a higher-order control for the question of what the control should be, and for the preparation of a corresponding higher-order feedback.

Although he did not discuss the self-organization theory directly, Amitai Etzioni considered a higher-order control for the mechanism that controls the environment and social systems, and grasped the "control of controls" as a positive involvement in society. He remarks that "man is not merely able to stand above the ongoing processes and review them, to choose between alternative courses of action and implement the choice. He also has the potential capacity to choose among criteria of choices, and to impose controls on controls."[11] Karl Deutsch analyzed systems from the viewpoint of message and communication modes, and proposed "feedback as consciousness" that processes the information on state changes inside the system – the secondary massage – as an index to the autonomy or capacity of innovation of the system.[12] Furthermore, Walter Buckley expressed the self-stability and self-organization of a society with the concepts of morphostasis and morphogenesis. He cited negative feedback to maintain homeostasis as a factor characterizing the former, and positive feedback that amplifies changes and innovation as a factor characterizing the latter.[13] Other trials implemented in various fields have similar characteristics to those of the trials cited above. In short, self-organization is expressed by feedback action and the control mode based thereon, in addition to original contrivances.

As will be discussed in detail in Chap. 2, it is possible to formulate self-organization from the viewpoint of the social development theory through work which has combined Ashby's studies on the principle of self-organization and the achievement of Parsons, who proposed the social system theory from the standpoint of functionalism. The starting point of this study is the following thesis by Ashby, namely, the analytical formulation of the self-organizing system requires the enlargement of self concept of the system, through which the system shall be connected with the sector where the second feedback is implemented with the environment. Otherwise, as he puts it, it will not be possible to avoid logical contradictions, even if a different approach is adopted in analytically dealing with the self-organizing system. What is called the second feedback above is information processing to investigate and modify the reaction of the system against the environment.

In Chap. 2, I define the sector having this function as the "self-organizing layer," and mainly discuss the control modes thereof, while classifying the modes of social system control into the following three types. The first is structural control (law, norms, etc.), or the control embedded in the social structure. The second is optimal control to select the means to input human and social resources and adjust the volume of their input, with the given social structure as a premise. The third is adaptive control to overcome difficulties due to environmental constraints by structural changes, making the social structure an object of control. Self-organizing is triggered by the action of the self-organizing layer equipped with the adaptive control of this third version. Regarding the second feedback with the environment, I combine value information and needs information, which characterize cultural and personality systems, respectively, to position them as action to inspect the validity of the social structure, and clarify that self-organizing activities to plan and control social changes appear as this action connects with adaptive control.

In formulating self-organization by a cybernetic method, my standpoint is to limit it to contrivances of control and feedback concepts. Then self-organization will become closely related to theories on development and planning.

However, cybernetic self-organization fundamentally contains a logical difficulty. This means that, despite the fact that the formulation of self-organization requires logic for the self to change itself, a self of such a kind cannot be determined through formal logic. If an attempt is made to describe self-organization by formal logic, it leads to the contradiction of self-nondetermination. As a second-best policy, therefore, Ashby could not help but introduce the concept of the *enlarged self*.[14] This is to analytically distinguish the self (the main self) from the part of the self which works upon the self (another self), and define a new self that contains these two.

Of course, this deviates from formal logic and falls into the paradox of self-reference, because it is not determinant whether the self working upon the self is the "self" or the "non-self." If the self working upon the self is recognized as the self, the original self cannot be the self. This is a contradiction. If the self working upon the self is prescribed as the non-self, a non-self element is contained in the self that combines the two selves (the enlarged self). This is also a contradiction. Irrespective of whether the self working upon the self is prescribed as the self or the non-self, therefore, it always constitutes a contradiction. Therefore the issue is indeterminate.

Ashby admits the impossibility of self-organizing from the viewpoint of formal logic, and states that the self-concept shall be used to an extremely limited extent in order to formulate self-organization. The concept of what he calls the *enlarged self* is a pragmatic compromise to deal with self-organization. In other words, he expressed his opinion only to the effect that systems which are not self-organizational in an intrinsic sense will become self-organizational if other parts are connected therewith.

The following is anticipated as a polemic from formalism against his remarks. Namely, the logical difficulty he has fallen into will easily be solved if meta-conceptualization of the self to control the self is introduced. Certainly, this is a solution. The cybernetic self-organization theory cannot help but adopt this standpoint to implement a pragmatic compromise against logical contradictions through meta-conceptualization. This is a sort of trial to make an approximate approach to self-organization from outfield bleachers, while keeping a distance from its essence.

There may be criticism that such a method is to avoid self-reference, and provides no solutions to the problem. It is necessary, however, to confirm that this approach is effective in guiding society in a desirable direction by plans and policies. Avoiding policy intervention in such a manner may leave the system unattended to destroy itself when it has fallen into functionally partial paralysis. When the self-referential action in autopoiesis is out of order (abnormality in auto-immunity or homeostasis in an organism), for example, autopoiesis will stop (die) unless corrective action is taken.

3 Synergetic Self-Organization

In the latter half of the 1970s, there appeared a new approach to self-organization in biology, thermodynamics, and chemistry to deal with the problems in self-referentiality and system fluctuations from various angles. For example, it includes research into autocatalytic action to create a new order through the amplification of fluctuations that have emerged within systems, the mechanism of self-recursion requiring the self to reproduce itself, and the circular cause and effect

3 Synergetic Self-Organization   15

network for a system element to produce other elements and eventually reproduce itself.

In concrete terms, there are the "theory of dissipative structures" by Ilya Prigogine, "synergetics" by Herman Haken, which has approximately the same logic, and the "autopoiesis theory" by Varela and Maturana, as cited above.[15] A specific feature common to these theories is the fact that they treat (1) self-referentiality represented by autocatalyst, self-recursion, and circular cause and effect, and (2) the amplification of fluctuations as an important factor for self-organization (except autopoiesis). They are different from the self-organization theory based on a control schema of cybernetics. Judging from their contents, therefore, it is appropriate to call them an *anticontrol paradigm*. Therefore, let us distinguish the self-organization theory focused on fluctuations and self-reference from cybernetic self-organization and call it *synergetic self-organization*.[16]

Fluctuation, a factor which compromises and shakes the foundations of events, means a phenomenon that cannot be contained in, or coped with by, the existing frameworks or conceptions. In natural science, fluctuation is defined as the deviation from the average value, or the state of equilibrium, which is generated in systems described by macroscopic physical quantities. This book, which deals with self-organization in social phenomena as the main topic, expands this deviation to mean phenomena that cannot be contained in the existing frameworks, or coped with by existing conceptions. In short, this book regards fluctuations as deviations from the equilibrium state of a system, or from existing frameworks in any extension.[17]

A principal point of synergetics is that fluctuations, which are quiescent in the stabilized state of equilibrium, are actualized in a nonequilibrium state and make an order parameter. Such fluctuations are called *critical fluctuations* and become *emergent information*. Under normal conditions, fluctuations are a minor and negligible behavior of systems, but in an unstable state they absorb other elements to make a large surge. Although multiple fluctuations emerge, it cannot be determined in advance which fluctuation (order parameter) absorbs elements, or where the random factors of self-organization creep in.

Synergetic self-organization features not only fluctuations, but also self-reference. In synergetics, the issue of self-reference is not explicitly discussed, but is dealt with only in the form of an autocatalyst and a self-accelerating response. What has addressed this issue head-on and greatly affected the social systems theory is the autopoiesis theory. Therefore, we now discuss first the issue of self-reference, and then that of fluctuations.

Logic of Autopoiesis

Varela and Maturana describe autopoiesis as a life machine, or as a machine that reproduces the self by itself, and not as a normal hardware machine. They formulate its features as follows.

> An autopoietic machine is a machine organized (defined as a unity) as a network of processes of production (transformation and destruction) of components that produces the components which: (i) through their interactions and transformations continuously regenerate and realize the network of processes (relations) that produced them; and (ii) constitute it (the machine) as a concrete unity in the space in which they (the components) exist by specifying the topological domain of its realization as such a network.[18]

Although this is abstract and difficult to comprehend, it may be understood if you compare an organism with a nonautopoietic machine such as a TV set or an automobile. Their parts are not produced through their internal processes, but manufactured in factories with which they have no direct relation. In this sense, automobiles are an allopoietic system (with "allo" meaning "other" in Greek).

In the case of organisms, in contrast, internal processes produce cells or components that generate and maintain the organism itself. The cells of the human body, which are renewed every few weeks, are produced inside, but not outside, the body. This means that the human body has a mechanism to generate cells in itself, and itself is composed of cells. In short, cells are reproducing themselves through a cell network, which is in turn composed of cells. Therefore, cells (components) are reproducing the network of the processes that produce them. Such mechanisms exist in all domains in the human body. In the case of the cells that compose a thumbnail or a brain, the cell network in which they are involved determines the domain of the nail or the brain. In short, the cells are not involved in the networks outside the domain of the nail or the brain. This ensures their existence.

This can be summarized as follows. The features of autopoiesis are the fact that (1) the elements composing a system are reproduced by the elements composing the system, and (2) this reproduction is closed as a recursive network that affects the autonomy of the system, whose action is characterized by the self-referentiality, or reflexivity, shown in a circular network process.

Sophistication of Homeostasis

Note that the autopoiesis theory basically investigates the mechanism which maintains organizations which are unchanged by the homeostasis of the system or the action of elements which compensate for perturbation. According to Maturana and Varela, "autopoiesis systems are homeostatic systems which have their own organization as the variables that they maintain constant."[19] Homeostasis maintains the value of the blood sugar and other basic variables within a certain range, and therefore maintains the organization of components at a constant level. As Maturana and Varela put it, autopoiesis means that "any deformation at any place is not compensated by bringing the system back to an identical state of its components...; rather it is compensated by keeping its organization constant."[20] In effect, autopoiesis maintains the production relation of components that keep their organization constant.

If it is said that a feature of autopoiesis is homeostasis, it may be thought that it is the same as the functionalist systems theory formulated by Parsons, because the satisfaction of functional requisites to maintain systems, as formulated by him, was invented with the homeostasis of living organisms as a clue. Is there any difference between the two? To state the conclusion first, the homeostasis of autopoiesis is totally different from that conceived by Parsons for the following reasons.

First, autopoiesis does not premise purposes or functions of systems. An aim or a target is a concept where activities are discussed from the outside, and belongs to the domain where an observer describes such activities but is not directly related to the immanent action processes of the system. According to Maturana and Varela, "The aim necessarily lies in the domain of the observer that defines the context and establishes the nexuses. Similarly, the notion of function arises in the description made by the observer of the components of a machine or system in reference to an encompassing entity, which may be the whole machine or part of it, ... Accordingly, since the relations implied in the notion of function are not constitutive of the organization of an autopoietic system, they cannot be used to explain its operation."[21] The upshot is that as the notion of aim or function does not refer to the process in which a phenomenon takes place, it does not have the value of an explanation. This means that teleonomy assuming an aim is not necessary. Teleonomy is nothing but another position with the same viewpoint as that of the observer, and which is therefore different from the inner viewpoint needed to investigate autopoietic organization. In this respect, autopoiesis diverges from functionalism.

Second, in relation to the above, autopoiesis does not give priority to systems, but attaches importance to the operation of components. The issue in which autopoiesis has the greatest interest is not the effect of the system on components, but the clarification of how the system is realized through the interaction between components. "A change in the relations that define a society as a particular social system can only take place through a change in the properties of the components that realize it. It follows that in a human society a social change can only take place if the individual properties, and hence conduct, of its members change."[22] From the standpoint which follows the social system theory by Parsons, there is no viewpoint for the *realization of the system* by the components, even though the maintenance of the system boundary may be emphasized. From the viewpoint of autopoiesis, the system boundary is in any event produced by the components. The boundary that demarcates the system is not given, but is determined each time by the operations of the components.

As mentioned above, the autopoiesis theory deals with the mechanism by which the network of production processes where elements are produced is continuously reproduced through the interaction and conversion of elements, and is maintained as a concrete unity. This is no surprise, even if the movement of self-reference comes to treat the same phenomenon as that which is called homeostasis in conventional systems theory. It may be taken rather as the formal formulation of the operation of conventional homeostasis. No noteworthy achievement has yet been attained, however, in regard to self-organization generating a new structure, because autopoiesis takes little account of structures.

Invariable Organization and Evolution

Autopoiesis does not take great account of the notion of structure, but also structures as being dissolved in the action process of components. As a special feature of autopoiesis, Maturana and Varela, for example, cite four factors, i.e., autonomy, individuality, unity, and the lack of input/output. The first three factors explain the maintenance of an organization by the operation of components.[23] Autonomy means that the organization is maintained even if the form (structure) of the system has changed. Individuality indicates that the organization is maintained in an unchanged state by self-producing components. The concept of unity determines the system boundary in the self-production process of components. A characteristic of the lack of input/output is not to formulate the system from the viewpoint of outside observers, but to narrate the system from an inner viewpoint that is related to the operation of the components. This characteristic also plays a role in dissolving the concept of structure in the concept of process.

The components (e.g., cells) of a biological organization that do not have consciousness can never recognize the outside influences which cause their operation as being input from the environment. They also do not know whether the results of their operation become output to the environment. They only maintain the organization as a nonreflexive totality through a chain of operations. Therefore, autopoiesis puts the subjectivity of components within brackets.

For the autopoiesis theory to contribute to the self-organization theory, it is necessary not only to convert perturbation and noise into the existing order, but also to develop a theory about the start of new eigen-behavior,[24] or to have a viewpoint about order formation through perturbation or noise. However, as yet the autopoiesis theory has no theory about a mechanism to convert perturbation and noise into a new eigen-behavior. In practice, it only introduces the concept of evolution theory into the start of new eigen-behavior. Nevertheless, this approach by Varela is suggestive in that it has presented a new possibility in the issue of evolution from autopoietic logic.

Varela lays more stress on *ontogeny* than on phylogeny as the evolution of species. Individuals have a history of the structural conversion of the unity of the species through the "dynamics of recursion," or phylogeny as an "internal image." This means that phylogeny is nested in ontogeny to create an internal image.[25] This is a fresh way of thinking. According to his thoughts, ontogeny is a process whereby individuals react with phylogeny at the species level, or the history of structural conversion. Therefore, the structure plasticizes in ontogeny and is subjected to changes all the time. This is thought to lead to the correction of the eigen-behavior of the system.[26] This is a phenomenon which has also been observed in the developmental process of human beings and social changes.

It is said that ontogeny repeats phylogeny. However, phylogeny should rather be regarded as being dependent on ontogeny. In ontogeny, external perturbation or noise is not necessarily dealt with by independent action or the dynamics of recursion learnt from the past phylogeny. Given the diversity of organisms, the number of events by the dynamics of recursion and eigen-behaviors amounts to an astronomical figure. What are selected from these events is largely determined by the past recursive history, and is mostly random depending on any new conditions. However, it is always true that autopoiesis converts perturbation and noise into order. Perturbation is converted into the existing order by morphostasis, and into a new order by morphogenesis. For the self-organization theory, the most important object of interest is the order conversion in morphogenesis.

Autopoiesis of the Society

Taking note of the autopoiesis theory, Luhmann developed the social system theory. He formulates the social system as an autopoietic system having communication as an element.[27] The economy, which is part of the social system, is a subsystem differentiated from the total society through communications using a medium of what is called currency, that is, a communication system composed of payment and receipt. This payment and receipt is reproducing the self through as interactive chain reaction, or producing an element (payment) that composes itself through the other element (payment) that composes itself. In short, the economy is an autopoiesis having payment as an element.

On the other hand, Luhmann defines modern society as a system that has achieved high-level functional differentiation. From the historical viewpoint, society evolved to functional differentiation in modern times from segmentation via stratification. At present, complete differentiation has been attained in politics, economy, culture, law, learning, and other functional subsystems, each having an autonomous "closure." Therefore, subsystems are only autopoietically reacting with each other, with no single one being able to control the whole society.[28] In a word, as the social system has functionally been differentiated to a great extent, it now lacks a center, or top. This bears a close resemblance to an autonomous distributed system. In practice, however, such a premise is a strategic contrivance to introduce the autopoiesis theory of biology into sociology.

The social system theory by Luhmann has characteristically connected the autopoiesis theory with functionalism (the functional differentiation theory, in particular) in sociology. In discussing social evolution and change, however, he deals with everything from the standpoint of functional differentiation, while abstracting the viewpoint of order conversion of perturbation and noise. He remarks that, as society has achieved high-level functional differentiation, the whole of society has fallen into an uncontrollable state which has resulted in nonunified conditions. However, difficulties lie in such a discussion, in that it has committed a category mistake in substituting theory recognition for actuality recognition.

Luhmann introduced the terms "equivalent function" and "reduction of complexity" to revise post-Parsons functionalism. These terms introduced, respectively, the concept of "equifinality" in general system theory, and that of the "law of requisite variety," a basis of cybernetic control, into sociology. For reference, the law of requisite variety referred to above means that the controller shall take at least the same number of distinguishable measures as those of the opponent, in order to succeed in controlling the opponent and ensuring effective results. If we admit that these two concepts have been introduced into sociology, theoretically functional differentiation should take place within the scope of society where the complexity of the society can be reduced, or excessive functional differentiation that deviates from the scope of society would not occur. In practice, however, this is not the case. As functional differentiation progressed beyond the boundary of the scope of society, it is recognized that society has fallen into an uncontrollable state. This means that the actual differentiation of society has progressed to the extent that functional substitution by the design of an equivalent function or a reduction of complexity cannot catch up. It is not correct to take this phenomenon as functional differentiation. This differentiation has exceeded the logic of function. This must not be taken as a result of high-level functional differentiation.

It is logically impossible to connect the autopoiesis theory by force with the macroscopic functional differentiation of society because autopoiesis rejects teleonomy that uses the concepts of aim and function, as seen in the above-mentioned views of Maturana and Varela. Cybernetics, a control theory, is a sort of teleonomy science. The reduction of complexity which is linked with control theory can never be connected with the self-referentiality of autopoiesis that does not blend with cybernetics, as the two are as different as water and oil. The differentiation having affinity with autopoiesis is *differencification* at the element level (ontogeny), and not functional differentiation at the social level (phylogeny).

As a matter of fact, Luhmann admits only the passive meaning of fluctuation, i.e., perturbation and noise that do not belong to the category of functional differentiation. From the viewpoint of functionalism, he formulated the meaning process as the reduction of complexity (control), and remarked that "a preference for meaning over world, for order over perturbation, for information over noise is only preference," and that the rejection of perturbation and noise is nothing but a problem of taste or choice. On the grounds that, even if we have chosen one, we cannot do without the other, he vindicates himself by saying that the "meaning process lives off disturbances, is nourished by disorder, and lets itself be carried by noise."[29] However, this is the same as the positioning of deviance and social order dealt with by Parsonian functionalism. In other words, this is the view that deviation is the perturbation of the social order and the source of the diversity of society at the same time. Even though we admit that there is a creative aspect to deviance, it is meaningless to discuss it unless we have a framework to theorize it. It lacks scholarly sincerity to regard perturbation and noise as an issue of taste and choice without clarifying how to make them a source of nutrition.

Yasuo Baba, who evaluates Luhmann's autopoiesis theory in a friendly manner, states that his way of thinking that modern society lacks a center and a top is similar to the rhizome theory by Gilles Deleuze and Félix Guattari.[30] Rhizome is an antifunctional system and a movement body of continued differencification. If this is so, Luhmann has indisputably betrayed functionalism by actually doing so. It is problematic to coercively connect the autopoiesis theory based on self-referentiality with social macroscopic functional differentiation. Such problems stem from the fact that Luhmann connected the concepts of the reduction of complexity and equifinality, a hint of which he obtained from cybernetics or control theory, with the self-referentiality of autopoiesis that stands in a completely opposite position to cybernetics.

Order through Fluctuations

The autopoiesis theory has formulated the logic for systems to convert perturbation into (the existing) order, but does not proceed beyond an interpretation from the viewpoint of evolution theory regarding conversion into a new order. In this sense, it remains in the domain of the morphostasis-type self-organization. To theoretically refine the evolutionary interpretation, it is necessary to address the issue of order through fluctuations. If we treat only fluctuations, however, we will at best be able to grasp the aspect where order breaks down, without obtaining any new knowledge. To discuss the issue of a new structure being created, it is necessary to prepare a paradigm of order formation incorporating fluctuations.

In the background of the rise of fluctuation science, there is a challenging movement of scientific thought – what is called the advent of new (age) science. This aims at establishing a new scientific idea which harmonizes with the life of human beings, while reflecting the view of science started by Descartes and Newton, i.e., reductionism, the dichotomy of subjectivity and objectivity, and mind/body dualism. Although the new sciences, such as *The Tao of Physics* by Fritjof Capra and *Supernature* by Lyall Watson, are confined within the realm of mysterious thought, the theory of *Dissipative Structures* by Prigogine and *Synergetics* by Haken, which are a extension of this flow in the broadest sense, focus on self-organization in order to try to turnround modern science and give a scientific basis to the idea of fluctuations.[31]

A dissipative structure in a thermodynamic system is generated when a system incorporating an autocatalyst moves to a point far away from the equilibrium state due to the amplification of the fluctuations. In synergetics, system components act cooperatively, triggered by fluctuations, and generate a macroscopic pattern. These two phenomena are in agreement in the sense that they emphasize the formation of a new order by the amplification of fluctuations. The amplification of fluctuations is also based on autocatalytic action, and is connected with the logic of self-reference in this respect. In effect, Prigogine and Haken clarified that fluctuations are self-strengthened to form a new order, and they subsequently raised fluctuations to become scientific subject.

Modern science stresses the importance of the formulation of system behavior while focusing on the equilibrium state. Hitherto, physicists, chemists, and other natural science researchers, as well as economists, sociologists, and other social science researchers, have tended to think that fluctuations and the nonequilibrium state do not contain significant information. This is because discussions on fluctuations do not provide significant information unless the analytical framework has a mechanism of self-reference. Even if we recognize that fluctuations are important, these could be no scholarly publication unless we have a method to deal with it appropriately. Therefore, serious scientists must refrain from giving a positive meaning to fluctuations.

Fluctuations as the Source of Order

According to Erich Jantsch, there are three prerequisite conditions for *order through fluctuations*, i.e., openness, far from equilibrium, and autocatalysis.[32] What is most important is the self-strengthening of fluctuations by autocatalysis, which makes systems unstable and eventually drives them into a new structure by crossing certain threshold values. In conventional equilibrium theory, fluctuations have been positioned as perturbations which threaten the existence of systems or dismantle their structures. In the self-organization theory, in contrast, fluctuations are not a factor which threatens or dismantles the existence of systems or structures, but a factor which drives systems to a different existence or structure. Microscopic elements containing fluctuations cooperate with each other to generate a pattern. A macroscopic reflection of this fact is the amplification of fluctuations.

In the equilibrium theory, fluctuations are regarded as random deviations from the *macroscopic equilibrium* state, and therefore as objects to be controlled in order to return the equilibrium state, whereas the macroscopic equilibrium state does not have an important meaning in the self-organization theory. Fluctuations are not randomly against equilibrium, but are uncontrollable objects having a certain directivity, and are a factor causing systematic bias in systems.

For modern reasons, fluctuations are governed by contingencies and stand beyond the range of determinism, and their emphasis seems to be the resurrection of irrationalism. Therefore, an emphasis on fluctuations means entrusting the world to chaos and randomness, which leads to the abandonment of science. Certainly, such criticism is significant for popular epistemology on chaos and fluctuations. Nevertheless, it is open to discussion whether an emphasis on fluctuations is directly equivalent to an insistence on randomness and contingency for the following reasons.

First, fluctuations, which may seem to be random from the macroscopic viewpoint, are sometimes rational and orderly actions at a microscopic level. In a word, randomness at a macroscopic level does not necessarily mean that we can assume randomness at a microscopic level. Fluctuations in the self-organization theory should be taken as the action of differencification from microscopic elements to the macroscopic whole, which is the opposite to controlled action from the macroscopic center of a system to its microscopic elements.

Second, we cannot necessarily determine whether fluctuations are random or contingent, as there are two types of fluctuation, i.e., random ones and those having a systematic bias. The fluctuations that do not connect with self-referentiality can be regarded as random, but others have a systematic bias (with a certain directivity) by a self-strengthening action.

3 Synergetic Self-Organization

Table 0.1 Characteristic features of synergetic self-organization

1. Fluctuations as a source of order
2. Preference of creative individuals
3. Acceptance of chaos
4. Nonrecognition of a control center

The idea of control has an implicit prejudice that fluctuations threaten systems, and therefore are something to be controlled. Therefore, we tend to make a mistake if we put together random fluctuations and those having a systematic bias without discriminating between the two, or to address the former alone while excluding the latter from recognition for the purpose of theoretically formulating controllability. However, fluctuations that seem to be random at a glance may lead to the formation of new order, if they are systemic. For example, a fashion that seems at first to be a random trial will become a great surge when bias is imposed thereon. A sudden attempt by one person in one place generates an autocatalytic action when another person appears who follows suit. This makes a fashion reality. Therefore, it is not justifiable to unilaterally determine that fluctuations are undesirable for systems.

Conventional equilibrium theory based on a system–environment schema regards fluctuations as random deviations from the macroscopic average, or the equilibrium state. However, it should be said that control theory comes into existence only when fluctuations are assumed to be random, since otherwise the conditions of controllability are not satisfied. As a matter of fact, the control theory of cybernetics separates fluctuations from the mechanism of self-reference. In synergetics, however, the macroscopic average, or the equilibrium state, has no important meaning. Fluctuations do not behave randomly against the average or equilibrium, but act with a certain directivity to yield a systematic bias in systems, and subsequently generate a new order parameter therefrom.

To sum up the above, one of the features of the synergetic self-organization theory is to regard *fluctuations as a source of order*. Fluctuations are a factor which drives systems to a different existence or structure. It is impossible to eliminate fluctuations from the world. Furthermore, it can be said that a society without fluctuations lacks vitality and is abnormal. In relation to order through fluctuations, there are three more features to be added. These are the *preference of creative individuals*, the *acceptance of chaos*, and the *nonrecognition of a control center*. Table 0.1 summarizes these four features of synergetic self-organization, and the three features introduced above are explained below.

Preference of Creative Individuals

When self-organizing is in progress, the macroscopic features of a system do not have any important functions, as the principle of creative individuals exceeds that of the system. In other words, fluctuations are positioned as a challenge of the operations of elements against the macroscopic whole, following the law of large numbers (which is a law of the probability theory which states that the probability of an event occurring becomes closer to a certain value as the frequency of the event increases). This proposition is critically important for the self-organization theory.

In metaphorical terms, fluctuations are a rebellion of monad against systems.[33] What accelerates the activity of monad is self-referentiality. It is true that in physical and chemical phenomena, monad as an individual acts according to the natural law and never intentionally acts in opposition thereto. However, this extinguishes the macroscopic principle of system. In other words, a number of elements interacting synergetically at the microscopic level generate a macroscopic pattern, the reflection of which is the self-strengthening phenomenon of fluctuations. The self-organization theory, as a science of fluctuations, gives a positive meaning not to the principle of the whole, but to the *principle of the individual*.

I will now explain the above by replacing it with social systems. The synergetic self-organization theory focuses on individuals, or microscopic aspects, rather than on a macroscopic aspect such as a society or organization, to emphasize that a new pattern is formed through the synergy of the differencification of individuals, or that the activities of individuals create a new meaning through synergy, from which a new order starts. This will lead to placing emphasis not on the roles played, or positions staged, by individuals according to social requirements, but on the activities not captured thereby and deviated therefrom. What causes fluctuations is the synergy of differencification by individuals. In this sense, therefore, the social norms or average patterns are not important. What are esteemed are the activities of individuals outside social norms or average patterns, or challenges by microscopic individuals against the system as a whole. In short, *systems are last*.

Defining individuals in this manner provides an appropriate relation between the parts and the whole of a system. The part–whole schema of the organismic theory that characterized the presystem theory was apt to emphasize the subordination of parts to the whole, and closeness under the name of wholeness. The system–environment schema, that made its debut in the middle of the 20th century, moved from the closeness to the openness of systems. Nevertheless, no significant changes were made on the issue of part/whole subordination as a result. Although it was often stressed that parts compose the whole, which in turn affects the parts, the interdependency between the two was harmonic, and no theoretical framework was prepared for the amplification of fluctuations through the interaction of parts to lead to a new structure. After the advent of the synergetic self-organization theory, which focused on a fluctuation schema, the significance of creative individuals was assessed correctly for the first time.

Acceptance of Chaos

The self-organization theory does not reject chaos, but positively accepts it. Conventional social systems theory focused on the equilibrium state to formulate the operation of systems, where the equilibrium state expresses a state where the goal has been attained or order is maintained, whereas the nonequilibrium state is positioned as a factor that leads systems into chaos or dissolution. Synergetic self-organization is significant because it insists that chaos, or the nonequilibrium state, is critically important, and the forces which generate a new order are not born without it.

In our routine life, chaos means a state where things are foggy, indistinguishable, and not clearly separated. In this state, we hardly know "what is what." Chaos in scholarly term is a state where, even if the status quo is correctly understood, it is not possible to predict what will happen in the future. It is thought that if we find the existence of a background law, we can predict or control the phenomena that will take place in the future. Chaos means that this conception is not necessarily justified.

The warning of chaos theory for conventional science is that neglecting small errors will boomerang as an incomparably serious retaliation. In indivisible calculations, we normally round the quotient to two to three decimal places, while believing that the rest can safely be neglected as the neglected figures will diminish or cancel each other out. Chaos theory insists that we should exclude such a belief.

In meteorological circles, there is a saying which symbolizes the features of chaos: it is called the *butterfly effect*. "If a butterfly stirs the air with its wings today in Beijing, it results in a storm next month in New York." This means that a difference that is normally negligible may bring about a great upheaval in the course of time. This butterfly effect is called "sensitive dependence on initial conditions"[34] in technical terms. We can cite several examples of the butterfly effect. A mistake in the initial stage of a criminal investigation causes confusion at later stages. If the first step in crisis control is wrong, it will lead to overwhelming results. The spirit of modern capitalism was created from the Protestant ethic that was thought to be heretical. The results of the presidential election in the USA, which people labelled "Decision 2000," were determined by a few hundred votes in the state of Florida and greatly affected the world order thereafter.

Chaos is generated by irregular interactions between heterogeneous entities. In society also, irregular interactions between minor events often form a new pattern. In this sense, chaos is a force which creates order, and which exists at the preorder stage or at the forefront of a new order. Hitherto, chaos has been regarded as a symbol of anti-order or anti-science. When a new order is being formed, however, the old and new orders are mixed to make a chaotic state. At any important turning point in society, it is essential to read the signs of the new order in the chaos.

Nonrecognition of a Control Center

The self-organization theory that gives a positive meaning to fluctuations rejects a control center or similar concepts or authorities, as well as the wholeness of the system. This is a viewpoint which overturns the subordination of individuals to the whole, and emphasizes the formation of order as the synergy of parts lacking a control center.

The systems theory which focuses on equilibrium analysis regards fluctuations as a controllable effect moving toward the equilibrium state of a system. Classical cybernetics, which has established control science, for example, sees the control operation as minimizing the deviation from the equilibrium state as a target value, as seen with a thermostat, in which the existence of the center to control fluctuations is a premise.

The social systems theory of functionalism advocated that the gratification or nongratification of functional requisites as a provisional aim of a system would ensure the continuation of, or changes in, the society, and emphasized that its mechanism was of the same type as that of cybernetic control. However, eventually cybernetics cannot help but assume the existence of a control center, given the composition of its logic. Even in cases where it cannot be explicitly expressed, a substitute must be still assumed in some form or other. The gratification of functional requisites (which is sometimes called the functional imperatives) in sociological functionalism is equivalent to this position. This is because the structure as an interactive pattern of the parts is inspected for validity based on whether or not functional requisites are satisfied. Although the inspection of validity in this manner does not assume the subject as the actual condition, it does execute a function equivalent to the control center in cybernetics, and therefore constitutes a concept of its de-substantialization.

Regarding the four characteristics of self-organization given above, in Chap. 5 I analyze the performance of the Kobe Steelers rugby team, who won the Japan championship seven consecutive times, as a case of noncontrol-type self-reformation. As discussed there, the images corresponding to the four characteristics described are the anti-sacrifice spirit and the thought of the team being last, the team making to break commonly accepted ideas, ad lib rugby, and the abolition of the supervisor system. These features do not lead the team (system) to destruction, but create a system full of vitality. If logic is carried too far, equilibrium destroys systems and nonequilibrium creates a new system.

4 Horizon of the Self-Organization Theory

Regarding the approaches to self-organization, two types of self-organization are discussed above, i.e., cybernetic self-organization based on a *control schema*, and synergetic self-organization based on a *fluctuation schema*. In its background, the former has a design idea which does not involve the factors that cause fluctuations, noise, or chaos, while the latter contains a spontaneous anticontrol idea laying emphasis on differencification. At a glance, the vectors of these two approaches are direct opposites and should cause a state of disruption. How is it possible for these two types of self-organization to construct togather a bridgehead for a united self-organization theory?

Difficulties of Self-Organization

In this context, what should be noted is that both types have theoretical difficulties. Cybernetic self-organization assumes that a new structure generated by self-organization is always prepared by a higher-order control, while synergetic self-organization is burdened with the risk of entrusting the formation of order to randomness, which is similar to mutation in evolution theory, by attributing the cause of structure generation to fluctuations. Susumu Kuroishi expressed these two difficulties as the "difficulty of *petitio principii* or taking in advance of arguing point" and the "difficulty of contingency," and stated that it is not possible to determine unconditionally which type of self-organization is superior to the other.[35]

Theoretically, as much higher-order control as possible can be added to prepare meta-control for control, meta-meta-control for meta-control, and so on. Endless repetition of placing a roof on a rooftop leads to an infinite controller, or Almighty God. This eventually makes self-organization fall into transcendentalism, which is known to God alone. In contrast, when fluctuations are praised excessively, systems become like rootless duckweed (rootless wanderers), entrusting themselves to contingency, and self-organization may be dissolved into blind evolution. It is a dangerous ideology to entrust the world to contingency or randomness, which can be criticized as chasing a will-o'-the-wisp.

It must be noted that the issue of self-reference is a vital point in the self-organization theory irrespective of whether it is based on a control schema or a fluctuation schema. The issue of self-reference is the best factor to break the difficulty of points being decided in advance by a higher-order control, or of contingency by the amplification of fluctuations. I believe that it is appropriate to position self-reference not as logic but as an operation, and in particular as an issue of self-reflexion when it is dealt with in social science, since it is possible to construct a bridgehead to conquer the above difficulties by the appropriate incorporation of self-reflexion.

Self-reflexion is to make the activities or operation of the self recur to itself. The working (e.g., knowledge) of society changes its character through working (knowledge activity) on the working (knowledge). This represents a circular process where (1) the activities needed to acquire information or knowledge of the situation in which individuals or the nation is placed reconstruct that situation by re-entering the society, and (2) the activities needed to acquire information or knowledge of that situation are repeated to re-enter the society again.[36] Self-reflexion must be distinguished from simple reflection. The term reflexion tends to cause misunderstandings, as it normally includes the moral viewpoint of regretting and reconsidering the activities of the self. Self-reflexion includes reconsideration as this type of consciousness process. In addition, it places emphasis on the aspect where the activity or operation of the self recurs to itself.

Self-Reflexive Control

To prevent placing a roof on the rooftop of cybernetic control, it is advisable to incorporate self-reflexion in the feedback control. Since the activities of human beings are not those of Almighty God, they often fail in an attempt to control, or have unintended results. As such results are the outcome of an accumulation of recursive activities, self-reflexion in such a mechanism stops higher-order control and provides a chance to review all control activities. What is required for nonreflexive activism, which is often equated with pan-design thought, is to incorporate self-reflexive feedback control, or *reflexive control*.

In Part II, I try to formulate a self-organization theory incorporating meaning and self-reflexion in the framework of structure and function. To be self-reflexive is to maintain an internal viewpoint at the level of meaning, and re-inquire about the self. Cybernetic adaptive control provides not only environmental adaptation, but also a mechanism of self-adaptation, where a robust autonomous subject is strictly assumed. To begin with, the concept of feedback premises the existence of a subject that collects information and corrects its actions. Even if changing the system structure by control is attempted, it will never be the case that the subject of change is simultaneously reviewed. Unless such a subject is decentralized with a confirmed inner viewpoint, the self-organization theory incorporating self-reference will not come into being. For this purpose, self-reflexive control based on self-reflexion is also required.

However, the course taken to reach that end is not simple. It is not sufficient simply to read adaptation control as reflexive control. In two chapters in Part II, a basic study of that statement will be made. There are two principal points. One is to establish a self-reflexive system theory which has meaning in addition to structure and function. This is attempted in Chap. 3. The other is to re-examine, based on the self-reflexive system theory, functionalized modern systems and individuals.

Self-reflexion also makes the self a main theme, which is possible by understanding the looking-glass self (Charles Cooly) or the self reflected in the eyes of others. George Mead succeeded in developing the looking-glass self, and advocated that the self was formed through interaction between the socially expected self (me) and the subjective self (I). The interaction between "I" and "me" is self-reflexive in the true sense of the word, because "I" becomes "self" through the interaction with "me," in an operation which is directed inward and not outward. As Herbert Blumer puts it, "with the mechanism of self-interaction the human being ceases to be a responding organism whose behavior is a product of what plays upon him from the outside, the inside, or both. Instead, he acts toward his world, interpreting what confronts him and organizing his action on the basis of the interpretation."[37]

The interaction with the self referred to above is nothing but self-reflexion. The *enlarged self*, which is indispensable for the cybernetic self-organization theory, must be understood in this manner, as discussed in Chap. 2.

Fluctuations and Self-Reflexion

On the other hand, synergetic self-organization can escape from the difficulty of contingency by incorporating self-reflexion. The social implication of fluctuations is differencification, which has the same character as that of mutation in the theory of evolution. Although mutation has been dealt with as a factor of contingency, evolution is not so blind or accidental as has hitherto been considered, according to the discoveries of modern life sciences. Although genes incorporate coded information to determine the structure of an organism, it is too complicated to be determined by the information of genes alone. Thus, it is not possible to determine the structure of an organism with the volume of information contained in genes. As a result, there is no alternative but to think that organisms are selectively using genetic codes for the purpose of self-organizing.[38]

Kinji Imanishi, who established a specific theory of evolution by criticizing Darwin-type mutation and natural selection, states that evolution is never a product of randomness or contingency, and that mutation is destined to occur according to its intrinsic directivity.[39] It is a deliberated process of life, and nothing but a process to make the self-determining structural program recur to the self, in which self-reflexion exists.

The issue of fluctuations can also be considered in the same way as for mutation in evolution. Synergetic self-organization deals not with the fluctuations governed by contingency, but with those having a bias connected with the mechanism of self-reference. It is an object that cannot be classified by the dichotomy of chance or necessity. Self-organization is a world consisting of reality, where necessity creeps in chance, and chance in necessity.

Fluctuations are an operation selected by the system's components in pursuit of their own stability under given conditions. Although intentional operations cannot be assumed for the elements of natural phenomena, a possible interpretation is that fluctuations are generated by self-reflexion and the differencification of elements against the equilibrium state of a system in the stage of being a living system and thereafter. Differencification stands apart from the existing systems of differences (cultures, institutions, knowledge, etc.), and is an activity to create new differences. The fluctuations that cause self-organization have a systematic bias. For fluctuations to have a systematic bias, it is necessary for them to revert to existing systems of differences or to implement reflection, with differencification not being implemented by chance. Its social implication is an activity to create a new rule or pattern from the reflexive power possessed by individuals. There exist actions which create ideas and added values which are different from those in the past and incorporate them into tradition. This is a movement for the formation of meaning through differencification, the transcription thereof to the structure, and the crystallization of differences as structure. Such a trial seems to be contingency or randomness only when viewed from the framework of existing systems.

As a result of the above discussions, a linkage will be foreseen between the control schema and the fluctuation schema. The design concept that is agreed upon by the control schema requires to read new values and desires in fluctuations, distinguish order parameters, and accelerate the synergy of component members. For the control method to take a high-handed attitude to determining a changing plan and impose it from the top on each member cannot be recognized as self-organization. What is required for the kind of anarchism implied in the fluctuation schema is not to play with differencification, but to review the structure and function of social systems and direct them toward deconstruction. To make differencification fruitful, it is essential to review structure and function by self-reflexion. Differencification is often dismissed as play or mere negligence of the establishment. To avoid such a situation, it is necessary to inspire synergy to lead to a new order formation by self-reflexion.

The horizon of self-organization, whether it is based on a control schema or a fluctuation schema, is a space where the structure of the self is re-examined by self-reflexion, with the work deployed with the aim of forming a new order. Although a united front between the two has not yet been established, a bridgehead for synthesis is visible ahead.

Part I
Origin of the Self-Organization Theory: Control and Social Development

Chapter 1
From Social Change to Self-Organization

The self-organization theory made its debut as a field of systems science, but its relations with the logic of changes in other fields, particularly cybernetics and functional analysis in sociology, are not clear. In this chapter, I will overlook a position of the self-organization theory in systems science and discuss the point of contact between self-organization and social change by focusing on the concept of structure. The essence of discussion is to consider the structural concept as a kind of control mechanism, not positioning it as a realistic concept. It was in the field of control theory that the self-organization theory appeared for the fist time. In the cybernetic theory of self-organization, problem of fluctuations and self-reference is avoided, and the problem of control by feedback mechanism is dealt with. However, the trial that positioned self-organization as a new paradigm is important.

1 Formation of Systems Paradigm

The term *system* is used not only as a scientific terminology, but also as a word in daily life, in referring to system kitchens, distribution system in the transport industry, online system of financial institutions, belt conveyer system, etc., for example. A reason why the term system has come to be used so widely across the world is its freshness of the idea and notion associated with this terminology, in that each element is dealt with not separated from others, grasped in an integrated whole and positioned in relation to others, to cite several examples.

A system is the whole consisting of a set of elements and their relations. Systems theory, therefore, aims at constructing a method to recognize and grasp each element in the organized whole, without separating it from others. As systems thinking is often compared to "all interdependent on all" syndrome, purpose of the systems theory is to clarify the complex interdependence between elements, while drawing a clear demarcation line against the standpoint to explain the whole by reducing it to elements.

Major concepts that characterize the system include wholeness, interdependence, emergent property that is not reduced to elements, hierarchy composition of complexity, goal directedness, adaptation, equilibrium, stability and so on. Interdisciplinary systems thinking has spread in social sciences, as represented by structural-functionalism in sociology, structuralism in anthropology and general equilibrium theory in modern economics. The approach common to all systems paradigms after World War II was to clarify phenomena mainly centering on the concepts of structure, control, adaptation, equilibrium and stability.

General System Theory

In the background of popularization of system concept, there is a movement to unify two different standpoints that have always been in confrontation against each other in the history of science. It is the advocacy of general system theory against the allelism between the paradigm of mechanistic theory and that of organismic theory, in which headwaters of modern systems science can be found.[1]

The mainstream of science from the 19th century to the first half of the 20th century was *mechanistic theory*. The radical claim of mechanistic approach is an analytical method by which it is possible to resolve the universe into components and know everything by clarifying the law governing them. This reductionism generates a claim that the whole can be obtained by simply aggregating its parts. This is why the classical mechanistic theory is called the science dealing with *organized simplicity*.

In contrast, *organismic theory* obstinately advocated an objection against mechanistic theory, emphasizing that the whole was over the sum of parts and could not be reduced to parts, while stressing the needs to focus on the wholeness shown by the aggregate of elements. The conception serving as the basis of this claim is a genetic cognition method that an object forms its property by interacting with other objects and the principle of emergent property that a new property will appear from the relations between parts. However, organismic theory or vitalism in biology in particular too hastily emphasized the wholeness different from the mere sum of parts and illustrated only a vague concept of wholeness because of excessive repulsion against mechanistic theory. This is the reason why the classical organismic theory was labeled as a non-scientific theory asserting *chaotic complexity*.

In such an antagonistic situation, Von Bertalanffy advocated a new discipline dealing with *organized complexity* on the basis of organismic theory and system concept – a general system theory.[2] General system theory aims at the unification of sciences by incorporating the characteristics of organisms, such as order, wholeness, goal directionality, growth and differentiation into the system concept, a compound entity composed of interdependence between elements, and using isomorphism existing between models in different fields as a methodological strategy. According to Kenneth Boulding, general system theory, existing midway between meaningless specialization and poor generalization in its content, indicates theoretical model building that has the optimum degree of generalization as a skeleton of sciences.[3]

1 Formation of Systems Paradigm

In 1954, Bertalanffy established the "Society for the Advancement of General Systems theory" (later renamed as the "Society for General System Research), together with Boulding (economist), Anatol Rapoport (mathematical biologist) and other researchers. While publishing the annual report *General Systems* in and after 1956, the society promoted what is called the *general system movement*. Thus, general system theory greatly contributed to the development of systems science with a perspective of organicism, with its effect reaching not only sociology but also various fields in social sciences.

Cybernetics

As if to respond to the advocacy of general system theory, Nobert Wiener made public cybernetics in 1948, a theory that significantly contributed to modern systems science.[4] Cybernetics is a science to systematically investigate the feedback mechanism in communication and control, with its term originating from the steering technology called "kybernetike" by Plato, a philosopher in ancient Greece.

From olden times, mankind has cherished a dream of making automatic machines, as seen with the "clock work" replacing manpower with roll screws in the Newton age, and with "steam engines" after the industrial revolution. However, either one was still an automatic machine based on materials and energy without changing the principle of operation. In contrast, cybernetics focuses on information processing and tries to make automatic machines from the viewpoint of "communication and control." Cybernetics is significant because it has established a mechanistic theory on the goal-directionality, adaptability and stability typical to organisms and enhanced information to a concept as important as materials and energy.

A feature of cybernetics in grasping systems is the fact that it has made the linkage between control and information a main theme, in contrast to the classical mechanistic theory centering on the relation between materials and energy. As described in Introduction, theory of negative feedback, a basic principle of control, represents a series of actions for systems to work on the environment to attain the predetermined goal, collect the information on the results, and measure and minimize the deviation from the goal. This control mechanism is not specific to individual objects, but commonly observed with machines, organisms, nature and human societies as seen with thermostats for household electric appliances, adjustment of blood sugar level in the human body and the action of game chasing predators, etc. As a matter of fact, this control was greatly expected in relation to the application of cybernetics to biology and social sciences for the reason that it is isomorphic with the homeostasis of organism and human behavior of goal pursuit.[5]

At first, Wiener expressed a negative view against the expansion of the methods of natural science to the domain of social science, saying, "This is too optimistic and seems to be based on a misunderstanding of the essence of science."[6] Despite that he was negative about the application of cybernetics to social sciences in this manner first, he later positively evaluated the application of cybernetics to social phenomena by manifesting a view that the feedback mechanism was also true for human beings and society would become understandable for the first time through researches on its messages and communication structures.[7] After that, Ross Ashby joined the information theory by Claude Shannon and Warren Weaver to cybernetics and contributed to its enhancement to the level of systems theory.[8] Thus, cybernetics, or a leading player of the modern mechanistic theory, systematically improved the mechanistic intervention for organismic characteristics such as goal-directedness, adaptation, equifinality, stability and self-organization. It is now being developed as a science to clarify the dynamics of social systems from the viewpoint of information and control.

General system theory and cybernetics provide the coordinate axes for modern systems science that have diversified and manifold disciplines, such as systems engineering, operations research, computer science, simulation analysis, information science and game theory, when we intend to properly arrange their phases. General system theory has made efforts mainly to formulate cognitive framework to grasp the object world as a system, while cybernetics endeavors to formulate analytical framework to clarify the system operation as a control process. When systems science is positioned as a paradigm quoted by Thomas Kuhn, general system theory and cybernetics weave a coordinate plane, with the former serving as the axis of *systems cognition* and the latter as the axis of *systems analysis*, and have improved systems paradigm, comprising various theories such as systems engineering, information theory and game theory.

Structural-Functional Analysis

A new paradigm declaration was made in sociology almost at the same time when Bertalanffy in biology and Wiener in communication engineering declared their paradigms. It is the advocacy of structural-functional analysis made public in 1945 by Talcott Parsons in his paper entitled "Present State and Prospect of the Systematic Theory in Sociology."[9] He is a sociologist who correctly introduced the theme what systems analysis should be in sociology into the sociological tradition without neglecting the consideration for empirical science. The above paper is the first trial for that purpose and synchronized in part with the intention of Bertalanffy, a proponent of general system theory.

As a cause that has hampered the development of social systems theory, Parsons pointed out the prevalence of the "factor theory" not premising broad empirical law or theories generalized with a specific social element as the axis. As seen with the differential equation system in analytical dynamics, the ideal form of a theory is the framework to dynamically analyze the interdependence between all variables composing a system. He remarks, however, it is meaningless if the framework is made to confine experience or victimize empirical comprehensiveness.[10] Thus, even the achievement of Vilfredo Pareto, who constructed a dynamic model of social systems by following general equilibrium analysis in economics, is stigmatized as insufficient in empirical comprehensiveness. It was the aim of structural-functional analysis envisaged at the beginning to scrutinize particularity and generality in theory construction from the viewpoint of empirical comprehensiveness, thereby constructing a social system theory having an optimum degree of generalization.

To attain above goal, Parsons kept an eye on the complimentary roles of *anatomy* and *physiology* developed to analyze organisms and extracted a structural category from the former and a functional category from the latter, by discarding mechanical models based on analytical dynamics. Structure is a concept to represent the arrangement or relation between system components that are patterned and relatively invariant, which is dealt with as a factor invariant in the analysis of system dynamics as well. In contrast, function is a concept to analyze the dynamics between components and between components and the whole under a certain structure.

To incorporate comprehensive social factors into structure, structural-functional analysis uses a cognition method called the *action frame of reference*. Then it constructs a general system of action and social system as a subsystem under what is called the "actor-situation schema" that represents the mode of actor's orientation to the surrounding situation by adopting the significant work of functionalists such as Emile Durkheim, Bronislaw Malinowski and Alfred Radcliffe-Brown, the action theory by Max Weber and the psychoanalysis by Sigmund Freud.[11] This became an original phase of systems theory in sociology after the World War II.

The system recognition of structural-functional analysis is located in the phase of systems science that has an organismic prospect in the sense that it inherits the work of Durkheim and Malinowski who followed the social organismic theory. In this respect, structural-functional analysis stands at the same position as that of general system theory. Moreover, the theoretical mechanism, the basis of structural-functional analysis, was the principle of homeostasis formulated by physiologist Walter Canon. This indicates that structural-functional analysis shares a common ground with cybernetics.

2 Social Change and Concept of Structure

Logic of Functional Analysis

Structural-functional analysis that represents systems analysis in sociology introduced the ideas of pattern variable, functional requisite, AGIL schema and boundary exchange with the action frame of reference as the axis after the Parsons' paper was released until the 1960s and walked through the way to the "normal science" (Kuhn) as an influential sociological paradigm. In this process, however, it was exposed to various criticisms, of which the most controversial was a criticism that this method was not able to analyze social changes appropriately and the counter-criticism against it from the standpoint of structural-functional analysis.

This dispute continued in the USA during the period from the second half of the 1950s to the first half of the next decade, and repeated in Japan after a 10-year interval therefrom with the advocacy of the theory of social changes by Ken'ichi Tominaga from the standpoint of structural-functional analysis as a momentum. After all, a period was put to this dispute with a conclusion that most of the criticisms against structural-functional analysis are only ideological or due to a misunderstanding of this method.[12]

When the development of structural-functional analysis is discussed in terms of the phase of systems science, it is required to notice the immanent discussions on functional analysis involved in the analysis of changes through the work to extract fundamental characteristics of this method, though not directly related to the dispute of the theory on changes. This discussion was triggered in several years after Parsons' advocating of structural-functional analysis by the attempt of Robert Merton to systematically improve and codify functional analysis in sociology in his paper entitled "Manifest and Latent Functions."[13] At the meeting of the International Sociological Association (ISA) in 1960, Merton expressed his view to oppose using the term "structural-functional analysis" that connected the terms "structural" and "functional" with a hyphen and proposed to simply use the term "functional analysis," for which Parsons manifested his opinion in support thereof. What should be noticed is the immanent development of functional analysis symbolized by this fact, the principal point of which is to position the structural concept in structural-functional analysis.

Systematic improvement of functional analysis by Merton was sophisticated thereafter by the formulation of its explanative logic by Ernest Nagel and Carl Hempel, which clarified that functional analysis had a logical structure to teleologically explain the contribution of parts to the whole. In response to the formulation of functional analysis by Nagel, Francesca Cancian investigated the logic of changes by functional analysis and distinguished the "change of the system" from the "change within system."[14]

According to Cancian, functional analysis consists of two factors. One is the system characteristic G (corresponding to functional requisites or system goal), which is necessary condition to maintain the system. The other is the state coordinates (a set of variables to express the state of the system) that determine whether G is realized or not. Suppose a situation where a state variable changes to inhibit the realization of G, and another changes to compensate for above change and realize G. This change is called the "change within system." Then, suppose that compensating changes on the state coordinates do not make it possible for G to realize, and a new set of coordinates appears to realize G. This change is called the "change of the system." She defined the former as a change not accompanying structural changes and the latter as a change accompanying structural changes, to make clear distinction between the two. The former is a change of variables that determine the state of the system or a *level change* and the latter is a change of the field that prescribes the state, or a *structure change*.

The above development clarifies that (1) the concept of function has explanative logic on system operation, which premises a sort of teleological explanation and (2) the concept of structure is regarded as a given condition on the explanation of system operation, which does not stand at the original position in explanative logic. This corresponds to the fact that the method of system recognition describes the relation or pattern between elements that are stable for a comparatively long period of time under the empirical comprehensiveness based on the concept of structure first, and then explains the mechanism to maintain boundaries from the viewpoint of self-adjustment by using a system-regulation schema based on the concept of function. Since the purpose of science is to explain phenomena, the concept of structure that describes the system under empirical comprehensiveness does not correspond to the concept of function at the same level.

In parallel with such development of functional analysis, Parsons' idea for structural-functional analysis changed. As he puts it, the focal concept is the *system*, and function determines the conditions that govern the duration or development of system under a system–environment schema. Function is an analytically higher order concept than structure. The concept corresponding to structure at the same level is process to execute a specific function.[15] Thus, Parsons split the structural-functional analysis connected with a hyphen into two to make functional analysis of the system rank higher than structural and process analysis. As a result, process under the present structure is inspected from the viewpoint of functional validity, with the basic premise for changes, a hypothesis that variability is required for the structure under the name of functional validity, placed at right position.

However, the above inevitably poses a problem in what meaning function is a superordinate concept to structure and process. In other words, the problem is how the structure is incorporated into the logic of function and how a position as an explanative concept can be ensured beyond the descriptive concept that secures empirical comprehensiveness.

In structural-functional analysis, researchers often use the expression that function is appropriately performed or not performed under the present structure. In addition, the relation of linkage between structure and function is emphasized by using such a phrase as "structure affects function and function affects structure."[16] Above problem requires that meaning of "under the structure" be clarified and that the mode of "linkage between structure and function" be formulated in consistent terms. How to position the concept of structure in systems theory is the watershed to determine success or failure of social systems theory including theory on changes.

Concept of social structure has been accepted for long years, without a positive prescription thereon beyond the social fabrication as a whole, however. It was only after cultural anthropology tried to introduce it from sociology that an attempt to exactly define social structure was made. Since Radcliffe-Brown published a paper "On Social Structure," the concept of social structure was actively discussed in the arena of cultural anthropology.[17] The concept of structure now used in sociology and its positioning from the methodological viewpoint in particular are presented in clear-cut forms in cultural anthropology.

Structure as Reality versus Structure as Model

Alfred Radcliffe-Brown stated in his book *Structure and Function in Primitive Societies* that his theoretical framework was based on the relationship between "structure," "function" and "process," and belonged to the 200-year cultural tradition represented by predecessors such as Charles Montesquieu, Auguste Comte, Herbert Spencer and Durkheim.[18]

The concept of structure by Radcliffe-Brown is a typical definition focusing on empirical reference. He puts it that structure is an empirical "set of various relations between existences" and social structure is a network of social relations that maintains its existence and continuity beyond individual members.[19] He maintains that social relations include systematically controlled and regulated relations, with the existence and continuity of social structure maintained by the "standardized modes of action" created by social institutions.[20] His social structure infinitely approximates the empirical reality by making a clear distinction from social institutions.

Concept of structure, which is at the opposite pole against the Radcliffe-Brown type definition of *structure as reality*, is that of Claude Lévi-Strauss who insisted on the *structure as model*. According to him, social structure does not directly relate to the empirical reality, but is a model created using it as a raw material. He maintains that social relations are what should be regarded as the raw materials therefor and social structure can, by no means, be reduced to the ensemble of the social relations to be described in a society.[21]

From the viewpoint of structure as model, Lévi-Strauss extracted as a mechanical model the elementary structure of kinship, which the inhabitants in primitive societies are not conscious of. The elementary structure of kinship is a system of marriage rules circulating women between tribes and a logical composition to create that system behind marriage relations (patterns) as the empirical reality.[22] Contrary to Radcliffe-Brown, his concept of structure is to emphasize the institutional rules that regulate empirical reality, thereby endlessly approaching logical composition.

A conspicuous contrast between Radcliffe-Brown representing functionalist anthropology and Lévi-Strauss, a founder of structural anthropology, is summarized as that concept of structure of the former is a tool to *describe* empirical phenomena, while that of the latter is a model to *explain* them. Since the purpose of science is not to simply describe phenomena, but to explain them, it should be concluded that concept of structure by Lévi-Strauss is superior to that by Radcliffe-Brown from methodological viewpoint. What attention should be paid to is, however, that the version by Radcliffe-Brown entrusts the explanative logic to function, with concept of structure positioned as a tool to empirically determine the object of explanation. Lévi-Strauss intends to radically raise the concept of structure to the logic of explanation. As a result, however, the tool to determine the object region specific to structural anthropology becomes weak. Structuralism, which presents a methodologically strong approach to position structure as an explanatory model, has a danger to make the object taken up only ad hoc one, where a reason why the trial to introduce structuralism into sociology is not so convincing.[23]

When Parsons once emphasized the necessity of concept of structure in sociology, he grieved that general equilibrium analysis in economics has completely liquidated concept of structure into that of process.[24] Contrary to general equilibrium analysis in economics, structuralism represented by Lévi-Strauss has radicalism to dissolve process in structure. Functionalist sociology intends to incorporate concepts of structure and process with concept of function as an axis into its range, while existing between these two concepts located directly at opposite positions, which is seen between the structural anthropology and neoclassical economics based on general equilibrium analysis.

Durkheim, who was considerably influential in introducing functionalism into sociology, once stated in regard to the meaning of social structure that "A structure is not only a certain mode of acting, it is a mode of being that necessitates a certain mode of acting. It implies not only a certain mode of vibration peculiar to molecules, but an arrangement of them that makes any other mode of vibration almost impossible."[25] This suggests the possibility that concept of social structure is bipolarized into (1) the Radcliffe-Brown style that emphasizes pattern of social relation and (2) the Lévi-Strauss style placing emphasis on the mode of existence (rules to produce relations). This is an insight to suggest the problem, which functional analysis will inevitably come across.

The trial to refine the concept of social structure, positioning it as "the background logic of empirical reality" or "a way of existing that necessitates a certain way of acting," from the viewpoint of descriptive term showing the pattern and constellation of social components to explanative term as a rule and logic that generate them is an appropriate work from the standpoint of scientific methodology. If this is excessively emphasized, however, the possibility of social change will be taken away. When structure is positioned like structuralism as only one basis to rely on in explaining social phenomena, social change defined by structural change will theoretically lose its home. In short, an explanatory concept of higher order is required in dealing with the problem of social change.

Functionalism utilized function as a concept with above condition. When Parsons used concept of structure, he emphasized empirical reference all the time, as he intended to provide concept of structure with a meaning to ensure the empirical comprehensiveness of theory. As mentioned above, however, he later emphasized that function is a concept having a higher order than that of structure and process. In the background of this attitude, he thought that structure should be incorporated in a consistent form into the logic of function as a concept of lower order. However, he failed to do so. As a reason for this, it can be pointed out that systems theory and cybernetics in particular, the importance of which he repeatedly emphasized, were not sociologically assimilated. In regard to cybernetics and systems theory, even Parsons who greedily absorbed widely ranged knowledge on economics, psychology, psychoanalysis and anthropology, not to mention of classical sociology, and systematized theories of these disciplines, was not able to get himself rid of the principle of classical homeostasis by Canon.[26]

3 System Analysis of Social Change

Structure as a Control Mechanism

Siegfried Nadel has introduced the idea of "degrees of abstraction," adopted the standpoint to set an intermediate stage between *structure as reality* and *structure as model* and defined the "orderly arrangement, system or network of social relations existing among individuals in their qualification to play the role interrelated with each other" as the most appropriate generalization of the concept of structure.[27] For Nadel, as associated with this definition, structural analysis is not a method of explanation, but only a method of description. A number of researchers in sociology adopt the definition and positioning of concept of structure based on Nadel's standpoint. Several trials were implemented, however, to modify this definition by asking why patterns and arrangements having relative homeostasis are required. These trials are typical of researchers who attempt to construct the theory of social system from the standpoint of systems science.

Marion Levy, who made efforts to improve structural-functional analysis together with Parsons, defines structure as "a pattern of action or operation" and function as "the state of conditions and matters generated from the operation through the time of structure," thereby setting the relation between structure and function in simple but distinct forms.[28] This idea is considerably close to the concept of structure in systems science. Oscar Lange, who formulated general theory of system from the standpoint of cybernetics, for example, regards the input-output combination of operators affecting other physical objects as the system and the network of linkage between operators as structure.[29] This definition is close to the Radcliffe-Brown type concept of structure as far as the connecting pattern is regarded as a structure, but is not a simple pattern or arrangement of social relations, as it includes conversion of input into output in operators. If the conversion of a set of inputs into a set of outputs by structure matrix of operator network is thought to be a performance of function by the system, Levy's concept of structure will be almost the same as that in systems science. He did not develop theory from the viewpoint of systems science, but oriented himself to prescribing structure as "the mechanism through which functions are fulfilled."[30]

Niklas Luhmann developed the evolution theory by connecting phenomenology and functionalism, introduced the idea of systems theory and energetically discussed structural-functional analysis in a critical manner. After studying sociology under Parsons at the Harvard University for a year from some time in 1960, he developed an original functional system theory. More specifically, on the ground that concept of structure was placed at an unduly superior position to that of concept of function in the conventional structural-functional analysis, he insisted on functional-structural analysis that had reversed the relation between these two concepts.[31] When chronologically viewed, Parsons positioned function at a central concept of the system–environment schema because he might be affected by Luhmann significantly.

Reduction of Complexity

Systems theory on which early Luhmann depended was cybernetics that Ashby enhanced to the systems theory by introducing the Shannon type information theory or the "law of requisite variety" in particular.[32] Here, early Luhmann means before his introducing autopoiesis theory into his own (until the 1970s). Cybernetics excluded the naive teleology that explains cause by effect (uses the purpose as a means of explanation) and made the purposiveness an object of explanation as a control process, thereby contributing to the improvement of teleology up to a science. For structural-functional analysis that requires the logic to explain system operation for the function, therefore, cybernetics provides a powerful tool, since structure will be enhanced from descriptive concept to explanative concept, if concept of structure is appropriately incorporated into the mechanism of system control.

The core framework of the early stage Luhmann theory is (1) "complexity" in the sense that the possibility of actualization higher than expected always exists for experience and action in the world, (2) "contingency" in the sense that the possibility of non-occurrence as expected depending on the environmental condition exists and (3) "structure of experience processing" to address and control these problems.[33]

The complexity and contingency of experience and action are inevitable problems for system to determine and maintain boundaries with environment. System cannot entrust itself to the contingency in which experience or action will misfire against expectation under the complicated environment. For system to maintain boundaries with environment, it must select realizable experience and action through the *reduction of complexity* and be able to fix them as expectable matters.[34] Concept of structure by Luhmann is to restrict experience and action to specific patterns through the reduction of complexity and enhance their expected values for realization, or select certain possibilities while implementing control to victimize others. Action system controls its process by its structure.

Now, social system is an open system, having a risk to increase the contingency of experience and action selected by structure as the complexity of environment increases. Therefore, system must reduce the complexity of environment as well. In other words, social system must not only control the process by structure but also implement control to overcome the constraint by environment. To reduce complexity of environment, however, complexity of system must be increased. To control the environment in effect, therefore, system must have at least the same complexity (variety) as that shown by environment or countermeasures.[35] After all, reduction of environmental complexity is for the system to control the environmental constraint (contingency of experience and action caused by the environmental complexity) by enhancing its own control capability. At this juncture, it may become necessary to select the possibilities not selected by the existing structure. It must be recognized, therefore, that structure has a possibility to change depending on environmental condition. Here arises the problem of social change.

Tamito Yoshida, who formulates society as an "information–resource processing system" from the standpoint of information science, is also one of the researchers advocating the necessity to grasp system structure as a control mechanism. In defining structure of social system, he considers descriptive structure as reality of Radcliffe-Brown type. In other words, structure is "a continuous and patterned relation between various elements composing social system."[36] For Yoshida who tries to reformulate structural-functional analysis as an information–resource processing paradigm, however, concept of structure does not have a central role in theoretical framework. According to him, what plays that role is structural control information, or *structural information* in short, that supports and controls the structure in above sense. This structural information has a function to generate a "continuous and patterned relation" (to structuralize the social system). Therefore, what he calls concept of structure is close to a rule to generate relations, the "mode of being that necessitates a certain mode of acting" by Durkheim or the structure as "background logic of empirical reality" of structuralism.

The Yoshida's theory can be summarized that structural information controls flow and stock of social system and their levels determine the attainment of functional requisites of social system. Therefore, it is possible to interpret that structural information controls the process of social system and the flow and stock output therefrom represent the functional performance. When set of this structural information is thought to be a system structure, structure is incorporated into functional logic as an explanative concept beyond the framework of simple descriptive concept.

Above discussed is the fact that there is an idea to incorporate structure into functional analysis, which is a variation of teleology, as a control mechanism. This is a feature common to the trials by Luhmann and Yoshida who intend to reconstruct structural-functional analysis in a criticizing manner from the standpoint of systems science. Then, structure is composed of (1) a mode of action ensuring functional achievement by controlling social system, i.e., the role as a normatively regulated rule of action and its composition and (2) rules to allocate manpower and resources required to actualize the activities. It is a problem of social change to consider the logic that changes structure as a control mechanism.

Structural Change and Evolution

When social structure is regarded as a control mechanism, its purpose is to maintain the functional output from social process within the scope where system boundaries can be maintained, or maintain the state of equilibrium in the sense of homeostasis. However, process control by structure programmed in the system does not always succeed against changes in the conditions inside and outside system. *Self-organization* is to try structural changes by itself when existing structure cannot maintain appropriate functional achievement in such a situation. Logic of social change deserves the naming as a theory by improving the mechanism of this self-organization.

Regarding the logic of change, functionalist systems theory has adopted theory of social evolution, which is isomorphic with evolution of species in biology. Since Herbert Spencer advocated the organismic theory of society following biological evolution theory by Charles Darwin, theory of evolution greatly influenced William Sumner, Lester Ward and other sociologists in the USA. After hovering low temporarily for a while, theory of evolution was rallied by Parsons.

If the logic of evolutional change is formulated at a high abstract level, a newly created *variation* will be *retained* in the system by artificial and/or natural *selections*.[37] Thus, evolutional changes are the enhancement of system capability for environmental adaptation by *selective retention of variation*. If this logic becomes stereotyped, however, it will cause a stop of scientific thinking. Evolution from "military society" to "industrial society" by Spencer, and "seedbed" theory of social evolution by Parsons have danger to fall into *Poverty of Historicism* (Karl Popper) in the sense that they intend to explain evolution with social tendency.

Luhmann formulates the logic of evolutional change as follows. Evolution is for the system to reduce environmental complexity and enhance its complexity to remove contingency of action, in case it cannot appropriately perform the boundary maintaining function (maintaining the morphostasis of the meaning linkage of action) when it has encountered environmental complexity.[38] If his logic is reinterpreted, it means that society stores possibility of action not selected by existing structure or new possibility found accidentally as a *pool of diversity*.[39] As these possibilities are not yet institutionalized, they are latent for society. Society selects an action that will potentially reduce environmental complexity from the pool of diversity and takes a measure to fix (institutionalize) it as a realizable object. This is the preparation of structure as a new selecting mechanism, which constitutes a structural change.[40]

However, pool of diversity makes a remainder category of structure and function in the theoretical framework of social system, which is equivalent to the abandonment of explanation by the theory. Therefore, it is logically at an isomorphic position as that of mutation in biological evolution theory. Although Yoshida applied a "free idea" to this area, there is no possibility that this relates to the working of self-organization of the social system. Even if there were, it may be an accidental result.[41] Moreover, it will be logically the same, even if any idea is applied to this area.

4 Toward the Self-Organization Theory

Systems science does not require the logic of change in the pool of diversity, but has tried to formulate it from the viewpoint of *information processing* of the system. Regarding the working of system, information processing which means collection, storage and processing of information focuses on the *feedback action* of information and the *mode of control*. Then, as will be discussed in detail in the next chapter, self-organization is shown by applying an original contrivance to these two concepts. Character of the system which makes the basis of discussion in this context is that complex systems have openness and a hierarchical composition without exception.[42]

Hierarchy of Control

Against classical cybernetic control, development of control science has formulated functional hierarchy of control, to represent the formulation of vertical division of control. This means distinguishing the following three types of process control.

1. Selection of acceptable action under the preset conditions (*regulation*).
2. Determination of the goal for regulatory control and control of disturbance (*optimum control*).
3. Selection of lower layer structure and function to realize the goal of the whole system (*adaptive control*).

Three layers that take charge of these controls are called *selection layer*, *adaptation layer* and *self-organization layer* in the order listed above.[43] Figure 1.1 shows the hierarchy of control layers and corresponding processes. In functional hierarchy of control, selection layer regulates process; adaptation layer controls this regulation mode in a optimum manner; and self-organization layer controls the modes of the optimum control through adaptive control.

I will explain above more in detail. *Regulation* is to regulate the interaction between elements so that the preset action is adopted. In this situation, the goal for regulation is not set by selection layer, but is given by the *optimum control* shown by adaptation layer. Therefore, selection layer receives contents and mode of desirable action from adaptation layer, based on which it adjusts the action. At this level, adjustment is performed by the existing structure. Therefore, regulation is nothing but to control the interaction so that function is appropriately performed by the given structure. This control is sociologically equivalent to the control by institutions and norms, or to the case where the action restricted by institutions and

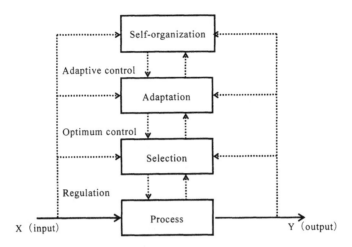

Fig. 1.1 Functional multilayer and control hierarchy

norms has become an unconscious habit in social process. When social process depends only on regulation, it becomes deterministic and mechanical.

In contrast, *optimum control* is a control to maximize the value of objective function or evaluation function for the system. Optimality is to make the evaluation function that represents the balance between cost and goal attainment take a most desirable value. This control weighs advantages and disadvantages of alternative ideas to attain the goal in terms of cost, selects the mode of action to maximize the value of evaluation function and inputs it into the selection layer. Even when the system ensures satisfactory performance through optimum control, however, it may be sometimes the case that optimality cannot be maintained due to new disturbances or environmental changes. Therefore, it is required to adjust the way of control in case the environment changes ceaselessly. Optimum control is to perform optimum decision-making, memorize the experience in the past and recognize environmental changes, thereby changing the input–output relation of the system.

Adaptive control provides adaptation layer with a model for optimum control. Adaptation is for the system to correct the criteria (evaluation function) or parameters for optimization in the interaction with environment and change system goal. Self-organization layer receives information on the internal state of system and changes its structure. As structure is changed irrespective of the state of layers lower than the control hierarchy, situations that cannot be dealt with by the lower layers may emerge, when the self-organization layer exerts its function.

Self-organization occurs (1) when a situation arises where system cannot maintain the self or attain optimum goal under the given structure, or (2) when it is required to introduce novelty to differentiate functions and embed it in the existing system. In this situation, system has reached a critical state either in a good or bad sense, where it cannot ensure self-maintenance or optimality. To make itself environment-adaptable or absorb the novelty (diversity) differentiated in itself, therefore, system exerts adaptive control to attain self-organization. This increases the complexity (diversity) of system, through which system changes the mode of working.

Parsons once tried to apply the hierarchy of control to social system for the four subsystems (cultural system, social system, personality system and behavioral organism) that constitute a general system of action. In this trial, however, based on the antagonistic relation between "information" and "energy" in the classical cybernetics, he only positioned vertically four subsystems from the high information–low energy cultural system to the low information–high energy behavioral organism through social and personality system. In other words, he typologically summarized that systems with relatively high-density information control those with low-density information while systems at relatively high energy levels determine the conditions of systems at low energy levels.[44] However, this remains only perfunctory.

Above mentioned control hierarchy formulated by the modern control science is applicable to (the self-organization of) social system, after some correction is made thereon.

First is the modification of selection layer and regulation located at the bottom of control hierarchy. In a case of small-scale enterprises and groups, regulation is based on the feedback information and directs to select appropriate action based on the result information, which is, therefore, nothing but a *posterior control* against disturbances. As for the social system, however, it is appropriate to think that acceptable action to be selected under the preset conditions is specified in advance by structure consisting of norms and institutions. Selection of such action is internalized for members through socialization. In this sense, social structure is thought to fulfill regulatory function as the *prior control* of social process.

Second is the modification of optimum control to determine the goal for regulation. The prior control (regulation) by social structure has a function to select and fix a certain possibility of action and victimize other possibilities. Therefore, there always exists a chance that the possibilities excluded by structure occur as deviant behavior. Control to attain functional achievement by the given structure requires a mechanism of infringement treatment. Since the purpose of regulation is to determine to what degree deviation as a disobedient phenomenon should be kept, the optimum control is required to determine the criterion therefor. Deviation as a disobedient phenomenon should be considered in a neutral sense that it has been excluded from the structural selection, which includes both the creative ones to enhance functional achievement and noncreative ones. Whichever the case is, existing structure is not prepared to address the excluded possibilities. Consequently, there is a possibility to cause tension and obstacles in purposive control aiming at functional achievement. To efficiently realize functional achievement under the existing structure, therefore, it is required to cope with this situation by redistributing manpower, resources and sanction to the role. This constitutes the optimum control in social system.

Third is the necessity of some modification on adaptive control shown by the self-organization layer, as a result of modifications on the regulation and optimum control. Adaptive control makes structure programmed in social system an object of control. This control increases the diversity of structure, in order to select action more than that selected by conventional structure, thereby aiming at the enhancement of control capability. Adaptive control is vitalized not only to correspond to the decrease in environment control capability due to the changes in environmental conditions, but also to trigger structural change by acquiring information of the state inside and outside the system in advance and setting or changing goals to attain higher functional achievement.

As seen in the above discussions, self-organization not only repeats the process currently in progress or selects action allowed by the structural framework, but also largely depends on the capability to impose "selection of selection criteria" or "control of controls." In other words, self-organization is a state where the power of self-innovation and self-determination including goal changing capacity are built in. Figure 1.2 expresses the case where functional hierarchy of control is applied to social system. In Figure 1.2, structural control represents the state where structure of social system works as a control device. Since structural control is a prior selection of desirable action, it is placed before the social process. The essence of structure is to designate the action selected at system level. Although laws and norms are in charge of this operation, they are symbols that are generally thought

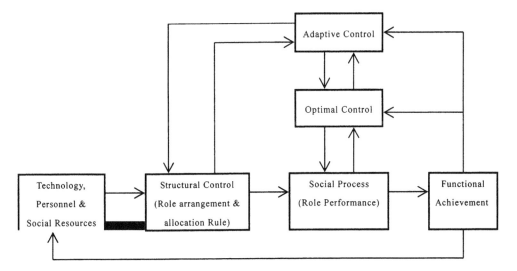

Fig. 1.2 Internal process of social system and hierarchy of control
Note: In the block diagram of the figure which displays operation mode of social system, each operation is hierarchically placed as follows. That is, adaptive control is placed at the top level, optimum control next, and the four block elements in the bottom. The arrow from the lower level to the upper level shows that the upper level element undertakes information-gathering from the lower level element. The reverse directional arrow shows that the upper level element exerts control action against the lower level.

to belong to cultural system. Since social system consists of interactions, it is required to consider the specified aspects of laws and norms in the phase of integration, such as rules to allocate social resources required for the role and its performance. Therefore, structural control is represented by the *role arrangement* as an assembly of roles and the *allocation rules* that assign manpower and social resources to the role.

Feedback Mode of Self-Organization

The second aspect that has been devised in systems science to formulate self-organization is the *feedback mechanism* in information processing. In the classical cybernetics, a feedback mechanism for error correction was thought first to measure the deviation from the desired value and direct a corrective action based thereon. However, it is not possible to correctly analyze the working of organisms or human societies by the error correction feedback alone, as seen with pattern recognition, learning and memory of human beings. When pattern recognition, learning or memory is implemented, system must be open not only for the environment but also for the inside of system itself. In addition, feedback mechanism should be discussed in relation to control hierarchy mentioned above, since there is a close correspondence between the two.

Structural control is a prior control to filter the social process to prevent it from becoming random by specifying action to be selected in advance. If the boundary maintaining function is performed only by this structural control, social system will become a simple state deterministic machine. This control does not have a feedback mechanism or memories except for those contained in system structure as self-evident ones.

According to economist Kenneth Boulding, there are four types of processes shown as time elapses, which are all included in the process of mankind, i.e., *random process, deterministic and mechanical process, purposive process* and *developmental process*.[45]

Random process is a process in which knowledge and records on the process do not enhance the probability to predict the future of the process at all. This unpredictability is based on the fact that information on the past does not have any contextual meaning of the course the process takes in the future. In other words, random process means the case where the process at the time t is independent of the processes before that. This process is not the object of control, which should be considered, while recognizing its randomness, as an unavoidable constraint in predicting future of the system.

Deterministic and mechanical process features that it correctly predicts state transition by recording a certain number of occurrences, on the assumption that the system, which is an object of consideration, does not change its structure over time. Therefore, it is presumed in advance that the aspect where stable state of the system is lost by disturbance can be neglected or excluded. In this situation, system is modeled not as an open system but as a closed system, which can be expressed by a state deterministic system. This system means a system having a characteristic to univocally determine the trajectory of its behavior when an initial state is given.

Purposive process is a process to correct action based on the goal to be attained. As seen with the feedback to pursue the goal, purposive control features that it compares the goal and the actual result of action, in order to modify and minimize the deviation from the goal. In purposive process, system corrects its action according to environmental changes or appropriately corresponds to unexpected changes. This is different from the case of deterministic and mechanical process. However, this correspondence is limited to changes in activity and presumes that existing structure does not change.

Developmental process is to direct system to a new organizing mode and complexity different from the existing ones. The novelty represents the disclosure of a cumulative novelty rather than that totally different from the past. Although existence of revolutionary processes that would overturn the existing process cannot be denied, a large change is normally an outcome of accumulated small changes.

Above four processes coexist in the actual social process. It should be confirmed, therefore, that they are analytically distinguished processes. Then, what relation exists between these processes and the social controls classified above?

Structural control that does not have a feedback mechanism works to enhance the random process to the deterministic and mechanical process. In contrast, optimum control performs error-correcting feedback to ensure the functional achievement, which is required to maintain system boundaries, under the contingency of action that cannot be dealt with by structural control. In short, social system overcomes infringement, environmental changes and uncertainty caused thereby by activity adjustment.

Social system incorporates information processing only when it has been modeled as having optimum control and error-correcting feedback. Information processing consists of three functions, i.e., (1) collecting information, (2) decision-making based thereon and (3) executing the action induced by decision-making. The first function (collecting information) is the cognitive aspect of system assigned to the detector. The second function (decision-making) is the evaluating aspect of system born by the selector. The third function (executing action) is the directive aspect, which the effector is in charge of. Optimum control collects information on the situation in and out of system and evaluates its conditions, thereby adjusting the system operation for improvement under the current structure. Adjustment of system activities by optimum control is equivalent, for example, to the adjustment of inequalities of service quality and apportionment of the cost therefor in the framework of social security system, which corresponds to what Cancian calls *change within system*.

Adaptive control to represent self-organization and its feedback mechanism are information processing related to Boulding's *developmental process*. The aim of this information processing is restructuring of the system, but not the activity adjustment observed in optimum control. Information on the structure is primary information that expresses the internal state of system. In contemporary societies where changes are a daily experience, what is important is the information processing to recognize self-evident and habitual structures in daily life as not self-evident.

Karl Deutsch, who introduced cybernetics into politics to formulate political information processing, considered a *feedback of consciousness* as the basis of self-organization. This feedback system recognizes and evaluates the massage on the state transition of the system or the secondary message. By having this function, system becomes highly autonomous and obtains self-innovative power.[46] He remarks that some organizations have a consciousness feedback mechanism to expedite changing the goal in its feedback processes, which sometimes brings about a fundamental change of the goal, and cites as an example the case where the Swedish political regime changed its goal from the pursuance of military power in the 17th century to that of social welfare in the 20th century.

By quoting the way of thinking by Deutsch, I refer to the feedback action in adaptive control as *feedback of consciousness* and information collected by this action as *structural message*. Then, information processing by self-organization is to recognize and evaluate the system structure, thereby performing function to intervene in structural changes. In relation to the control of social structure, adaptive control connotes optimum control. As a matter of course, therefore, it retrieves information on what is called social problems such as unexpected phenomena output from social process and action or conditions to arouse public interest. However, it is different from optimum control in the sense that it translates such information into a structural message and solves the problems at the structural level. To construct the self-organization theory, it is required to study the mode of such information processing more in detail. It is also indispensable to discuss the cause of change and process from its start to a settlement, or the pervasive effect and stabilizing mechanism of changes.

The history of modern society since the Industrial Revolution has been a process, where the self-conscious adaptive control becomes increasingly superior. This type control is developed, in the postindustrial and information societies in particular, where theoretical knowledge and technologies perform central functions. Systems engineering, a field where systems science is applied or implemented, has erected a milepost in system designs through integration of *measurement theory* and *control theory*. Social planning that designs changes for social development will solidify its ground by the social engineering of institutions through synthesizing *social indicator theory* and *policy science*. Social indicator theory is related to the measurement of structural message collected by the feedback of consciousness. Policy science is related to implement adaptive control in the form of intervention in structural changes. Synthesis of both theories into social planning theory is one of the most important subjects of the self-organization theory. In the next chapter, I will give a basis to the theory of social development based on the principles of self-organization and discuss planning and control of social development.

Chapter 2
Principles of Self-Organization and the Theory of Social Development

The theory of development has been improved mainly in economics. Economic development means that the output of domestic product increases as a result of the innovation of technologies and productivity. Economics is mainly interested in the output that is measurable in monetary term. Therefore, it tends to develop the theory of development from the quantitative viewpoint and relegate roles, institutions and other structural viewpoints. To make social development an object of study, it is required to keep in view the improvement of functional achievement through changing structure, or to study it from the quantitative and qualitative viewpoints. While succeeding the theory of functionalism in a critical manner, this chapter formulates the theory of social development from the viewpoint of self-organization and connects it with the theory of social planning. Self-organization referred to in this chapter means cybernetic self-organization, unless otherwise specified.

1 What is Social Development?

In sociology, social development generally refers to the fact that society shifts to a more desirable state by changing its structure. This represents a position to grasp social development from the two aspects, or the *change of social structure* and the *value orientation* as a more desirable state. However, attention must be paid to the latter aspect, or the value orientation, because it will potentially make value judgment creep in the concept of social development.

Definition of Social Development

In functionalism, social analysis is normally approached from two aspects, structure and function. The value orientation of society is assessed with increases in the *functional achievement*, which is a low level of value judgment. Functional achievement is a concept that expresses to what degree the existing system has solved system problems for it to continue. Social indicators contributing to the life and welfare, such as the levels of income, consumption, health, public safety, education, culture, living environment, labor, leisure and social security, are typical examples of functional achievement. By using this concept, it can be defined that the *social development is for society to increase the functional achievement through structural change*. For reference, the increase in the functional achievement without accompanying structural change is called social growth, which is distinguished from social development.

Considering social development with structural change and increase in functional achievement is more general than that of economic development. Economic development generally means the state where economic output (national income, GDP, etc.) increases as technological and institutional production methods change, with a focus on the increases in productivity by the innovation of technologies and institutions. The primary function of economy is to produce disposable goods required for social life and allocate them to different applications. Thus, the increase in the production power corresponds to the increase in functional achievement. Technological and institutional innovation is to introduce a new mode of productive activities into economic process, which leads to changes in social structure in the sense that the method of activity hitherto not used is newly organized and structuralized.

Improvement of functional achievement is multi-dimensional including that of economic achievement. Talcott Parsons, for example, views social system with the AGIL schema, where economy is positioned as a subsystem in charge of adaptation in the whole society. This sector of adaptive function (hereinafter referred to as function A) procures and provides various means required for social activities, or acquire and prepare instruments or means for goal attainment from the outer world. In a highly differentiated industrial society, function A is performed mostly by enterprises. In addition to this function, social system has political function to execute goal attainment of society (hereinafter referred to as function G), the integration function (hereinafter referred to as function I) to enhance social solidarity and the pattern maintenance or latency function (hereinafter referred to as function L) that executes tension management and socialization of members.[1]

To effectively promote goal attainment, the political function G adjusts collective efforts, as typically seen with the activity of the government to mobilize various resources to attain social goal. The sector of function I adjusts activities of different sectors so that they do not cause conflicts, obstruct or offset their efforts, thereby establishing cooperative relations. This adjustment is performed through setting a criterion to allocate resources and rewards distribution, supporting for politics and forming public opinions, in order to create solidarity between sectors working for social division of labor. As the sector that performs this function, Parsons cites "societal communities." This is a generalized concept to include concrete units such as voluntary associations, local communities and cultural organizations. The sector of function L ensures motivation to role activity by managing the tension that emerges in social system and internalizing social norms and values to members. Its concrete units are typically families, schools, and religious groups. Social development includes increases in the achievement of these functions and problem of the balance in between.

Modern economics tends to avoid the use of concept of structure as far as possible. In defining development, therefore, expressions of quantitative change and qualitative change are used in place of the increase in functional achievement (increase in output) and structural change (technological and institutional innovation). To correctly trace the theory of development, however, it is essential to prepare definite conceptual tools. Since the concepts of structure and function, among others, provide a framework indispensable in clarifying social phenomena, it is particularly important to improve the theory of development by using these concepts.

Structure and Functional Requisite

In sociology, method to analyze society from two aspects, structure and function, has been called structural-functional analysis. The postulation by this method is that *functional requisite* imposed on the system must appropriately be gratified for social system to be maintained. When this postulation is satisfied or the functional performance is ensured under ongoing structure, therefore, social system can continue to exist without changing. In case this postulation is not satisfied for some reason, however, the system stands on the verge of dissolution and is forced to change its structure as a result. This is the essential logic of social change in structural-functional analysis.[2] Therefore, the skeleton of social development theory is how to successfully connect structural change with the increase in functional achievement.

However, these two concepts cannot be connected so easily. Structural change premises that social system falls into functional disorder on one hand, and social development premises structural change on the other. This means that social development does not realize, unless the system falls into functional disorder. It is an extremely passive attitude, however, to expect that development realizes as functional disorder has taken place. In the first place, development is for the system to positively enhance its functional achievement irrespective of whether functional disorder occurs. Even if the functional requisite is gratified, social development will deserve its name only when the system causes social change to enhance functional achievement further. For this purpose, it is required to adopt player who causes social change without being satisfied at the status quo as the study object.

From the standpoint of social systems theory, this is to incorporate a sector that implements self-organization into it, or to build *self-organization layer* in the system which evaluates the system from the viewpoint of increases in functional achievement, determine the direction in which the system will proceed and change its structure. This self-organization layer is a comprehensive concept to include function of reformer in the theory of social movement, function of institutional innovation by administrative authorities and ability of entrepreneurs who perform organizational innovation. I believe that a theory of social development that really deserves its naming will be established, if a model of social system having a built-in self-organization layer is connected with functional analysis. In the following sections, therefore, I will clarify the basic logic of self-organization, digest it sociologically and try to improve the theory of social development.

2 Basic Logic of Self-Organization

In theorizing social development based on the self-organization theory, what should be done first is to confirm what self-organization and its logic are. This is not a concept devised in a specific scientific field, but an abstract one emerged from general system theory, logical and mathematical automata theory or control theory. Since it does not embody special conditions of individual sciences, it is the most important subject for the self-organization theory how to connect its logic with the conceptual device or analyzing frameworks of individual sciences.

Organization as Mapping

Therefore, we first discuss the concept of *organization* when self-organization is referred to. This concept has been used in wide ranges to indicate the organizations that are bureaucratic, corporate, religious, school-related, criminal, political, official, non-official, organic and mechanical. To make the concept of organization a theoretical one, however, a definite definition must be established.

According to Ross Ashby, theory of organization has a common point with the theory of mathematical function having two or more variables. Existence of organization between various variables is the same as the fact that *constraints* are in the product space as a combination of all relations logically taken by variables.[3] This means that restrictions exist so that some relations exist while others do not in a set of relations of variables. When this is applied to social system, interactions constituting the system are not random, but are relatively patterned under some constraints.

Where interactions are patterned, there is a structure. Thus, the essence of organization means the existence of structure. Self-organizing is to modify the structure or to newly perform structuration. In this sense, self-organization includes the logic of structural changes. Then, how is the system having a constraint or a structure expressed? To answer this question, it is required to fix a certain structure first and show the deterministic state of the system under that structure. It is a misunderstanding to think that flexibility of structure can be expressed analytically at the

2 Basic Logic of Self-Organization

very beginning. If flexibility is to be shown, there will be no alternatives than incorporating a sector to change the structure in the model.

Therefore, we express the system first keeping an eye on rigidity or regularity without considering uncertainty of the system. Suppose that the system is composed of variables $x_1, x_2, \ldots, x_n$, with the values taken by the variables, or the set of states, denoted by $X_1, X_2, \ldots, X_n$ ($x_{ik} \in X_i$) respectively. Then, the system is expressed as a proper subset X_s ($\subset X$) of the direct product space (set) $X = X_1 * X_2 * \ldots * X_n$ of $X_1, X_2, \ldots, X_n$.

The state where the system is a proper subset of the product set X means that specific relations can be specified between system variables $x_1, x_2, \ldots, x_n$ and that any variable cannot determine a state randomly or independently of others. More specifically, it means that some relations can be selected from the total set of logically possible relations. Suppose a taxation system composed of two variables, income and tax rate, with income having a domain from 0 to infinity and the tax rate from 0% to 60%. In this case, there are infinite combinations of income and tax rate as an infinite set of products. In actuality, however, certain relations are specified between income and tax rate, in that the tax rate is 37% for a yearly income amount of 18 million yen in Japan 2003, for example, which cannot be discounted to 20%. The tax rate is 20% for an income of four million yen per year. The product set between income and tax rate includes all combinations of the domains of these two variables. The taxation system (proper subset) is established by setting constraints on this set. Narrowing the product set to a proper subset is a constraint or a structure essential for the organization.

Then, how is this structure expressed? Generally speaking, the system as an organization is an open system to implement interactions not only between components, but also with the external world or the environment. To express the organization, therefore, it is required to consider a set (denoted by I) representing the input from external world, in addition to the set S ($= X_s; X_s \in X$) representing internal state, when the behavior of system is determined by the *mapping f* from the product set $I * S$ to the set S. In other words, the system existing under a state S_i takes an input I from the external world and changes to the state S_j after interactions within the system. What changes the state from S_i to S_j in this manner is the mapping f that determines how the interactions between variables are to be implemented.

According to Ashby, mapping f determines organization between different parts, which changes as f changes. "In other words, the possible organizations between the parts can be set into one-one correspondence with the set of possible mappings of $I \times S$ into S. Thus 'organization' and 'mapping' are two ways of looking at the same thing."[4] Mapping referred to here is a mathematical expression of the concept of structure now under consideration.

When the mapping f is regarded as a mathematical expression of system structure, structural change, which is a feature of self-organization, is a change in the mapping f, which means that the structure is not a constant but becomes a variable, or that the organization itself becomes a variable. Since regarding the system as a deterministic entity rejects that f changes depending on the state of the system, organization cannot be self-organizational in this sense.

However, self-organizational features can be observed even with machines that are a deterministic system. "Homeostat" can change its circuit by itself. Computers can write programs by themselves. Automaton can make and change machines by itself. These facts mean that the system must be supposed to start from a state, with the mapping f changing to g, for example, and experience a structural change. Then, what is the condition to make the change possible?

Enlargement of Self Concept

A fundamental feature of machines is that they can be *connected* with others or two or more machines can be combined to compose a machine, which is the condition to make self-organization possible. In this situation, the structural change can be formulated as a system expressed by S is connected with a different system α and S has a structure f first, which changes later to g, under a function $\alpha(t)$. In this manner, even a deterministic system that cannot inherently be self-organizational can be self-organizational when a different system is connected with.

> If the system is to be in some sense "self-organizing," the "self" must be enlarged to include this variable α, and, to keep the whole bounded, the cause of α's change must be in S (or α).
>
> Thus the appearance of being "self-organizing" can be given only by the machine S being coupled to another machine (of one part):

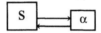

> Then the part S can be "self-organizing" within the whole $S + \alpha$.
>
> Only in this partial and strictly qualified sense can we understand that a system is "self-organizing" without being self-contradictory.[5]

To consider the system as self-organizational, the above requires (1) connecting a sector to perform special functions with the existing system and (2) a trial of *enlargement of self concept* through this connection.

Social system is an integrated whole, therefore it does not allow dismantling parts or connecting with others unlike machines. Since the system is an abstract model based on specific recognition, it does not represent actual world as it is. By using a new cognitive framework, it is possible to additionally extract factors that were not in system model in the past and connect them with the original system. In other words, it is possible with social system as well, to increase the order of cognitive framework for system recognition, thereby enlarging self concept and implementing system connection different from that of machines.

The cognitive framework of *system maintenance* in structural-functional analysis is to inspect functional validity of structure from the viewpoint of gratification of functional requisite or goal of the ongoing system. This leads to a proposition that the system is forced to undergo a structural change when it has fallen into functional disorder. Although this logic describes inevitability of structural changes to maintain the system, it does not include the logic to separately extract a sector

2 Basic Logic of Self-Organization   59

having a function to modify structure or restructure the system and connect it with the system in order to enlarge the self concept.

In contrast, cognitive framework of *system development* premises the existence of self-organization layer or a sector to evaluate, diagnose and modify the structure from the viewpoint of the increases in functional achievement of the system. Therefore, it is possible to connect self-organization layer α emerged from the cognitive framework of system development with system S modeled from the cognitive framework of system maintenance for enlargement of self concept.

If the feature of self-organization layer α is expressed in simple words, it is an exogenous factor to cause structural changes of social system S and simultaneously implement interaction by feedback with S. The fact that self-organization layer α is an exogenous factor means that structure of social system S is changed not by any factor existing in S, but by the factor α that works on S as an input. Since α receives feedback information from the social system, however, it is not a genuine exogenous factor that affects the system one-sidedly. As far as it performs interaction with social system, it is an endogenous factor in some sense. In this manner, self-organization layer acts following internal mechanism sometimes, and goes out of the system to evaluate and diagnose it at other times. In short, self-organization layer has a characteristic of compound eye to have visual fields inside and outside the social system, as a sector positioning not at an inner or exterior point, but at its boundary point.

The Second Feedback

Ashby developed discussions persistently with focusing on machines, which are the deterministic systems, and remarked that "machines develop a functional structure homologous with 'adaptive organisms' to the extent allowed by their scale and complexity."[6] A functional structure is an "organ" adaptive to the environment or self-organization layer referred to above. He calls the system that develops a functional structure homologous with "adaptive organisms" an "ultra-stable system" and defines it as follows.

> Two systems of continuous variables (that we called "environment" and "reacting part") interact, so that a primary feedback (through complex sensory and motor channels) exists between them. Another feedback, working intermittently and at a much slower order of speed, goes from the environment to certain continuous variables which in their turn affect some step-mechanisms, the effect being that the step-mechanisms change value when and only when these variables pass outside given limits. The step-mechanisms affect the reacting part; by acting as parameters to it they determine how it shall react to the environment.[7]

Here, important characters of self-organization are described exactly to the point. To promote discussions along social system theory, we read the "reacting part" as social system S and the "step mechanism" that changes mode of reaction of the "reacting part" as self-organization layer α. In this case, the first feedback

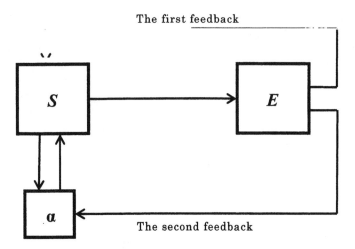

Fig. 2.1 Two levels feedback in self-organization system

in normal sense exists between the system S and the environment E, with mechanism of purposive control working to pursue the goal. In the enlarged social system $S + \alpha$ as a self-organization system, however, the second feedback exists between the environment and self-organization layer α. Self-organization layer α evaluates and changes structure based on the second feedback and feedback from the social system S, thereby trying to increase functional achievement.

Figure 2.1 shows the above feedback mode observed with self-organization system. The second feedback that increases functional achievement through structural changes corresponds to *adaptive control* discussed in previous chapter and makes system structure a control object. In contrast, the first feedback adjusts deviations from the goal value by activity change. The feedback that ensures functional achievement with changing activities corresponds to *optimal control* and makes activities an control object.[8]

Self-organization system changes its structure and improves functional achievement through above two-stage feedback control. A model equipped with only the feedback function in normal sense without a built-in self-organization layer α can effectively analyze only *structurally stable system* that performs optimal modification of activity under the ongoing structure and reaches a new equilibrium state.[9] To assume society as a structurally stable system is to assume that it is controllable against any factor that disturbs equilibrium. Of course, uncontrollable states often occur in actuality. In such states, this model cannot perform effective analysis, but only describes the crisis of system collapse.

In contrast, self-organization system recognizes structural stability only in part, in the following two meanings. First, when a critical state exists where the system cannot return to equilibrium by control action under the ongoing structure and will dissolve if abandoned, the step mechanism works to change structures such as control rules and evaluation criteria to recover new equilibrium. Second, even when it is in the state of stable structure with equilibrium maintained, the system pursues higher functional achievement to create new goals or enhance them increasingly to cause structural changes. The first structural change is a passive adaptive control, while the second is a positive adaptive control based on the capabilities of changing goals and self-innovation. This positive adaptive control is appropriate as a basis of social development.

Through work to strictly pursue the fundamental logic of self-organization above, I have discussed conditions to model the self-organization system. When these widely ranged discussions are summarized, it is evident that the focus of self organization studies is on the problem of system structure and control. What should be done next, therefore, is to study structure and control of social system from the viewpoint of development theory. In Chap. 1, I tried to position structure with control from the viewpoint of cybernetics. In the following sections, we discuss it sociologically more in detail.

3 Structure and Control of Social System

There are two meanings that can be distinguished for self-organization.[10] First is self-organization as a change for mutually independent parts to connect with each other in order to form relations, or a change from an unorganized state to an organized state. Second is self-organization to change from an organization to a better organization, when it is advantageous to change the state of ongoing organization in order to perform functions more efficiently.

When a whole society is the study object, self-organization of the second meaning is focused on, as it is not pragmatic to assume an entirely unorganized state. Self-organization of the second meaning is nothing but the social development. It also includes self-organization of the first meaning, because changes to a better organization accompany the introduction of new system elements by innovation or development of new contrivances without exception and constitute an unorganized state with existing elements.

Structure or Rigid Control

When the mode of relatively patterned interactions in a social system is extracted, there exists a structure. We define the characteristics to cause these relatively patterned interactions a social structure.[11] That interaction is patterned means that it is not implemented at random, but a rule (norm) on actions is institutionalized. Institutionalization of a rule on actions means that it is accepted by the members of society, which sociologically indicates a state where the rule is internalized into members' personality and provided with legitimacy, with a criterion of sanction established against actions to violate the rule.

Interaction means a process for the members of society to enter into relations with others by using various instruments, and provide others with the opportunities for needs gratification and accept the same in return from others. Therefore, institutionalization of actions means that the mode of mutually expected actions is institutionalized between people and a mechanism to adjust mutual activities has been formed. The mode of action regulated by institutionalized rule (norm) on actions is called *role*. Expectation by others or society for role is called role expectation. Consequently, role is a characteristic to bring about the mode of relatively patterned interactions and *role arrangement* as a construction of various roles is the first characteristic of social structure.

Another characteristic of social structure is *allocation rule* on how to allocate limited personnel and social resources among various roles. Social system ensures functional achievement by executing various roles. The role is a symbol to specify what is expected, what must be done and what should not be done. It is not specified, however, who takes the role and how to allocate resources and means required for executing the role. In other words, it is sort of a material particle without mass in physics, which does not provide social activities as a momentum. Working of the society becomes possible only when *personnel allocation* and *resource allocation* have been performed for the role.

To summarize above discussions, it can be concluded that social structure is a mechanism to control social activities by role arrangement and rules to allocate personnel and social resources thereto. As the role arrangement controls how the social relations should be, so the allocation rules control personnel and social resources as a vehicle for social relations.[12]

Now, we call the operation of social structure as a control mechanism *structural control*, which expresses that control is incorporated institutionally in social system. In economics, there is a concept called a built-in stabilizer that expresses an institutionally created financial system to automatically suppress changes in effective demand and national income to some extent. Typical examples of structural control are the withholding tax at source and the progressive tax in taxation system. The *Elementary Structures of Kinship* in uncivilized societies, which was discovered by Claude Lévi-Strauss, represents the mode to allocate women as scarce goods among different tribes based on their marriage rules. The marriage rules function to create kinship relations and strengthen the solidarity between tribes, representing a typical case of structural control of personnel allocation. In this manner, structural control regulates the allocation of social resources and personnel, entrusting it with social norms and institutions, in order to ensure the functional performance required for existence of the system. Therefore, it is sort of rigid control, which is stereotyped against the changes inside and outside the system.

Hot Society and Optimal Control

Actual society is not a cold society that will function by structural control alone. In particular, industrial society is a *hot society* where optimal control and adaptive control are performed to aim at ensuring functional achievement efficiently. Optimal control is tried for a situation that cannot be coped with by structural control and adaptive control or *control of controls* is applied to control the structural control and the optimal control.[13] Then, how are these controls possible?

In the above, I defined social structure as a characteristic to cause relatively patterned interactions. The relativity of this patternization shows that structural control is not rigid but has room of uncertainty. This uncertainty implies (1) possibility of discretional activities to a certain extent under the ongoing structure and (2) possibility of structural changes. The former uncertainty premises optimal control to correct activities under a certain structure, while the latter uncertainty assumes adaptive control accompanying structural changes.

The problem of optimal control is to select means input and adjust the amount of input to maximize or minimize the value of objective function under given constrained conditions. When this is applied to social system, it means adjusting the allocation of personnel and social resources under certain role arrangement and allocation rules. The role is performed by personnel having an adequate ability and functional contribution is outputted when social resources are allocated thereto. It is possible, therefore, to regard the role as a type of conversion mechanism. Since the role as this conversion mechanism is executed by real human beings, different personnel have different capabilities of contribution. Adjustment of personnel allocation is to change role players through reshuffling.

As optimal control assumes that the ongoing structure remains unchanged, reshuffling is implemented within the framework of social system that prescribes allocation rules. Typical examples are reshuffling of personnel within the frameworks of representative, bureaucratic and market systems, such as changing Diet members after the dissolution of Diet and implementation of general election, promoting employees based on their performance and reallocating labor to cope with changes in supply and demand. The government, enterprises, markets and different groups in communities adopt different rules on personnel allocation. However, reshuffling of personnel in these sectors is summed up to constitute the reallocation of personnel in whole society. Similarly, in the case of wealth, authority, knowledge, prestige and other social resources input into the role, the resources allocated in different sectors are totaled to make resources input in whole society. When society is viewed as a whole, therefore, it can be said that there exists a huge control apparatus to select and implement the optimal input in pursuing functional achievement. In short, social system is a huge-scale optimal control apparatus embracing certain role arrangement and operates it to overcome environmental constraints in order to realize functional achievement.

Structural Instability and Conflict between Requisites

When the social system implements efficient functional achievement and gratifies functional requisites, it is in the state of *structurally stable* equilibrium, where the term structurally stable means a state where no force works to cause structural changes. However, social system cannot always succeed in implementing control in this manner. Even if efficient functional achievement has been realized, social system sometimes does not reach the level to gratify functional requisites, when it falls in the state of structurally unstable equilibrium and accumulates a force to cause structural changes.

However, structural instability is not the same as structural change. To make a structural change start, it is required to clarify what part of the ongoing structure has a problem and what the problem is, and then design and execute a changing program. After structural change, it should also be evaluated and inspected whether the functional requisites have been satisfied. Even if a force has been accumulated to trigger a structural change, however, no changes will take place in actuality, unless self-organization layer is built in the system to implement such work. In this situation, structural instability remains a necessary condition for structural changes. In the conventional structural-functional analysis, this was not distinctly clarified. Instead, the non-gratification of functional requisites was illogically considered as the occurrence of a structural change. This is the reason why structural instability does not successfully connect with the self-organization theory.

The concept of equilibrium referred to below must be discussed now in relation to structural-functional analysis. In using the concept of equilibrium, variables or indexes that balance with each other should definitely be specified, in such a manner as what is balanced with what. Typical examples of variables or indexes to be specified in classical mechanics are the action and reaction of force, and those in economics are the volume of demand of goods to maximize the utility function of consumers and the volume of supply to maximize the benefit function of producers. The concept of equilibrium used here is defined for functional requisites that should be gratified by social system. In other words, society has not only the economic function but also multi-dimensional functions such as to deal with tension management, ensure social integration and develop motivation of members. Therefore, equilibrium among these functions must be considered.

Functional achievement that should be realized by social system is originally multi-dimensional as seen with the AGIL schema referred to above. Therefore, system evaluation cannot be measured with a one-dimensional scalar measure (as a directionless quantity). Thus, a multi-dimensional vector evaluation measure shall be used instead, together with a vector objective function. Generally speaking, vector objective function does not perform total ordering (linear ordering) unlike the one-dimensional scalar function and causes a partial order relation. We take the AGIL functional requisite as an example and consider two vector solutions, one being superior in regard to the functional requisite A (economic achievement) and the other being superior in regard to the functional requisite I. Then, partial order relation imposes a condition that cannot determine hierarchical ranking between these two solutions.[14]

3 Structure and Control of Social System

In this situation, the vector solution of functional achievement is given as a set of solutions that are not inferior to any other solution under the partial order relation or as a set of Pareto optimal solutions. When social system reaches the Pareto optimal state in this sense, it has realized efficient functional achievement under the ongoing structure. This is a state where social system should decrease other functional achievements, if it tries to increase a specific functional achievement, or a state where the gratification of various functional requisites is at equilibrium. This is the meaning of the equilibrium of social system.[15]

Generally speaking, there are plural cases of such equilibrium state. In any case, however, when at least one functional requisite is not gratified sufficiently, there is a sector that lacks *functional validity* in the ongoing structure. In this state, it causes tension. This tension is not generated by contingency or an emergency state, but by the existing role arrangement or allocation rules. In this sense, therefore, it is called the *state of structural tension*.[16] The state where tension is accumulated as energy to trigger a structural change is the state of *structural instability*. Therefore, structurally unstable state of equilibrium expresses a state that connotes tension due to non-gratification of requisites, despite that the social system has implemented the optimal personnel and social resources allocation under the ongoing role arrangement and allocation rules.

In the period of high economic growth, for example, Japan followed a process in which higher economic achievement was attained in the Pareto optimal solution set of equilibrium. Therefore, other functional achievements were victimized to accumulate various tensions, such as those seen in community movements pursuing new social solidarity, distrust in politics, collapse of GNP adherence and antipollution campaigns, which emerged as the opportunity of needs gratification in non-economic fields decreased as a result of lowered social integration, political and latent functions.

To shift in the Pareto optimal solution set to different positions with priority placed on economics is a development as far as from the viewpoint of economic monism. From the standpoint to consider the society as a system having multi-dimensional functions, however, it is by no means a development as a whole, as there are no hierarchical relations between various states of equilibrium contained in the Pareto optimal solution set. To carry logic to extremes, the high economic growth of Japan was attainted as the multi-dimensionality of society was reduced to the monism of economics. It was sort of a visionary growth, therefore. For the social growth or development to be acknowledged, society must depart from the present state of equilibrium and shift to a more desirable state of equilibrium at least without losing any functional achievement realized in the previous state of equilibrium.

In the above, I formulated the concept of structure sociologically, and discussed optimal control, stability/instability of structure and the equilibrium of social system based thereon. What should be done next is to scrutinize these concepts and analytical framework in relation to self-organization layer and adaptive control and to discuss the skeleton of theory of social development.

4 Conditions for Social Development and Adaptive Control

The essence of social development is the active control to perform structural changes to enhance various functional achievements one after another without being satisfied with the status quo. This means that society is not pleased with the structurally stable state of equilibrium, but departs therefrom to grope for a more desirable equilibrium. For social development, therefore, the value or needs that esteem such attempt must be accumulated first of all in the system.

The equilibrium state of social system means that gratification of various functional requisites is in the Pareto optimal state under the present structure. It is not possible, therefore, to try to depart from this state or shift to a more desirable state with the present structure maintained. Thus, society cannot help but undergo a structural change. For the society to develop, therefore, it must have an attitude routinely prepared to accept structural innovation with the value or needs. Self-organizing actions start with such attitude formation as a prerequisite. Therefore, what becomes a problem first is how the self-organization layer relates with such value and needs.

Value and Needs: Identification of Development Vector

Value is an equivocal concept. Sociologically, it is an idea of the desirable state of society cherished by its members and an element of symbol system shared as a criterion for the selection of social goal.[17] In contrast, *needs* are the energy that motivates the action of individuals, which are not dissolved simply at the individual level, but provides energy to express intentions to require the opportunity for needs gratification received from society through their contribution to the system. In short, value provides a criterion for the selection of course (goal) for social system, while needs work as a motive force.

Therefore, value or needs become a constituent element of *development vector* that displays in what direction and to what extent the social system shall desirably attain the functional achievement. Japan in the high economic growth period, for example, is characterized by the development vector to enhance opportunity for needs gratification in the direction to endlessly increase economic achievement. After the high economic growth, however, development vector gave way to the clamor to improve social welfare and strengthen social solidarity. For a society to develop, it is required first to identify the social development vector corresponding to changes in value and/or needs. Therefore:

> (1) The work of self-organization layer to induce social development is to receive the information on changes in value and/or needs of members and their speed, identify development vector and create a future image of society.

4 Conditions for Social Development and Adaptive Control

Then, how is development vector defined? In discussing the equilibrium of social system in previous section, I stated that functional achievement to be realized is multi-dimensional and society is a multi-purpose system. A multi-purpose system means that the objective function or the evaluation scale is not one-dimensional but is given in a vector form and that the number of vector elements is the same as that of functional achievements. In addition, vector becomes an indicator value having direction and magnitude in the multi-dimensional space. Therefore, development vector becomes a concept to specify the achievement to be enhanced, together with its degree of enhancement, among various functional achievements that have been realized and shown in the present state of equilibrium. In this situation, value provides a criterion to decide the ratios of different functional achievements to be enhanced or the direction of development. An example of this is to concentrate on the improvement of welfare with economic growth rate suppressed to zero or attain a welfare level twice as high as that in the past with economic growth rate kept low. The needs of members are to determine to what degree the attainment is required in that direction.

In the social systems theory that starts at action and considers using it to bridge systems theory, the bases of value and needs are in cultural system and personality system, respectively. In parallel with social system, these systems constitute a general system of action, which is a relatively demarcated subsystem.[18] Therefore, value and needs are environmental factors in the action system. In short, social system has an environment in the action system (internal environment) in addition to the environment in normal sense (external environment).

I described above that self-organization layer is a sector located at the boundary area of social system and implements second feedback to and from the environment. Self-organization layer collects information on the changes in value, needs and their speed through the second feedback. In this manner, self-organization layer monitors how the formation of value progresses, clarifies changes in value for the members and accelerates value formation, thereby acquiring knowledge in advance on the direction of social development on one hand, and collects changes in requirement level for the opportunity for needs gratification and determines the realization level of functional achievement on the other. In this manner, it identifies the development vector.

Development vector is a future image drawn with value and needs but it is a mere sketch showing what innovation is acceptable. It is so-to-speak a track along which society proceeds. Social system is an action system based on the goal distinguished from value and needs.[19] To put the first step along the wide view of development vector, therefore, it is required to input a goal in concrete terms. In other words:

> (2) The second work of self-organization layer is to modify or change the existing social goals to a new one along the track of development vector and input it into social system.

Role Differentiation and Institutionalization of Allocation Rules

When a goal is input, the system falls into a structurally unstable state, as present structure (role arrangement and allocation rules) cannot attain it. In this state, the necessity of innovation increases for the social system to become a resource conversion device with a higher capability for performance. Although the term "innovation of resource conversion device" strongly smacks of a technology-based principle associated with images of productive function and technological innovation in economics, it is an innovation of role and institution sociologically. Therefore, requirement for innovation means that formation of new *role expectation* progresses among members responding to the plea to innovate the ongoing role arrangement.

Role expectation is to expect actions required for social units at special positions in society, such as enterprises, administrative organizations and educational institutions. Therefore, formation of new role expectation means that requirements become stronger to change the mode of conventional role action and acquire a new one. This is equal to differentiation of a new role in the conventional role arrangement. Differentiation of a new role will not necessarily be sufficient, if role expectation alone exists. Role expectation is nothing but expecting actions. To actualize it, however, an allocation rule must be institutionalized to ensure human and material resources required for its execution.

Social expectation required for new role differentiation does not have definite contexts at the beginning, but it normally accompanies ambiguities. An indefinite role prescription makes adaptation to the role insufficient and acquisition of necessary output difficult. When new role expectation is imposed on an enterprise, for example, such as responsibility for society or equal participation by men and women, it is difficult for an enterprise to adapt itself to the role, unless what role performance it means is clarified in concrete terms. In other words:

(3) The third work of self-organization layer is to differentiate the role required for the attainment of a new social goal, clarify role prescription and institutionalize allocation rule to ensure the personnel and social resources required for role performance.

To perform new role requires knowledge, technologies and human resources having appropriate capabilities. It is needless to say, therefore, that the ability development and resource exploitation are essential for social development. In return, such development sometimes triggers new role differentiation or institutionalization of an allocation rule. This means that (1) role arrangement, (2) allocation rule and (3) personnel and social resources that characterize social structure are mutually dependent, making it impossible to univocally determine the change in which of these three concepts is the determinant factor for social development. To deal with social development, therefore, it is required to address the interrelations between these three factors. Even if this situation is taken into consideration, however, it may be allowed to explain social development by focusing on a specific factor. To do so, I adopt role here for the reasons that it is an important factor to gratify functional requisites and that I intend to consider social development in relation to their gratifications.

Control of Structural Incongruence

The third function of self-organization layer is to perform structural changes that express the process of adaptive control based on the second feedback. However, it is rarely the case that self-organization layer succeeds in structural innovation by implementing a trial only once. Although changes in the environmental condition are conceivable as one of the causes, a more important one is a problem generated within the system. As roles and allocation rules are mutually dependent, a change that takes place at a part inevitably affects other parts. Therefore, it is not always the case that an achievement along development vector is realized, but deviation from the track is normally generated. To correct it, a control is required to congruently embed a new allocation rule or role arrangement in the ongoing structure.

If new role differentiation and institutionalization of allocation rule are thought to be the first stage of adaptive control, above control problem is the work to incorporate newly formulated roles and allocation rule into existing ones and adjust the conflict and discrepancy between roles and between allocation rules. This constitutes the second stage of adaptive control.

Regarding the pervasive effect of newly introduced structural characteristics, it is effective to analyze it based on the *structurally indispensable requisite*. A structurally indispensable requisite, which is sometimes called the requisite for compatibility, requires that conditions imposed by some structural characteristics are congruent with those imposed by other structural characteristics.[20] If the role types that characterize the occupational structure of industrial society are given, for example, most of the role types that have supported kinship system will lose its adequacy. As a matter of fact, conventional extended families forced to undergo a change to nuclear families composed of husband and wife and their children as industrialization progressed. In this process, adjustment was implemented to make the old structure adapt itself to a new structure. The same logic applies not only to large-scale structural changes such as industrialization, but also basically to partial structural changes. Simultaneous existence of incompatible structural characteristics is an obstacle for functional performance, as far as structure is a device to realize functional achievement.

Now, we call the obstacle generated by non-gratification of structurally indispensable requisites a *structural conflict*. Then, two types of structural conflict are distinguished. One is the *conflict of role structure* caused by role arrangement and the other is the *conflict of allocation structure* caused by allocation rules.

The conflict of role structure expresses the state where a new role is not compatible with other roles, or the performance of a new role obstructs the performance of other roles, with functional contribution by the new role offsetting that by others so that goal is not attained. As a problem of social structure, Parsons cited two aspects, integrative and allocative, and discussed the conflict of role structure referred to above as role disintegration.[21] Role disintegration is the state where role arrangement does not function well or functional performance is not appropriately ensured, which causes conflict of role structure.

In contrast, conflict of allocation structure expresses the state where the allocation rule institutionalized as a result of new role formation conflicts with the existing one and personnel and resources required for role performance are not appropriately obtained. At the initial stage of industrialization, for example, conflicts were observed between the ascription/particularism principle allocation rule on occupational roles and the achievement/universalism principle allocation rule due to specialization and bureaucratization.[22] Another example is a situation where the allocation rule of achievement principle, on which priority is placed for the purpose of economic growth, makes it difficult to ensure social resources and personnel required for creating family ties, enhancement of community consciousness and other measures to enhance social solidarity. As far as functional achievement to be realized by social system is multi-dimensional, there always exists a case where the allocation rule applied on a preferential basis to enhancing a specific achievement conflicts with the allocation rule to realize other achievement. The control purpose of change is to adjust new and existing structural characteristics and try to ensure structural congruence, thereby aiming at solving these conflicts. Although conflicts that occur between the allocation rule and role arrangement are logically conceivable, we continue discussions on the assumption that optimal allocation rule has been determined to perform a particular role.

The conflicts of role structure and allocation structure feature that the causes are (1) immanent for the structures themselves and (2) mismatching between roles and allocation rules, with functional performance not appropriately attained as a result. This means that structures are not congruently constructed. Therefore, we call the social state that generates these conflicts the state of *structural incongruence*, and the innovation to a state where necessary achievements are ensured through the solution of conflicts *structural harmonization*.[23] In this respect, structural harmonization becomes a process of adaptive control that is indispensable for social development. Therefore:

(4) The fourth work of self-organization layer is to control structural incongruence caused by new role formation and institutionalization of allocation rule and to direct social system toward structural harmonization.

Adaptive control toward structural harmonization is represented by the modification of role prescription, abolition of unnecessary roles and adjustment of allocation rules. This function eventually resolves itself into changing the conventional mode of action and establishing a new one. Since the final units of actions are individual members, structural harmonization is eventually to perform control so that the actions of members converge into a new mode of action, when the disturbing factors for control purpose are deviance and what is called anomie, such as the resistance and defending behavior of members who cannot adapt themselves to the new mode of action and advocators of vested rights and interests. These disturbing factors cause various problems in social life, such as those of unemployment due to technological innovation, medical service and pension for aged people, juvenile delinquency, which are often referred to as a social problem.

Embedding of Amplifying Feedback

An equilibrium state that deserves development is brought about by adaptive control aiming at structural harmonization. However, developmental phenomenon includes increases of continuous achievement that do not end in goal attainment only once. Therefore, a system embedded with a development vector must have the operation to accelerate this continuous process. In other words:

> (5) The fifth work of self-organization layer is not to constantly stabilize the system by goal attainment, but to input a new goal along the track of development vector and trigger amplifying feedback for goal attainment.

This *amplifying feedback* shifts the social system again from structurally stable state to that of structural instability and accumulates the force to cause a new structural change. In this manner, social system reciprocates between the states of equilibrium and nonequilibrium in a ceaseless structural change to enhance functional achievement. Of course, the amplifying feedback for goal attainment is a challenge for a new possibility and an investment action. An investment action always accompanies risk, without which the way toward development will not be opened. Since social development is eventually to control external environment and expand the opportunity to gratify diversified needs of members, the work of self-organization layer described above is to enhance control ability of social system against various environmental constraints.

Generally speaking, the work of the system to succeed in control of the environment and attain effective results is to decrease the uncertainty of results caused by environmental constrains and ensure the output required for goal attainment. For this purpose, there are no alternatives for the system than increasing its variety of the measures against external disturbance and decreasing the variety of environmental disturbance. In any event, however, the policy should eventually resolve itself to enhancing control ability against the environment. Therefore, it is a prerequisite condition for social development to refine the system structure as a control device.

5 Application to the Theory of Social Planning

Theory of social development is closely related to that of planning. Five workings of self-organization layer are to formulate the innovative actions for its own structure and method of functional performance, which are also to plan and control social changes. In this section, therefore, I apply above discussions to the theory of social planning.

Planning and Control of Social Change

Robert Mayer defined social planning as a plan of social changes and tried to theorize it from the standpoint of structural-functional analysis.[24] He constructed the planning of change from three aspect (1) social problems, (2) structural phenomena and (3) intervention means into structural changes. This is to intentionally try changes, which is one of the work categories inevitable for social development.[25]

The first item "social problems" is to constitute actions and conditions to raise public concern among people in some form or other, which is represented by the phenomena to make dependent variables in the planning of changes, such as poverty, crimes, discrimination and poor living conditions. The second item "structural phenomena" consists of such aspects characterizing social structure as roles, statuses and personnel, which are phenomena adopted as the object of operation by planners in solving social problems. They are at the position of intervening variables in the framework of planned changes. In contrast, the third item "intervention means into structural changes" is a control means in social relations used to change structural phenomena that are regarded as independent variables. Thus, the problem of planning changes is composed of two series, i.e., the work (1) to translate social problems (dependent variables) into structural phenomena (intervening variables) and (2) to closely examine conceivable and appropriate methods as an intervening means into structural phenomena (independent variables).

In short, the point of Mayer's aim is summarized as a remark that social problems are translated into structural phenomena and solved by structural changes. Based on this point, he addressed a case study of city communities and tried to generalize it in a middle range. However, his point is greatly suggestive in conceptualizing a more generalized theory of planned changes, because the work to translate social problems into a structural phenomenon can be regarded as the problem of the second feedback that characterizes self-organization. In addition, social problems, a concept of middle range, can be repositioned as the *system problems* in the general system of actions.

Therefore, we start discussions from the work to generalize social problems as system problems. Social problems express that actions or conditions to inspire public interest in some form or other have actualized, having tension that cannot be left unattended. From the standpoint of viewing society at structural and functional levels, the existence of such tension means that an obstacle has occurred in functional achievement required for system maintenance, since a state that cannot appropriately be controlled under the ongoing structure has emerged. Furthermore, this state means that disturbance has occurred in the social expectation indispensable for the crystallization of social structure. Social expectation is the integrated element of needs disposition of people and cultural value orientation on the aspect of mutual interaction. Therefore, occurrence of disturbance in the social expectation means that a change has occurred in needs disposition and/or value orientation. Thus, change of needs disposition in personality system and those of value orientation in cultural system can be cited as the most common source of social tension.

The structural characteristics, such as role arrangement and allocation rules of personnel and social resources, are a factor to crystallize the social expectation. Therefore, non-preparation of structural characteristics for changes in the social expectation causes an obstacle in structural control aiming at functional achievement and subsequently generates tension.

To avoid positioning tension in a passive manner, it is effective to define social tension as a deviation from the existing value orientation and needs disposition. Tension is generated not only when a state to worsen the status quo has occurred, but also when an attempt is made to lead the status quo to a better state through creative activities. The expression of social planning conceives a desirable society in the future in its background and assumes involvement in an active society to attain it purposively. The tension caused by the fact that direction of desirable social state is different from that of the present state actualizes as a social problem or a social movement. This is typically represented by community organizing movements to enhance social solidarity through participation, trends to require improvement of social welfare and security, various movements to call for the social responsibility of enterprises and women's liberation movements aiming at their social advancement. Heated and ideological arguments are often implemented on these movements, trends and campaigns. For the insistence in these augments to be accepted by society, however, discussion should be promoted from the comments at tensional dimension to the design problem at structural dimension.

We specifically use the term *planning of change* to indicate the process from the social tension dimension to design problem at structural dimension, and the term *control of change* to refer to the aspect of control process against various disturbances generated in the process after a change is introduced into society until it pervades and stabilizes. Planning generally contains both of these two aspects. As seen in the expressions "a plan in the air" or "a plan on the desk," plans designed in advance encounter various obstacles and resistance during the implementation process. This normally requires modification or adjustment of plans in some form. If modification or adjustment is not implemented properly, plans will not be accepted by society. To emphasize the importance of this aspect in particular, I dare separate control of change from planning of change.

Making of Cognitive Schema for Change

The work to plan a social change and embed it in the ongoing society is an action of investment into society or an institutional investment. This requires the work to minimize uncertainty by gathering correct information on the conditions inside and outside society.

For planning of change, the important activity to gather information is first to grasp information on the changes in cultural value orientation, which is a general source of social tension and those in the needs disposition of members. This is because planning of change inevitably requires information to determine the *direction* of change and that on the conditions of *motivation* to drive that change. As mentioned before, value is a symbolic element that is shared as a useful criterion when selecting a specific option from conceivable alternatives and a factor to define the direction of social change. In contrast, needs disposition expresses what opportunity for needs gratification people are interested in and a factor to compose motivation against social changes.

The second information gathering activity, which is also important for planning of change, is to know what expectation is being formed in the society as value orientation and needs disposition change. It is difficult to directly observe the social expectation that is newly being formed. Since structural characteristics to realize such expectation is not prepared in the ongoing social structure, disturbance is generated in some form or other in expectation system and actions emerge to pursue the gratification of needs, which is different from and incompatible with that obtained from the present society. In other words, social problems or movements that cannot help but arouse public concern appear. Therefore, information on the new social expectation will be obtained by the work to systematically collect and analyze the information on social problems and movements that inspire public concern.

The third information gathering activity is to know how much functional achievement has been realized under the present social structure. Although it is difficult to implement this activity separated from the second one, these two should be distinguished from each other analytically, because the third one is related to the social output information with present structure assumed, while the second one is to gather information on the gap between social output under the new structure and that under the present structure. The third one should be emphasized in particular, because it makes an evaluating criterion for the planning of change.

Above three information gathering activities express the second feedback that is indispensable for self-organization, because they are to make a *cognitive schema* of changes with the focus placed on the validity of structure and its refining. When an attempt is made to consider function of self-organization shown by adaptive control from the aspect of information processing, these information gathering activities are equivalent to *detector* in the theory of communication and express a cognitive aspect of self-organization.

There are normally two more aspects in information processing. One is *selector* for decision-making based on the cognitive schema. The other is *effector* to execute the option selected by decision-making. Selector in self-organization has a function to set the goal for changes and propose a structure design as a means necessary therefor. In contrast, effector has a function to embed the designed structure in present society and make changes executed. The former is evaluative aspect of self-organization and the latter is directive aspect.

Structure Design

The function of selector is to identify changing direction of the system, confirm functional attainment whose realization is desired by social expectation and input a goal to fill the gap with present functional attainment based on the cognitive schema obtained by the activity of detector. The goal input aiming at social development premises the functional achievement that cannot be realized by the allocation rules or role arrangement of the ongoing structure. As a means for goal attainment, therefore, a *structure design* toward changes should be presented.

Structure design includes three problems, i.e., those on (1) role composition, (2) allocation of personnel to perform role and (3) allocation of social resources required for role performance. Structure design is rarely conducted by a single role design, but normally with the institution to have fabricated and integrated plural roles into a complex as a unit. In the problem of role formation in structure design, therefore, there are two problems, (1) setting role type that contributes to functional achievement adopted as a goal and (2) design of role arrangement to appropriately fabricate and connect roles so that they properly mesh with each other.

The setting of role type is to clarify role expectation and rights and duties for roles. In contrast, design of role arrangement is to integrate roles so that compatibility between roles is ensured. Allocation problems of personnel and resources to roles are to ensure personnel required for operating the institution as a role complex and procure resources. This is also a problem to make role taker learn and internalize role expectation so that the role fits with capability and needs of him and motivate him for performance by reward management, thereby ensuring commitment to the role. Therefore, allocation rule of personnel and resources should be designed also from the viewpoint of acquiring ability required for role performance and motivation therefor.

Implementation and Control of Change

The subject next to the setting of goal change and structure design is a method to effectively implement the draft of designed structure change. An issue of major concern in drafting process of the plan is to pursue a structure design that is most appropriate to attain the change set as a goal. Problem in executing the plan dealt with in this process is only to discuss the possibility of plan, but not to determine a concrete or practical method or procedure for implementation. What addresses this subject is the effector function of self-organization.

Implementation of the plan is to start action to embed designed structural characteristics into the ongoing structure, which is exceedingly a problem of policy.[26] As a basic method to create policies, Charles Lindblom distinguished four concepts. They are administrative coordination, legislation, judicial decision and civil pressure.[27] On the ground that these methods of creating policies resemble the means to intervene in structural changes, Mayer generalized intervention means included in nine case studies and cited five concepts, public expenditure and political power added with the first three concepts by Lindblom. He also remarked that it was more appropriate to call civil pressure, which was not included in the case studies, social movement.[28]

In the background of this discussion, there is the standpoint of Mayer that planning of structural change is not necessarily limited to political intervention by the administrative authorities. For this reason, he used concept of intervention means into structural changes without using the term of policy. This idea is approvable, as self-organization is a comprehensive concept that includes social movements and the function of administrative authorities to innovate institutions. However, there is room for contrivance in regard to the types of means to intervene in structural changes, because the classification by Mayer is a generalization of empirical cases having duplicated contents and, therefore, it does not satisfy the conditions of typology sufficiently. As Mayer himself adopts structural-functional method, it is required to present an axis of classification from this standpoint in order to maintain theoretical congruence. I do not have enough time to systematically deal with this problem, but the following method is conceivable as a solution for contrivance.

It is to reinterpret the schema of four functional requisites (AGIL) jointly devised by Parsons and Robert Bales from the viewpoint of self-organization. In structural-functional analysis, this schema is the typified functional requisites that must be gratified by the system to maintain itself, which represents a standpoint to regard the four functional requisites as an object hypothesized in the system.[29] However, this is only appropriate to formulate the social system at self-stability level. To formulate it at self-organization level, higher order recognition is required for the object at self-stability level to change to a means. Therefore, the problem of requisite gratification can be regarded as a means to guide changes at the level of planning change, when the characteristics of each of four functional requisites (AGIL) can be positioned as a strategic factor to trigger a structural change. Therefore, we adopt here generalized symbolic media in AGIL sectors such as currency, authority, influence and value commitment to consider the classification of strategy of change.[30]

Strategy of Change

As an object of control, the currency deals with the flow of economic goods or the flow of generalized resources used for various applications in a broad sense.

5 Application to the Theory of Social Planning   77

Therefore, making it a strategy of change is equivalent to manipulating facilities. Thus, we call it *strategy of facility*. The strategy of facility is an effective means of intervention, when problem consciousness or the necessity of change has penetrated sufficiently into the recipient side of change or the client. A typical example is the inducement of changes by public expenditure.

Power makes compulsory obedience an object of control. Intervention by power is an effective strategy, when strong resistance against changes should be conquered, when a change should be implemented before resistance is deployed; or when a change is imminent. Typical examples are the exertion of political power by organizing a pressure group, administrative regulations by official authority or exertion of power through social movements. Such means can be named *strategy of power*.

Influence addresses the consensus formation by persuasion as an object of control. Its phenomenal form is social control by communal norm having legitimacy. Thus, we name such means *strategy of persuasion*. This strategy is effective at the stage where the clients judge whether they accept the change or not; when they justify the change or when the social effect of change is unknown, as represented by judicial arbitration or enactment of law.

Value commitment adopts value internalization, motivation and other issues of socialization as the object of control. Since the term enlightenment is appropriate as a mature expression corresponding to socialization, we call this *strategy of enlightenment*. This is effective when the change is ignored or consciousness thereof is lacking; when the change requires skill and knowledge for the clients or when the change is not so imminent. This is represented by campaigning activities, public relations and exercises.

Above is a simple sketch of four strategies. These four strategies as a means of intervention into structural changes are only analytically distinguished from each other, with which one-to-one correspondence does not necessarily hold against those in actual society, since a mixing strategy to combine these four strategies are normally adopted depending on the situation. When he classified the intervention means based on empirical cases, Mayer stated that there were duplications with each other in some cases. The trial of classification at the analytical level is not to leave the duplication unattended but to clarify the viewpoint to get it to the bottom.

Resolution of Structural Conflict

Structural changes triggered by the effector function of self-organization cause various ripples in the existing social structure. The most important subject for the control of change is to effectively treat and settle these ripples. What is important in dealing with the problems of social change is to analyze ripple effect of the change, including first adjustment at the stage of introduction. Adaptive control of the ripple effect of a change is a key to determine whether the change settles in the system. As planning of change aiming at the design of a new structure is thought to be the first stage of adaptive control, so the work to control the conflict between existing structure and new one and ensure integration of the two is the second stage of adaptive control.

Regarding structural conflict caused by the introduction of new structural characteristics, following three solutions are normally conceivable. First solution is to make old structure adapt itself to the new structural characteristics; second is to make new structural characteristics adapt themselves to the old structure; and third is to make the structural characteristics of the former adopt themselves to those of the latter and vice versa. However, third one is the most common and frequent solution.

In the theory of industrialization, researchers mainly analyze the process where existing roles and allocation rules change to conform to those of the modern occupational structure. However, occupational structures of different countries have settled in diversified forms. This indicates not only the fact that conventional social structure changed to conform to the modern occupational structure but also the fact that new occupational structure and conventional social structure changed to conform to each other. It is thought that perhaps a *core value* exists in each country, which tends to prevent infringement and governs what structural change should be. Even if the blueprint of socialism is the same, for example, the pattern to attain it has been processed differently by different countries. In this sense as well, the third solution is common.

Control of change deals with allocation rules, roles and other structural characteristics as its object. Then, what is usable as evaluation information to judge the results of control? To answer this question, it is required first to select phenomena that are observable and appear under the structural conflict. Following two actions can be pointed out as the phenomena that satisfy this condition. As already mentioned, they are (1) resistance by people who insist on vested rights, and (2) defending action by those who cannot adapt themselves to the new role. These phenomena are useful as the information that becomes an evaluation parameter in changing process of allocation rule and role modification, because a control circuit is formed, as this information is fed back to the detector of self-organization layer to make the cognition schema modified and structure design reviewed by the detector. In the same way as market mechanism aiming at optimal resource allocation functions with the price as a parameter and adjusts supply and demand, adaptive control aiming at structural congruency functions with the defense action and resistance insisting on vested rights as a parameter and adjusts conflict between the new and old structural characteristics. Success in this control makes the planned social change settle and stabilize in society.

As far as social development can be attained only by the purposive efforts of people, it is an important subject to plan and control social development. To vivify such conception and make it fruitful, it is essential to establish the theory of social development including an economic view while maintaining a viewpoint of planning simultaneously. For this purpose as well, it is required to prepare conceptual device to grasp social development and analytical framework at a general level.

The trial in this chapter is to connect theory of self-organization with the theory of social development. Such fundamental work will connect with (1) contrivance of indicators on the multi-dimensional functional achievement, which is a scale for development, and (2) improvement of information that manipulates the control of change, to become a guide that leads a positive plan for social organization. The logic of self-organization developed in this chapter makes it possible to integrate the disrupted viewpoints of social movement theory and planning theory in regard to social reorganization. Self-organization layer, which has been extracted strictly as an analytical concept, does not require that its five operations be borne always by one and the same actor in the self-organizing process. Self-organization is taken an active part by (1) the prior acquisition of value, acceleration of value formation, setting of the social goal and other aspects that have been emphasized mainly from the viewpoint of social movement theory and (2) differentiation and prescription of roles, setting and modification of personnel and resource allocation and other aspects that have been emphasized mainly from the viewpoint of the planning theory. Self-organization theory includes the viewpoint that social reorganization is executed through organic cooperation in between. Theory of social reorganization should not be disputed for the difference in viewpoint, but shall be improved by creating a common ground at the analytical dimension.

Part II
Elaboration of the Self-Organization Theory: Metamorphosing of System and Individual

Chapter 3
Signification and Reflexive System

In the foregoing two chapters, I developed the self-organization theory that relies on cybernetics. Cybernetic self-organization is a powerful paradigm to formulate social planning and development focusing on structure and function of the system. However, self-organization is not limited to such an intentional and deliberate concept. There is self-organization having another important aspect, or the performative and spontaneous self-organization, which is based on the reflexion of human beings. The former is top-down self-organization, while the latter bottom-up self-organization.

In the latter half of the 1970s, a new paradigm made its debut to focus on the behavior of elements and deal with order formation from their synergy in the field of systems science. As summarized in Introduction, it is the synergetic self-organization theory that includes theories of dissipative structure, hyper-cycle and autopoiesis. Sociology also experienced changes in parallel with systems science, in that it saw a rise of meaning school in opposition to functionalism and critical sociology. Symbolic interactionism, ethnomethodology and phenomenological sociology denied the actor image embedded in the macroscopic system logic and advocated an approach that constitutes the actual society with microscopic individuals. It focuses on the formation of institutions and norms through the synergy of individual actors.

To apply synergetic self-organization to sociology, it is required to take in the claims of meaning school. The work required for this purpose is to embed fluctuation and signification in the social system theory constructed centering on structure and function. In this chapter, I formulize such self-organization as a reflexive system.

1 Linguistic and Semantic Turn in Social Theory

From the latter half of the 1970s to the 1980s, a large wave of changes washed sociology, in that the regime of confrontation between critical sociology (including Marxism) and functionalism that had led sociology after World War II collapsed and caused confusion and multipolarization in sociological paradigm. What was in the background of this trend was a change called a *linguistic and semantic turn in social theory*. This turn indicates the trial to create a new social theory by taking in a proposal of meaning school which appealed the loss of reality against the above two dominant sociologies.[1]

Suffering of Paradigms after World War II

Functionalism that had led the sociology after World War II was in a honeymoon relation with theory of industrial society that made orderly prosperity the spirit of an age and naturalism or positivism that advocated methodological improvement of exact science. This relation reached a climax in the period of high economic growth when orderly prosperity lasted, or in the age of Pax Americana in international scenes, when functionalism established a position of main paradigm in sociology to seemingly constitute what is called "normal science." However, as mythology of growth collapsed and effectiveness of industrialism was lost, honeymoon relation started to decay. This is not because of the limit of functionalism, but because theory of industrial society represented by modernization, urbanization or industrialization no longer played a role to delineate coming society. As functionalism was a paradigm to support the theory of industrial society, it also withered. In short, theory of social change held up by functionalism was the same as that of industrialization.

I make it a rule to use the term *zation-phenomenon* for a phenomenon of "such-and-such-zation" represented by industrialization.[2] The zation-phenomena, such as modernization, urbanization, massification, democratization and popularization of higher education, indicate that changes proceed continually with certain direction. This is an application of the principle of uniformity, a premise of inductive logic, to social changes. In other words, it premises the principle of uniformity that changes in certain direction will continue in future. Therefore, it is weak or rather of no use in the discussions that a symptom of change starts or uniformity of change ends. When a change to predict order formation in the coming society is a problem in particular, its analyzing power loses effectiveness. What is required in this situation is a method to approach new reality construction.

Challenge by the Meaning School

I regard *meaning school* as a general term for phenomenological sociology, ethnomethodology and symbolic interactionism. The significance of meaning school is to have thematized the problem of reality construction. This undermined the basis of structural-functionalism that had been at the position of main paradigm, and attacked it by holding up the reinstatement of reality missed by functionalist school.

I understand that different researchers in meaning school insisted in common that actors must be grasped not simply as purposively rational existence but more than that as talented existence to conduct meaning construction in ordinary world. Self-control toward goal attainment alone is not the working of human beings. Fulfilling and reflecting meaning are also extremely important working. The schools of functionalism and critical sociology fell into reality loss, as they were not able to properly theorize this aspect. What should be done is to return to the individual action level and reconstruct the action theory from the viewpoint of signification, which is the first problem raised by meaning school.

The advent of meaning school undermined not only the ground of functionalist school but also that of critical sociology, and proclaimed that the paradigms after World War II had become antiquated and moss-grown. In other words, it nullified the regime of confrontation between functionalism and critical sociology that had been a typical phenomenon during the period of high economic growth, or the cold war structure of paradigms. The curtain was drawn down for the age where two major paradigms were antagonistic to each other. This is the second problem raised by meaning school.

Challenge by meaning school was significant in the sense that it raised an opposition to functionalism and Marxism that had been dominant schools in sociology in the past and pointed out that their defect was the lacked treatment of *meaning*. However, it can hardly be said that this school appropriately theorized the sociality and public nature of meaning, because a large scene of what is called society does not appear, despite that it correctly rediscovered the ordinary world and common sense that had been missing in conventional sociology. It is possible, for example, to have convincing discussions on the aspect where the society works as an oppressive apparatus for individuals or the process of reality construction in small groups, but a noteworthy theory has not been established on the whole society. Meaning dealt with by meaning school is subjectivistic and lacks the institutional and structural viewpoint. Nevertheless, it can be highly evaluated with respect to its inquiry about the importance of meaning construction against social theory where the function is superior and its proposal of life world based on meaning in contrast to social system based on function.[3]

Response from the Orthodox School

Responding to the problem lodging by meaning school, a strong tendency arose to conceive a theory of society that takes in the linguistic and semantic perspective. This started from the dispute on system theory between Jürgen Habermas and Niklas Luhmann, in which a heated argument was developed on meaning in the social system theory, communicative action and interpretation.[4] This made a turning point of the linguistic and semantic perspective for social theory thereafter. As a matter of fact, major social theories advocated in and after the 1980s were all baptized in some way or other by this perspective.

Habermas who had once developed critical sociology from the standpoint of Marxism completed *The Theory of Communicative Action* in 1981, for example. While aiming at a critique of functionalist reason, he sets communicative action oriented to reaching mutual understanding against the purposive rational action. He also prepares *system* to characterize the society composed of purposive rational action oriented to success on one hand, and *lifeworld* centering on communicative action oriented to reaching mutual understanding on the other.

Habermas remarks that the modern society separated system from lifeworld and used the former to promote the colonization of the latter, which has distorted the consensus formation and intersubjective meaning formation through discussions to a large extent. What he calls communicative action aims at reaching mutual understanding with others against purposive rational action that often falls in solipsism. In this sense, it draws a line of demarcation against the conventional functionalist theory of action in particular. Habermas states that reaching understanding through discourse alone is the intersubjective meaning formation that does not fall in solipsism (not contaminated by subjectivism), and that the intrinsic entity of modernity is to direct a reflexive viewpoint through such work to selfish action of individuals and establish a new action mode. As Yoshiyuki Sato puts it, this view is worth attention in the sense that it turns "instrumental reason" on which the conventional functionalism relied to "dialogical reason."[5] Communicative action and dialogical reason are achievements of Habermas to symbolize the linguistic and semantic turn in the standpoint of critical theory.

Luhmann published *Social Systems* in 1984 that mainly dealt with meaning and self-referentiality. Luhmann, who has elaborated functionalist social theory through a dialog with general system theory, also addresses a semantic theory and positions the social system as a semantically constructed system via communication. He brings in meaning concept from phenomenology and represcribes it from the viewpoint of function to escape from the fallacy of subjectivism. In other words, he regards meaning as a strategic concept to introduce selection behavior under uncertainty and have a function to reduce complexity by stabilizing the differences between the inside and outside of the system. However, *reduction of complexity* is logically the same as "law of requisite variety" by cyberneticist Ross Ashby as pointed out in Introduction. This corresponds to the fundamental principle of control.

With dispute with Habermas as a momentum, Luhmann added self-referentiality to a key concept of the theory of social system. By doing so, he positioned meaning as the self-referential loop of *differencification* (not functional differentiation in a macro societal level but the activity differing the established order) and indication. Meaning is interpreted as treatment by difference to force itself to changes.[6] The view to make meaning a movement body of self-differencification is significantly different from the former standpoint to regard meaning as a reduction of complexity. As far as the schema of reduction of complexity is followed, social system cannot help but become functionally monistic and be connoted in control thought with meaning and structure becoming subordinate concepts. In this sense, Luhmann's social system theory in the past was coherent as functionalism. However, he adopted schema of self-referentiality to bring *recursive movement of differencification* into the mechanism of meaning.[7]

In addition, Anthony Giddens in the UK develops theory of structuration that takes in the linguistic theory, while discussing meaning school in a critical manner. In Japan as well, Daisaburo Hashizume aims at establishing a social theory relied on the language game by Ludwig Wittgenstein.[8] A trial common to Habermas, Luhmann, Giddens and Hashizume is to theorize the sociality and public nature of meaning. Although I do not think that their trial has succeeded sufficiently, their presentation of a new direction in sociology is significant.

As explained above, situation of sociological paradigms became uncertain as meaning school gained power and was forced to make a linguistic and semantic turn. However, no adequate languages yet have been found to narrate and conceive the coming society, or no languages exist to speak of meaning socially at the moment.

Meaning school tried to formulate the human beings as talented existence that makes meaning construction in ordinary world, and aimed at a revival of the image of human beings as an existence to form and maintain social order by themselves, irrespective of whether it may be subjectivism or confirmation of existing order. It was also a trial to return to the reality and excavate a language to conceive a new society therefrom. As mentioned above, it is by no means possible to sufficiently prepare a language to conceive a society, however, due to the fallacy of subjectivism and lack of institutional perspective. The most important cause of this fallacy is in the image of actor that pursues meaning alone. It is true that society draws a line of demarcation by meaning against other physical and biological systems. However, it is a necessary condition and not a sufficient one. If meaning stands alone, what results therefrom is metaphysics of society.

What is required for meaning is a work to add significance equivalent or superior to structure and function that have been hitherto a core concept of sociology respectively. As far as captured by the modern conception, however, it is not conceivable how to realize it, since modernity has excluded the sociality and public nature of meaning and confined them in a field of subjectivity and privatism. Therefore, there are no alternatives than reviewing the modern conception from scratch. This should be deconstructed (disassembled and reassembled) from the aspects of meaning and fluctuation. Theory of self-organization is a powerful paradigm for this purpose.

2 Reflexion and Scientific View

A scientific view of self-reference is indispensable for social theory from the viewpoint of self-organization. However, avoidance of self-reference is not a problem simply specific to functionalism. Most of modern sciences have made a detour to avoid this problem. Therefore, discussion on this problem is to raise a problem for modern sciences at the same time. In this chapter, I will discuss functional theory and scientific view in detail to solidify the ground of reflexive self-organization.

Logical Contradiction in Functionalism

The first cause of decline of functionalism is unclarity and lacked strictness of functional logic. Functionalism has kept pace with naturalism. Naturalism makes the nomothetic explanation of phenomena an ideal of science. Exact discussions through formalization of theory are essential even if they do not proceed ideally. However, satisfactory results are not obtained, even if functionalism is formalized according to this scientific view.

The essence of functionalism is eventually to *explain maintenance and change of social system with the gratification/nongratification of functional requisites*. The functional requisite referred to here is a necessary condition to be gratified for the maintenance of social system. It is also allowed to read the maintenance and change of social system as those of social structure. As it is immediately noticed, above logic includes tautology. As functional requisite is defined as a condition to be gratified for the maintenance of social system, it is natural according to the definition that social system is maintained when the requisite is gratified and changes (or is dissolved) when it is not. Therefore, above statement is another expression of the definition, rather than a proposition. As the logic is a tautology at its basis, the same results will be obtained even if it is elaborated in detail.

Structural-functional analysis started by Talcott Parsons was improved in formal logic after introduced into Japan, mainly led by Ken'ichi Tominaga, Tamito Yoshida and Naoki Komuro. In consequence, as a feature of Japanese structural-functionalism, it is added with the idea of "interrelation analysis" (Komuro) in general equilibrium theory in economics and that of "evaluation analysis based on an ordinal scale" (Yoshida), which followed the model of the social choice theory by Kenneth Arrow.[9] The former aimed at escaping from the tautology connoted in functional theory and the latter at formally elaborating functional requisite theory.

However, it was discussed by Daisaburo Hashizume, Kiyoshi Shida and Naoyuki Tsunematsu that such formalization contains a contradiction.[10] By prescribing that the essence of structural-functionalism is to explain the structure and changes of social system by functional evaluation, they criticize it from the standpoint of formal logic. Their insistence is summarized as the following three points. First, explanation of society by functional evaluation is not compatible with the idea that functional requisites interrelate with each other (AGIL schema). Second, assumption of plural functional requisites leads to a contraction. Third, explanation of social change by functional evaluation is not significant.

According to my understanding, the criticism by Hashizume and others is to insist that the introduction of interrelation analysis and evaluation analysis based on an ordinal scale aiming at formalization of structural-functionalism has revealed a logical contradiction against its intention. In other words, they say that it is fruitless to borrow evaluation analysis based on an ordinal scale from economics in order to formalize structural-functional analysis. I interpret that logic of structural-functionalism cannot escape eventually from the aforementioned tautology. The third point in the criticism that the explanation of social change by functional evaluation is not significant should be interpreted in this way.

I am ready to admit significance of their criticism. Their article extends a full-scale criticism for structural-functional analysis. Among the criticisms developed in Japan, there are no rivals superior thereto. Nevertheless, their criticism is too much contaminated by formalism. It may favorably be evaluated that they criticized functionalism relying on formalism. However, they denied possibility of a theory of social change as a result. As far as they rely on the general equilibrium theory type of formalization, problem of change is meaningless and has no significant contents. In the last analysis, their insistence means that social sciences must restrain passions for the problem of change. This may be a discerning standpoint. As far as changes are routinely happening in actual society, however, abstinence from the problem of change is nothing but a deed to rob social sciences of their effectiveness.

Scientific View of Self-Reference

Then, what must be thought of the problem of change? The answer is to escape from the formal logic. For this purpose, it is necessary to redefine scientific view that has been elaborated by modern sciences from scratch, and review what science is and what methodological rule should be applied to prescribing science. After that, we should present the horizon of widely ranged scientific methodologies including the improvement of theories by formal logic as a part of scientific standard. This point is related to the second cause of decline of functionalism. In one word, the logic of function makes reflexion, or an important feature of the action of human beings, missed. This is the most important point raised by meaning school as mentioned in the previous section.

Problem of reflexion is equivalent to that of self-reference in the theory of logic or science. Therefore, relation between reflexion and self-reference corresponds to that between social theory and the supporting scientific view thereof. In addition, self-reference conceives a cumbersome problem to lead formal logic to a paradox. As pointed out in Introduction, problem of self-reference has fundamentally given rise to the paradox of a "Cretan liar," paradox of the theory of sets found by Bertrand Russell and incomplete theorems by Kurt Gödel, for example. Modern sciences have evaded this annoying problem, which is typically represented by the prohibition of circular argument. For the reason that it leads formal logic to a contradiction, circular argument is unduly shut out of the system of logic. Even an illusion has been created as if circular argument itself is unjustifiable. Here is violence by the scientific view elaborated under the name of modernity.

The problem of self-reference positions at the limit of formal logic and provides a strategic basis to escape therefrom, which has not been noticed by meaning school, however. Therefore, it fell into the fallacy of subjectivism and was not able to construct its own theory of scientific methodology against naturalism. To escape from the formal logic, it is required to establish a *scientific view of self-reference*. Since this is an extremely elusive concept, however, it is not determinate at all, even if its necessity is simply insisted upon. A good key is necessary to start discussions. A concept to be noticed for this purpose is self-organization.

Self-organization premises scientific view of self-reference, because self-organization is a phenomenon for the system to change its structure by itself and *self-reference* exists at this point, where the self is related with the self. In addition, it is not the case that self-organization has its features only in the problem of self-reference, but it attaches importance to the problem of *fluctuation* jutted out of existing organizational state and *symptom* that takes new organizational state in advance. In the world of self-organization, individual and particular events are important, as seen in order conversion of fluctuation and symptom of change. The ontological problem of self-organization is not the experience existing around the corner, but the experience of the completion of existence which realize someday somewhere.

In effect, the reality specific to self-organization is characterized by three concepts, *self-reference*, *fluctuation* and *symptom*, all of which have been weak points of hitherto modern sciences. As it prohibits circular argument, positivism or naturalism excludes self-reference. In addition, it expels fluctuation out of the visual field as it regards exceptional phenomena as useless for science, and expels symptoms as it makes the "sense data as presence" a basis of experience.

As far as self-organization phenomena are out of range of the modern scientific view of naturalism, sciences that make them an object must climb over naturalism.[11] In other words, what is required is a scientific view that is able to make self-reference, fluctuations and symptoms an object. A key to establish this scientific view exists in the tradition of interpretative science or hermeneutics that has been forced to be resigned at the position of a minor science. Interpretative science has been refined in the history from the classical hermeneutics by Wilhelm Dilthey and Max Weber to the ontological hermeneutics by Martin Heidegger and Hans-Georg Gadamar via the phenomenology by Edmund Husserl. The standpoint of this methodology is also a scientific view relied on by meaning school, although it has been indifferent to the important publication *Being and Time* by Heidegger and cannot take into consideration its suggestive sociological implications.

Naturalism has been skeptical about the methodological feature of interpretative science. However, this standpoint has a scientific view that is appropriate to deal with above three characteristics, or the reality of self-organization. More specifically, it has a methodological basis in hermeneutical circle (self-reference), adopts a method to grasp meaning by attribution to and estrangement from tradition (fluctuation through differencification), and lays stress on the experience as completion of existence of meaning (symptom). Therefore, it is essential for scientific view of self-reference not to doubt feature of interpretative science, but to establish a methodological rule to positively accept it.

Triangle of Methodology

To expand the basis of conventional sciences, I define scientific method as a procedure of reason to connect the cognition of phenomenon with existence. In short, science is the *connection of cognition to existence*.[12] Based on this standpoint, sciences are constituted by the tradition of rationalism and empiricism, or the basis of naturalism, and that of hermeneutics or the basis of interpretatism. It is integrated with the *triangle of methodology* that connects cognitive stance of hypothesis, observation and meaning with existence (experience), which is refutable, verifiable and understandable, by the methodological procedure of deduction, induction and interpretation respectively. Reason implementing science emerges as a *transformative reason* that freely behaves on this triangle. Only the transformative reason is appropriate to make the basis of scientific view of self-reference. Adopting reflexion in social theory after securing self-referentiality at the level of scientific view – this is to scientifically make the basis of self-organization theory.[13]

A supplementary explanation thereof is that the scientific view of transformative reason insists that the world of scientific methodology is composed of three methods, *hypothesico–deductive*, *observatory–inductive* and *meaning–interpretative*, and that scientific activities consist of the reason freely moving on the triangle of methodology made of these three methods without bound by strict rules. Each of the methodologies composing of the triangle represents one of the three modes of procedure of reason in science, which is a unique existence that cannot be reduced to others. The *observation* that is related to the observatory-inductive method referred to in this book expresses measurement of social events in the massive observation in social survey researches or repeated experiments. Other than the observations of this category, there are those including participant observation to minutely survey particular fields or observation of individual cases aiming at extracting the distinctive meaning or essence of things, which is not an inductive method but one specific to the interpretative method. The observation referred to in this book is limited to that premising inductive generalization.

The methodology that has supported modern sciences can broadly be classified into positivism and hermeneutics, both of which had crystallized into three types through the transition from classical to modern stages until the middle of the 20th century. Hypothesico–deductive and observatory–inductive methods differentiated themselves from the genealogy of positivism through the advent of logical positivism. Meaning–interpretative method, which originated in

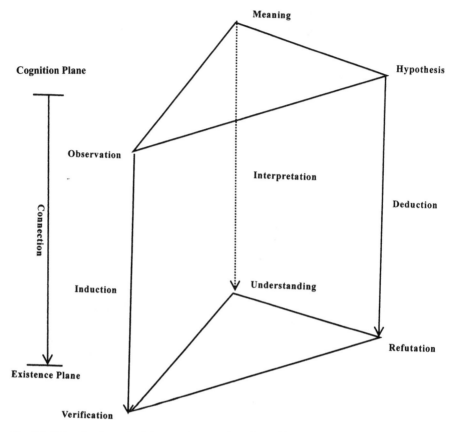

Fig. 3.1 Triangle of menthodology and connection of cognition to existence

hermeneutics, was completed with the ontological hermeneutics via phenomenology. Hypothesico–deductive method connects hypothetical cognition with refutable existence by the procedure of deduction. Similarly, observatory–inductive method connects observatory cognition with verifiable existence by the inductive procedure. In addition, meaning–interpretative method connects meaning cognition with understandable existence by the procedure of interpretation.

Figure 3.1 illustrates structure of the triangle of methodology. Three methods composing the triangle are those of pure type. In actual research activities, working is implemented while rather freely shifting on the cognition plane of hypothesis, observation and meaning and on the existence plane of refutation, verification and understanding. It constitutes so-to-speak a transformative structure expressed by the turn of equilateral triangle.[14]

To sufficiently clarify the phenomena in human society, all methods should be mobilized in some form or other. Consider a condition necessary to determine that a suspected person is a murderer, for example. It is composed of three requirements, i.e., *material evidence* to prove that the suspect has committed murder, an *alibi break* to prove that the suspect was at the site when murder took place and a *motive* for committing murder. The material evidence, alibi and motive compose a structure extremely close to the triangle of methodology in science. Material evidence is to induce (generalize) the occurrence of criminal act by thorough investigation at the scene (observation) and determine the existence of criminal act as verifiable. In contrast, alibi break is to establish a hypothesis that the suspect could be at the site of criminal act when it occurred based on logical (deductive) inference and infers it as correct as far as it is not refutable. The investigation of motive is to understand why the criminal act occurred (could exist) through meaning interpretation of the context of human relations where the suspect was placed. When these three requirements are satisfied, the suspect is determined as a criminal. This is exactly the determination of criminal reality by wholly mobilizing the triangle of methodology.

In the background where I became to conceive the scientific view of transformative reason, there is method of interpretative science (*Verstehende Wissenschaft*) by Max Weber, for whom understanding is a cognition method in which deduction, induction and interpretation are a complete whole. This can be inferred by his notion of the three types of subjective meaning. He defined that understanding is to interpretatively grasp meaning or meaning interrelation and distinguished three types of meaning as those (1) thought realistically by individual action in historical considerations, (2) thought averagely and approximately in sociologically massive observation and (3) constructed as a pure form in ideal type grasping.[15]

Pure economic theory and the Gresham's law that "bad money drives out good" can be cited as an example of the third meaning or that of the ideal type grasping. Methodologically, this is equivalent to the hypothesico–deductive method. The second meaning is an average meaning based on massive observation in social surveys and equivalent to the observatory–inductive method. The first meaning or the realistic meaning in historical considerations is one included in individual and particular action, which is equivalent to the meaning–interpretative method. To deal with all phenomena that are the object of social sciences integratedly at the dimension of meaning, Weber regarded the cognition started from hypothesis and observation as a form of meaning understanding. I think that he aimed at integrating social sciences adopting the methods of natural science and humanities as well. Therefore, a method of understanding is insisted to establish a complete whole by such terms as explanation, interpretation, elucidation, massive observation and chance.

In the next section, I will discuss the reflexive system to make the basis of self-organization theory and model the reflexion at social level as the *self-referentiality of structure mediated by action*. For this purpose, a methodological horizon is required to freely shift from analytical methods such as deduction and induction to an interpretative method focused on reflexion. In this respect, the transformative reason whose basis is the triangle of methodology is indispensable in order to grasp the reality of self-organization.

Recognition of Unique Factor

The three methods that compose transformative reason have different methods to grasp reality. Hypothesico–deductive method features deducing a proposition from an abstract hypothesis and extracting universal reality that transcends space-time. Observatory–inductive method features collecting concrete data and generalizing the analyzed characteristics over the whole population. Meaning–interpretative method features selecting individual and often particular cases and perceiving the essence of social events thereof.

Actual phenomena do not appear dichotomically, like individual versus general, particular versus universal or concrete versus abstract, but occur with generality intermingled with individuality, universality with particularity and abstractness with concreteness. In short, the dichotomy in each combination is a convenient method to approximate reality. To sufficiently grasp reality, therefore, all of the three methods should be mobilized. It is a case, for example, to perceive first the essence of individual and particular cases; then to formulize a universal and abstract law based thereon; finally to implement concrete and generalizable verification based on the data obtained from experiments or questionnaire survey researches.

What should be emphasized is that reality of research subject in the field of self-organization is not only the universal and generalizable reality that is appropriate for nomothetic cognition but also the reality incorporating individual and particular factors. An example is the approach giving due rights to factors that have been positioned as a disturbance by the conventional method, such as fluctuation, noise and chaos, which are therefore individualistic-particularistic events for the system.

The modern science of the Galileo-Newtonian type has placed stress on reductionism, determinism, time reversibility, equilibrium and stability, and makes it a work of science to extract order ($\approx$law) from this world, where is a background hypothesis insisting that it is possible to articulate the order distinguished and existing separately from chaos. Unlike the Galileo-Newtonian type science, however, self-organization paradigm in a broad sense that arose toward the end of the 1970s emphasizes emergent property, nondeterminism, time irreversibility, nonequilibrium and instability, and researches are being promoted in the opposite direction to that of modern science. In such sciences, there exists a background hypothesis to regard that essence of the world is order formation through chaos, interpenetration between order and chaos, and a state paradoxical at a glance that is "not orderly nor chaotic" or "orderly and chaotic." In other words, it is a scientific view that the world is nothing but a nonstationary system fluctuating across the boundary between order and chaos. Order and chaos have a subtly fluctuating boundary in between and cannot be separable distinctly. There is a tendency to theorize what this nature is.

The mainstream of the modern science from Galileo to Newton has been the science of equilibrium system that deals with the dynamics of steady state, where perturbation is nothing but an object to be controlled to return to equilibrium or an object to be disposed of as an *error*. However, the new paradigm emphasizes that perturbation or error contains important information on the system behavior and tries to clarify that it triggers the genesis of significantly different behavior and order. Nevertheless, it does not ignore the universal and generalizable reality, because it does not discard the description of equilibrium system, but sets a model incorporating a perturbation term and clarifies that it leads the structure (order) of the equilibrium system to that of different mode depending on the condition, where there is a trial that goes over dual opposition, or the superiority of universality to particularity or that of generality to individuality.

This suggests a method to approach the reality incorporating both normal and unique factors into view. *Normal factors* exist not distinguished from *unique factors*, but implement synergy therewith and the changes thereof come up depending on the condition. In chaos theory, for example, the importance of the *sensitivity to initial conditions* is emphasized, which symbolically indicates that a minor difference in the initial value that would normally be treated as an error will cause a significantly great difference in the system behavior thereafter. The catastrophe theory, which takes into consideration splitting factors in addition to normal factors, indicates that normal factors gradually and continuously change (quantitative change) when splitting factors are small, and discontinuously jump (qualitative change) when they exceed a certain value.

The upshot of the above is that researchers cannot be indifferent to particular and individual events in grasping self-organization. It is necessary to discover the start of self-organizing in fluctuations and symptoms of changes, though they are events to be neglected or controlled from the viewpoint of maintaining the system. For the system, a fluctuation is a particular and individual event, while order is a universal and general event. Therefore, order transformation of fluctuation is for an individual and particular event to be transformed into a universal and general one. It is unreasonable to treat such a problem only by formal logic. At this point as well, transformative reason is required to freely shift from the meaning–interpretative method that treats particular and individual reality to the deductive or inductive method dealing with universal and/or general reality.

3 Theory of Reflexive System

Social theory of self-organization addresses theoretical construction from two levels, action and system, based on the scientific view of self-reference, and adopts reflexion in functionalism to aim at cross-linking between structure, function and meaning that are key concepts of social theory.

The most important issue in conventional functionalism is the lack of *reflexion*. After World War II, functionalism has maintained a position of orthodox school, while being criticized by Marxian sociology and critical sociology. Its basis did not shake even when criticized as it was "biased too much toward integration and equilibrium" or "insufficient in dealing with conflict and opposition," because it can formulate conflicts and disequilibrium functionalistically. A criticism cannot be genuine, unless it problematizes issues related to more fundamental views of human being and society. It should become a problem related to a large historical current and will extend to an inquiry into skepticism and criticism against modernity. As the basis of modern scientific view is shaken by self-referentiality, so the modern views of human beings and society are also being shaken by confronting the problem of self-reflexion.

Reflexion and Social Theory

Max Weber typed the actions of human beings as traditional, affective and instrumentally rational (which is referred to as purposive-rational in Japanese) and value-rational actions and found the process where instrumentally rational actions excel others as a destiny of modernity. As a matter of fact, industrialization that characterizes modernity was a process where instrumentally rational actions were released from the norm of traditional system and penetrated into various areas of daily life. Instrumental rationality places priority on the value of the instrument based on technological rules and has power to go over cultures specific to different countries and radicalism to change values and norms shared by people into a simple instrument at its extremity.

The rationalization process that characterizes modernity integrates things as a *means–end schema* and makes the value of instrument to attain goals superior thereto. This is the preference of instrumental activism advocated by Talcott Parsons. This code of action brings about the importance attached to goal-attainment process, where is a contact point between the logic of function and that of action and the basis of the idea of control. What Weber calls rationalization process is also the penetration of idea of control. The modern times are an age of control, with the essence of functionalism existing in the idea of control (see Chap. 2). However, rationalization process promoted in the modern times is now being reinquired, with the limit of idea of control being recognized. A typical representation of this event is the problem of *meaning*.

While holding up the subjective sense-making in action and reality construction in lifeworld, meaning school raised an objection to the functionalist theory of social system. As typically seen in the phenomenological sociology by Alfred Schutz, it insists on non–Parsonian development of Weberian theory of action. When he formulated the theory of social system, Parsons abandoned the voluntaristic theory of action of the initial stage, by trivializing the significance of Weberian theory of action with Durkheimean functionalism. In contrast, meaning school does not dissolve the action of human beings into the means–end schema, but tries to capture it by the meaning–expression schema. However, this standpoint is also to trivialize the Weberian theory of action, as it is subjectification of society.

The concept of meaning used by meaning school is ambiguous and relies too munch on the self-apparency of everyday life. I consider meaning by dividing it into descriptive concept and explanative concept, and seek its significance in reflexion thought for control thought. Descriptive concept of meaning is *difference* and explanative concept is *reflexion*. Meaning originates in difference. As meaning emerges when an object is distinguished from others, grasping what the difference is constitutes description of meaning. In contrast, a difference is recognizable only as the differencification from the existing system of differences. To recognize the working of difference, therefore, it is required for differencification to return to the existing differences. This means that reflexion is necessary because a difference cannot be a difference by itself and its existence can be confirmed only in the systematic operation of differencification. This means that meaning can be meaning only by returning to the existing meaning system. Therefore, the explanative concept of meaning that interprets the working of difference cannot help but be reflexion for the difference to return to the existing system of differences.[16]

If the concept of meaning is formulated as above, it will be possible to establish a bridgehead that takes meaning into social theory without falling into subjectivism. It is also evident that meaning is decidedly related with the problem of self-reference. At present, the logic of industrial society is at a stalemate and the control thought can no longer maintain its effectiveness. In the age when directivity of society must be reviewed to grope self-organizing, effectiveness of control thought lowers. This problem requires reflexion and differencification from the conventional institutions and values. At this point exists the significance of meaning. Theory of *reflexive system* is a theory taking reflexion into the conventional functionalism after confirming the significance of meaning in social theory as mentioned above.

Although social theory must connect the dimension of action with that of system, important point for the theory of societal self-organization is to formulate *self-referentiality of structure mediated by action*. What this problem implies is surmounting of the antinomy of "action and structure" or "individual and society" that is a classical problem for social theory. Structure is constituted by action while regulating action. Individuals are formed by society and vice versa. What the theory of self-organization aims at is to clarify such problems from the viewpoint of self-reference. Then, how is the self-referentiality of structure via action formulated? To answer this question, conventional action and system theories must fundamentally be reconstructed from the viewpoint of structure, function and meaning.

In my book titled *Self-Organity: Revitalization of Social Theory*, I formulated this work as a model of *complex spiral movement* between action and system, by the following procedures. First, I typed social actions as conventional, rational and reflexive ones, with each becoming circulative while being put in question by others, and formulated a model of *spiral movement of action* with the order of this circulation becoming higher. Second, I formulated the movement of system dimension, which is in parallel with the spiral movement of action dimension, as a model of *spiral movement of system* between structure, function and meaning. This is a model in which structure is put in question by function, function by meaning and meaning by structure. Third, I formulated a model of complex spiral movement in which each of the spiral movements of action and system dimensions penetrates into the other. This is a mutual penetration model of action and system in which structure penetrates action and vice versa, which formulates the self-referentiality of structure mediated by action. This complex spiral movement model makes the basis of reflexive system and constitutes a *cross-linkage paradigm* between split structuralism, functionalism and meaning school, as outlined below.[17]

Spiral Movement of Action

To formulate action theory that makes the basis of self-organization, Weberian action theory should be developed in a direction different from that adopted by Parsons. Action must not be treated simply by means–end schema. It is not sufficient either to dissolve it into the subjectivistic meaning–expression schema emphasized by phenomenological sociology and ethnomethodology. I conceive a *meaning–reflexion schema* incorporating reflexion by actors as the basis of action theory on self-organization.

Action is to obey and use rules and attain a goal while putting meaning of obeying rules in question. By this definition, *self-control* toward the purpose and *reflexion* to review meaning can be taken into the action theory. The self-control toward goal expresses the aspect of rational action to select optimal instrument for goal-attainment. In contrast, reflexion to re-inquiry meaning is related to the action to return to the original action and inquire the reason, or reflexion, in case an unintended consequence of action has resulted. Rational action is to make the means–end schema superior, while reflexive action is to make the meaning–reflexion schema superior.

Synergetic self-organization should be formulated as a paradigm to integrate the dimensions of structure, function and meaning. Therefore, a typical action type should be adopted to correspond to each dimension. Rational action based on means–end schema is typical of functional dimension, and reflexive action based on meaning–reflexion schema is typical of meaning dimension. The action type corresponding to structural dimension is conventional action. The essence of structure is rule. Action obeying the structure as a rule is nonreflexive against rules, which can be called conventional action in the sense that it follows accustomed conventions. Accustomed conventions have their basis in the routinization of obeying rules. Routinization is a concept at the same level as that of the self-control in rational action and reflexion in reflexive action. Conventional action can be regarded as the action to which attribution to the traditional institutions and values is superior or action based on the tradition–attribution scheme. Thus, the action theory incorporating reflexion is composed of conventional, rational and reflexive actions, each corresponding to structure, function and meaning at system dimension.

The process of concrete action generally contains conventional, rational and reflexive actions. It is allowed to distinguish analytically these three action types. In constituting a theory, however, a model must be considered to integrate these three action types. A theory to model the society from specific aspects of

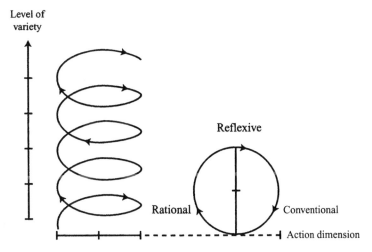

Fig. 3.2 Spiral movement of action

conventional, rational and reflexive actions is nothing but a snap shot that has stopped the passage of time.

The spiral movement of action is a model having conventional action with superior routinization inquired by rational action in which self-control is superior; rational action inquired by reflexive action in which reflexion is superior; and reflexive action returning to conventional action in which routinization is superior. This relation is not two-dimensional but makes a spiral movement to shift to a phase of higher order after one circulation (see Figure 3.2.).

To sum up, the conventional action in which attribution to tradition was dominant at the beginning is transformed into rational action, when people become conscious of the control instrument against purpose. When the rational action comes to its limit, however, reflexion by meaning is vitalized to grope new meaning formation. This meaning cuts in on existing rules to ensure a position for its existence and is added as a new tradition to the existing institutional traditions, thereby reaching a tradition having a higher order (variety of higher level) than that of existing tradition. In this sense, the three types of action are connected with each other by an upward circular movement or a spiral movement.

Of course, such a movement of the action dimension is observed only when self-organization competence vitalized. It is thought that, when unintended consequences of action or social problems do not exist, a lower circular movement of conventional and rational actions alone is developed while skipping reflexive action. In this state, social system repeats only reproduction of existing meaning to become an autopoietic system of meaning. Since structure is not intervened by the meaning, only homeostasis (reproduction) of meaning alone is implemented by existing structure.

Spiral Movement of System

Incorporation of reflexion in the action model makes it possible to apply signification borne by language and symbol to action theory. As the basic concept of social theory, I add meaning to structure and function, and formulate system spiral movement of structure, function and meaning that corresponds to the action dimension. The causes of equivocality and disputes on structure, function and meaning that are observed in hitherto social theory can be summarized as the difference whether they are positioned as descriptive concept or explanative concept. To avoid confusion of concepts, I use structure, function and meaning by dividing each into descriptive and explanative concepts.

As suggested by the foregoing discussions in this book, structure becomes rule when used as explanatory concept or pattern when used as descriptive concept. Similarly, function becomes control or performance and meaning becomes reflexion or difference. The relation between descriptive and explanatory concepts is expressed as the fact that rule generates pattern; control ensures performance; and reflexion operates difference. If these concepts are not distinctly distinguished, discussions cross each other. Meaningless antagonism between structuralism; and functionalism on the concept of structure is caused by the fact that the former refers to structure as a rule (structure as model) and the latter refers to structure as a pattern (structure as reality).

Efforts have been made to put in order the concepts of structure and function in some form or other. This is not the case with meaning, however. As already mentioned, I divide meaning into difference (descriptive concept) and reflexion (explanatory concept) in order to make the basic concept of social theory with meaning in parallel with structure and function. To study self-organization in particular, it is required to formulate the self-referentiality of structure mediated by action. For this purpose, it is necessary to theorize the operation which meaning as difference shall inevitably return (reflect) to structure by meaning as reflexion. Meaning school falls in the error of subjectivism and lacks the institutional perspective, as it misses this aspect of meaning.

Systems theory incorporating reflexion questions structure as rule with function as control and questions function with meaning as reflexion. In addition, these three concepts have a circular relation, each being questioned by others. In other words, as structure is questioned by function and function by meaning, meaning returns to be questioned by structure, as if the head and tail reverses with a Moebius strip. In short, meaning works systematically with difference and reflexion and emerges as a structural problem as pattern and rule. Furthermore, when self-organization occurs, circulation movement of structure, function and meaning is not in one plane, but spirally increases its level of variety (see Figure 3.3).

Now, we explain system spiral movement starting from function as control. For a system to control the environment and ensure desirable performance, it must have variety equal to or higher than that of the environment. To put it simply, the player must have strategies equal to or more than those of the opponent in order to win

3 Theory of Reflexive System

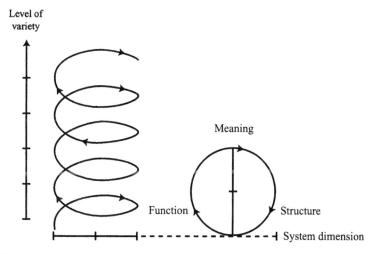

Fig. 3.3 Spiral movement of system

the game. For social system to ensure its performance in the diversifying environment, there are no other alternatives than increasing its own variety. Metaphorically, a system is a creature to eat disorder or entropy only by increasing its variety. Therefore, function as control always proceeds in the direction to increase variety, or systems that cannot increase variety shall stagnate or be dissolved. If the variety of control increases, it will be incorporated into the spiral movement of structure, function and meaning. This increases the variety of reflexion and rule, and that of difference and pattern prescribed in this work, thereby increasing the order of system spiral movement.

Structuralism, functionalism and meaning school have hitherto insisted on their legitimacy and been in opposition to each other. This is because they are captured by narrow-minded reason in that they question structure with structure, function with function and meaning with meaning alone. The system spiral movement is a model that has deconstructed such reason.

Complex Spiral Movement between Action and System

The spiral movement of system dimension and that of action dimension penetrate each other to be coupled and form a new spiral movement, which is a complex spiral movement to formulate self-referentiality of structure. For the convenience of discussion, we model it first below (see Figure 3.4).

Contemporary biology or bioholonics in particular, has formulated an interesting hypothesis on the relation between part and whole, which advocates that

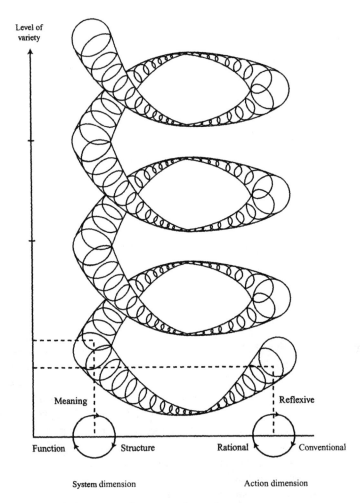

Fig. 3.4 Complex spiral movement between action and system

whole is contained in part. I cannot discuss it in detail here. If this proposition is applied to social science, however, society as whole enters the actor as part to make a *nested relation between whole and part*. Of course, mass or energy of society cannot enter the actor. Therefore, society referred to here is that as information or semantic information in particular. In other words, the actor has society prescribed as meaning in itself. In addition, this *meaning* is not a subjective meaning but one as self-reflexion of difference that makes rule a reference point. I do not deal with meaning with subjectivity or objectivity, because subjective and objective meanings cannot strictly be distinguished. Meaning is nowhere but in the movement of difference and reflexion that makes rule a reference point.

3 Theory of Reflexive System   103

The nested relation between part and whole is maintained at the information level. Part corresponds to action dimension and whole to system dimension. Therefore, for the society (system dimension) to penetrate the actor (action dimension) is for the spiral movement of structure, function and meaning to penetrate that of conventional, rational and reflexive actions. The actor takes the spiral movement of structure, function and meaning as an internal image of system, and transforms it into that of conventional, rational and reflexive actions.

Incorporation of the spiral movement of structure, function and meaning of system dimension into that of action dimension should be taken as different from individual to individual. Individuals are a copying machine of society having different types and quality. Some sensitively respond to structure as rule and others to function as control or meaning as reflexion. The present situation where personalization and diversification are clamored and people are sensitive to meaning as differencification indicates that the actor has become a copying machine sensitive to meaning. In this situation as well, however, individuals are greatly different from each other depending on what aspect of meaning they are sensitive to. In short, what I want to say is that the spiral movement of system dimension does not enter action dimension entirely. Each person has a reduced copy of society and is implementing a spiral movement of action while responding to the internal image of society. This means that the spiral movement of system dimension is differently reduced from person to person and transformed into the spiral movement of action dimension. This reducing process is expressed as a tapering-off spiral in complex spiral movement.

The reducing method reflects the individuality and personality. Actors having a reduced copy focused on structure as rule have personality placing emphasis on attribution to tradition and conventional action in compliance with rules. In contrast, we can consider the personality that attaches importance to the rational action using rules and/or strategic thought of means–ends analysis, when function as control is focused on. When meaning as reflexion is focused on, however, it becomes the personality that attaches importance to the reflexive action motivated by differencification and/or requestioning of meaning. Of course, these three personality types are owned by all actors to different degrees.

The fact that the spiral movement of system dimension, which has once been reduced is again expanded at action dimension means that spiral movements of a number of actors synchronize with each other to compose a large spiral movement. Then, the spiral movement of action reduces again and tapers off. This express the fact that the movement of action dimension is reduced again and transformed into that of system dimension.

Meaning–reflexion is inspired by the occurrence of unintended consequences of actions and social problems or changes in the values between generations. This brings about differencification from the conventional action governed by routinization. The new difference generated by this differencification reflectively intervenes in the system of differences maintained under the conventional structure. As a result, differencification from the original difference takes place. Although it is minor differencification at the beginning, it triggers the spiral movement of structure, function and meaning. The difference generated through the amplification of that spiral movement is transformed into a new structure. Thus, structure as rule is institutionalized. In parallel, function as control becomes more powerful equipment, with meaning as reflexion enriched. The shift of spiral movement from action dimension to system dimension expresses this movement. When the complex spiral movement is formulated as above, structure prescribes action and is represcribed by action, to facilitate understanding of the self-referentiality of structure appropriately.

Complex spiral movement between action and system is significant as a *protomodel* of social theory. The complex spiral model to formulate self-organization of social system will become the basis of social theory to integrate structuralism, functionalism and meaning school.

4 Language Game and Self-Organization

An interesting attempt has been made to theorize sociality and public nature of meaning from a standpoint different from that of this book and from an angle different from that in the field of orthodox sociology. It is an attempt to address the problem of meaning and understanding based on the theory of *language game*. To pursue the same purpose, my theory of *self-organization* takes in the problem of meaning missed in conventional structural-functionalism and formulates a hyper loop to add meaning to the loop of structure and function. Then, does the reconstruction of social theory by language game replace that of self-organization?

Theory of Language Game

Theory of language game advocated by late-Wittgenstein radically urges requestioning of modern reason as an influential standpoint. It was a dramatic turn for him, given the fact that he strongly promoted logical positivism as a founder at an early stage. It may be said, however, that he pursued the modern reason to its extreme, had a strong doubt on it and desperately groped for departure therefrom. Conceptualization of social theory from the standpoint of language game is to inherit such problem consciousness of Ludwig Wittgenstein.

According to Daisaburo Hashizume, various properties of language game are induced from the "fundamental fact that language game is a performative state."[18] Therefore, social theory of language game is to insist that performative action of people, which is not intentional or based on consciousness, forms the rule or social order often as an unintended consequence. It means that, since the essence of language game is in the rule, playing a language game is continuous execution of a rule-governed behavior. In short, features of social recognition suggested by language game is "... a performatively generated conventional state, a tacit state that cannot reasonably be referred to or a normative state that cannot be attributed to individuals."[19] This is a description made by Hitoshi Ochiai to summarize the essence of social theory of conservatism represented by Friedrich Hayek, Herbert Hart and John Austin. This is not directly related with language game. However, its features hold true of language game as they are. Therefore, it can be said that a common ideological basis exists between theory of language game and social philosophy of conservatism.

To tell the truth, here exists the point where self-organization parts from language game. However, we pursue the way of thinking in language game for a while. According to Hashizume, "the language game is as amorphous as, or more amorphous than the everyday life of people, repeating birth and death continuously to make a whirlpool of various language games. It is impossible to command a full view thereof."[20] In other words, his standpoint is to state that it is impossible to describe all rules. It may be possible partly to do so. Since describing whole rules theoretically is to start a new language game, however, it will constitute a whole of language games a new including the description itself. This makes it impossible to escape from the world of language games, but means starting performative action according to a new rule by definition.

> The "language game" is not based on anything. In this sense, it is totally arbitrary (willkürlich). To abolish or overcome a language game, therefore, a new language game superior thereto should be started and disseminated, which will make it possible to go out of any language game. However, this is done in exchange for entering another language game. Therefore, it is by no means possible to go out of the total of language games.[21]

What Hashizume wants to go over in language game is superiority of the subject of recognition to the object of recognition assumed by modern reason. To put it plainly, language game cannot distinguish the observer's standpoint from the observee's standpoint. According to modern reason, observer transcends the standpoint as a concerned party and recognizes the object. Therefore, it could not help but exclude self-referentiality for the self to speak of the self.

In actual world, however, such self-referentiality is not a contradiction but exists as a common phenomenon. Therefore, it is no longer possible to rely on the dichotomy between the two, subject versus object, to regard the former as superior to the latter. At least, the conception of social theory complacently relying thereon is to exert cognitive violence. In this sense as well, it can be said that theory of language game is a requestioning of the modern reason. It contains raising of a question that is the same as construction of self-referential logic questioned by theory of self-organization, on the assumption that language game cannot go out of (or recognize) the whole of language games for not falling in the paradox of self-referentiality.

Arbitrariness of Rule

A contact point between language game and self-organization is in the treatment of rule. Language game is conducted by the rule following behavior. Therefore, it seems impossible at a glance to change the rule. However, this behavior is not conscious and intentional as generally accepted but performative. In other words, it follows tacit rule of which linguistic expression is not necessarily possible, though its existence is known. In short, human beings are free to always follow a new rule tacitly. Therefore, human beings have the freedom to generate rules they tacitly observe, frame up rules and neglect old rules.

Such a view of language game is interesting. It seems that this theory is developing discussions that crush the feasibility of social planning or controllability as a premise of modern rationalism. Language game offers the base of a counter-argument against thought of progressive enlightenment that controls society based on planning and leads it in a desirable direction. However, there is an important problem. This means that acceptance of language game will make one fall into the trap of *arbitrariness of rule*. Hashizume also recognizes this point or seems to be positively accepting it, as he states that anybody can make a rule and observe it.

Arbitrariness of rule is eventually to admit that there are different language games for different people. As Wittgenstein remarks, however, people cannot obey rules privately. To abolish or overcome a language game, therefore, they cannot help but develop and disseminate a language game superior thereto, as stated by Hashizume. Then, how shall a language game be disseminated? Theory of language game does not have means to answer this question at the moment. If a language game hit upon by somebody is disseminated in a society, a new rule will be structuralized. It is logically the same as self-organization that creates a new order from an arbitrary and contingent fluctuation. However, language game does not clarify its mechanism.

Self-organization theory focuses on clarifying autocatalytic process of fluctuation as self-referentiality. Occurrence of fluctuation due to differencification is at a position logically equivalent to that of starting arbitrary language game. A problem exists ahead, however. Self-organization does not occur by a simple play of differencification. Difference ensures its position in traditional system of differences (meaning fulfillment is implemented) only after experiencing a struggle or reflective movement of differences. Dissemination of an arbitrary language game alone is nothing but a simple fashion.

Narrowness of Action View

Above is related to the narrowness of action view assumed by language game. Performative action is a conventional state of affairs. It is true that this effectively denies the superiority of rational action. However, it may not eliminate the possibility to exclude rational action as a result. If so, rationality cultivated by a great deal of efforts by modern society will totally be denied. It is required not to exclude rational action, but to formulate action that goes over its limit. What language game theory relies on is the performative action, which is to be considered before rationality. Modern society has made the faith in rationality prevail more than necessary. To correct this bias, therefore, it is effective to emphasize the importance of performative action before rationality. It does not mean, however, that society is composed of performative action alone. Theory of language game has succeeded in stopping the faith in rationality in modern times, but has consequently emphasized too much the performative or conventional action.

My theory of self-organization incorporates performative action as conventional action, and does not exclude rational action. In addition, it positively incorporates reflexive action to make superiority of rational action relative. I believe that the circulation movement of these three categories of action is the action in actuality. To make the argument easier, about 80% of people's action are conventional and rule-governed. In everyday life, however, they are implementing not only rule-governed action but also rational action, in order to efficiently attain the goal. The latter may account for about 15% of the total. Remaining 5% are reflexive action to requestion the rule itself. In relation to the rule, there are three categories of action, rule-governed, rule-utilizing and rule-questioning. The ratio between these three categories is at least my assumption when I developed self-organization theory, though there is not precise empirical evidence.

Modern society placed too large an emphasis on rational action among the above three. It continuously spread an illusion as if this action is everything. Modern society has made rational action superior and degraded performative and conventional action. For this reason, therefore, language game and the insistence by neoconservatism are accepted as having strong persuasive power. Nevertheless, rational action cannot be denied. Denial of rational action is too one-sided. Self-organization theory does not return to the stage before rationality, but adds reflexive action to the conventional view of action in consideration of rationality beyond.

In my view, rational action is not rule-governed action, but rather rule-utilizing action. Therefore, rational action need not be grounded with the rule but has only to use it pragmatically. Rational action shows involvement in the rule at best to that extent. In short, rational action has radicalism to make even the rule a means of action. Nevertheless, it does not have a motivation to question the rule. For this reason, therefore, the viewpoint of reflexive action is required.

Grounding of the Society

In language game, it is assumed that a language game can be started quite simply. On what basis can it be said so? If the language game is grounded only by continuous execution of action, there are no other alternatives than grounding the start of a new language game also by performative action. If so, a new language game starts accidentally and mutationally without any reason. As a result, it can be said that language game theory does not provide a basis to the start of a new game at all. Therefore, it cannot be said that a new language game can be started any time.

When a new language game starts, differencification from the existing language games and reflexion are working. It is true that language game premises that people have freedom to start a new rule and observe it. Even if people have such freedom, it will end in a castle in the air unless there is grounding to put it into implementation. For this purpose as well, reflexion is indispensable. Of course, theory of language game may insist that society itself is composed on groundlessness from the beginning and be trying to open a new viewpoint toward theory of power for the reason that actual society does not look groundless because a power mechanism is working. If grounding does not exist to start a new language game, however, even the language game of power becomes groundless.

Grounding of the society by self-organization theory is *reflexive competence*. Language game is possible as human beings have this ability. Reflexion is one of the most important characteristics to distinguish human beings from other animals. When the language was selected as the object of language, language game became possible for the first time. At the same time, thinking became possible, followed by culture and society. The human world distinguished from the animal world made its debut not because human beings had language, but because they acquired a language to refer itself, which premises reflexion competence. Human beings acquired this perhaps in the ancient times. Human beings became to be able to continuously question the present state by developing self-referential language.

Modern civilization did not have a theory to appropriately evaluate reflexive competence of human beings. As a result, human beings have become to place emphasis on control ability. However, what is questioned now is reflexive competence of human beings. Reflexion thought behind the theory of self-organization contains a basic problem related to the grounding of human beings and the society.

Chapter 4
Self-Organization and Postmodernity

The theory of self-organization has something in common with that of postmodernity. In advanced industrial societies withdrew frontal discussions on modernization or modernism in and after the 1980s. Except for antiquated modernists or historians on modernization, there are no researchers who publish a book holding up the term "modernization" or "modernism" as a title. Even when dealing with modern society, it is normally the case that they use passive expressions such as "modernity" or "reflexive modern" in place of active terms of "modernization" or "modernism." This reflects the necessity to re-inspect the engine of modernization due to the advent of postmodernism and a start of reviewing modernity. What is required is not discussion on postmodernity as a fashion but sincere and intellectual working to clarify its reality and polish theory thereof. This chapter discusses that theory of self-organization has affinity with that of postmodernity in relation to situations of the times. The essential point is that both theories have a viewpoint of deconstruction of modernity.

1 Fluctuation of Modernity

What is the Modern?

As expounded by Max Weber, the essence of modernity is rationalization process of society. For him, modern times are liberation from the relief by churches or sacraments or from superstitions and the numinous, that is *disenchantment*. The rationalization to promote disenchantment is to (1) exclude the judgment based on whimsicality, arbitrariness, emotion, the numinous, tradition and specific human relations and the mechanism based thereon, and (2) theoretically assess the reality as a correct and abstract concept and generalize things for systematization.[1] What Weber calls rationality is not limited to purposive rationality or formal rationality as calculability such as routinely used efficiency or optimality, but includes value rationality or substantive rationality to realize values and belief. However, modernization progressed with the former exceeding the latter. Modernization pushed history to a world governed by formal rationality that was not related to values or belief but predicted and calculated technologically.

While inheriting the concept of Weberian rationality, Karl Mannheim also proposed the concept of *functionalist rationality*.[2] It is similar to formal rationality. Mannheim advocated that, as industrialization progresses to increasingly develop division of labor and organizations, areas of human activity are functionally rationalized more to enable prediction in advance. In addition, functionalist rationalization incorporates the viewpoint of relations between individuals and organization and between parts and whole. Nowadays it is a generally accepted view that organization will not survive or develop appropriately, if the rationality of individuals alone is discussed. Introduction of functionalism induced discussion on the contribution of individuals to organization, adaptability of organization to the environment and organizational equilibrium distinguished from individuals. In this sense, functional rationalization has advanced the Weberian theory of rationalization one step further.

Based on the above discussion, I define modernity abstractly as the process of establishing a society with *function primacy* that attaches importance to efficiency and rationality. The concept of function primacy means primarily orientation towards ensuring performance with control, or construction of a society with a *control-performance* schema.[3] According to this definition, it is possible to assess systematically most of the features of modernity such as technocracy (technologyism) and industrialism, as well as the rationalization process of society.

There are a number of theories for defining modernity, such as those that regard it as the process of the penetration of technocracy, the rationalization of society as symbolized by bureaucracy, the penetration of mechanized factory production and industrialization where its effect pervades society and culture, and democratization to realize freedom and equality. Each of these definitions is correct, but none can be used to assess modernity systematically. Even when democratization is regarded as the essence of the modern age, for example, it does not explain industrialization, or vice versa.

Using the above abstract definition, however, we can comprehensively grasp modernity. Technocracy just means seeking efficiency and rationality. Bureaucracy means promoting the rationalization of jobs and personnel affairs. Industrialization means mass production with efficient factory labor and mechanical technologies. Although democracy is apparently beyond the definition, the idea of function includes the logic of democratization. The functionalist idea implies the motto of universally adopting human resources and treating them according to performance (the principle of achievement), irrespective of family background, sex, race or other ascriptions. Establishing a society of function primacy, therefore, includes the principle of equal opportunity. Although democracy includes fundamental human rights, social rights and other principles that cannot be deduced directly from the functionalist idea, ensuring and protecting human rights is implied by it if we understand that they are indispensable for the functional operation of society and the rights are guaranteed for that purpose.

In fact, it is no exaggeration to say that what modern democracy has attained is a partial realization of equal opportunity. Democracy in the modern age that aims at realizing freedom and equality has often been subject to the function primacy, or has been recognized only to the extent that it does not compromise efficiency or rationality. This is because, once efficiency has fallen, causing economic stagnation, economic activities which reduce welfare or ignore human rights often prevail. In the modern age, democracy should have controlled industrialism, bureaucracy and technocracy and restrained runaway efficiency and rationality. However, the truth is that different "isms" ran in different directions causing chaos beyond the control of the carter, democracy. In practice, therefore, the essence of modernity is to construct a society with function primacy that respects efficiency and rationality, whatever its ideal may be.

Consequently, above definition of modernity covers the broadest range. This is in precise accord with the way that modernism is understood in architecture, where modernism is equivalent to functionalism. Modern architecture is equal to functionalist architecture, or an idea of thoroughly eliminating waste, play and decoration. The well-known propositions of modern architecture, "Form (Structure) is subordinate to function" and "Beauty (Meaning) is in function," precisely express the concept of function primacy. In other words, the essence of modernity is to functionalize the social formation (structure) and culture (meaning).

Fading Function Primacy

Since the 1980s, the term *fluctuation* has been popular. Fluctuation in this context means undermining or compromising the basis of things, or a phenomenon that does not fit or cannot be treated using established framework or mechanisms.[4] This popularity, which was largely caused by stalemated modernism, indicates that phenomena unsuited to the ideas of modernity are taking place everywhere. The term was not heard during rapid economic growth, when the same phenomena were called deviations, perturbations or protests. They were undesirable for sustaining orderly prosperity and, therefore, had to be controlled in order for the equilibrium to be maintained. In other words, there were definite standard models of people and society when the economy was growing rapidly. The same phenomena, however, are now called fluctuations. This means that the conventional standard models no longer fit the situation. Furthermore, the standard models themselves are also fluctuating.

Modern society has pursued the realization of an affluent society by trying to improve productivity, by valuing efficiency and rationality and creating growth-oriented control devices. We now have innumerable terms related to function, such as efficiency, rationalization, management, control, plan, optimization, productivity, equilibrium, growth, development and so on. People can think only by using their own vocabulary and ideas. Phenomena outside these frameworks are regarded as cumbersome or undesirable. In fact, phenomena that deviate from the functionalist idea have been degraded by being called perturbations, deviations, resistance or noise. They are merely the objects of control from the viewpoint of modernity.

However, the coming of an affluent society has caused the people's values to diversify and their lifestyles to become personalized. Diversification and individuation represent a state in which behaviors and values cannot be decoded precisely using the predetermined standard models. A situation in which diversification and individuation are excessive incubates a fluctuating society. It also reflects the fact that people have become suspicious of social and personal values which indicate preference toward *function primacy*. Today, people tend to think that they cannot obtain true happiness merely by pursuing efficient and rational methods. Some people have become disillusioned with the rigorous efforts required. Most people are doubtful of the point of their efforts: whether they have intrinsic worth or promote enrichment of life. For that very reason, diversions, playing with difference and other postmodern phenomena have become fashionable.

Promoting social functions based on efficiency and rationality is not all that people do. Importantly, they also create new lifestyles and cultures by seeking and questioning the meaning of life. Conventional modern society, constructed mainly to pursue function, has lost momentum as it has failed to reveal respect for the need for meaning fulfillment.

Postmodernity and Signification

Postmodernity is a term to express the situation that comes after modernity or goes over it. It is a concept to give a generic name to the feeling of reality in and after the age when modern conception lost the power to capture reality. Its origin goes back to the nihilism that made its debut as the skepticism against the progressivism in the West. Nihilism expresses the unstable and groundless sense against reality, with postmodernity existing on the extension thereof.

I define postmodernity as the *re-injection of signification into society after the rationalization process of modern times*.[5] As modern society addressed the problem of signification, which is important working of human beings, from a functional viewpoint, it degraded the social significance of meaning not in conformity with function. Thus, it locked signification out of public fields and expelled to the field of private life or culture. In other words, modern society effectively utilized human beings at the functional aspect, but established a system to waste them at the meaning aspect. Postmodernity was generated as a reaction to such a tendency, which linked itself with nihilism at the initial stage. However, the essence of postmodernity is not limited to nihilism, but is to dissolve functionalist reason and reconstruct it as a different rationality. It is understood as a movement to recover the semantic space, which was dissolved by modernity, from the viewpoint of existential life.

Postmodern Syndrome

There is the poststructuralism as a predecessor of the postmodernism. Poststructuralism appeared as a reaction against structuralism, which was represented by Lévi-Strauss, to have excluded violence, noise, happening, and difference from the concept of structure.[6] Structure is not as strict as structuralism considers it to be, but accompanies the distortion and cleavage in many parts of itself. The cause of this feature lies in the forces of heterogeneity and differentiality. Therefore, differencification from the establishment becomes the key idea in poststructuralism.

Differencification is the movement of coexisting with heterogeneous differences and causes cracks and cleavages in structure. It is akin to the concept of fluctuation. In addition to this, poststructuralism does not only stress differencification, cracks and cleavages of structure, but also emphasizes reconstruction work after disjoining it as is observed in the idea of deconstruction. According to Jacques Derrida, *deconstruction* does not mean simple destruction and negation, but means that it will reconstruct the structure of an issue through analyzing, dissolving and modifying its structure.[7]

Following Barry Smart postmodernism has a longer history as it is argued.[8] But it was after the late 1970's when a British architect Charles Jencks used the term of postmodernism that the contemporary thought of postmodernism came to prevail widely.[9] The thought of postmodern architecture means the movement which declares criticism of the functionalist (modernism) architecture that excludes luxury decoration and wastefulness as much as possible, and which takes in play, symbolic expression, and free idea. After this movement, postmodernism became a key concept representing one of the main streams in contemporary thought with fashion, literature, philosophy and social sciences prevailing over the architecture.

Jean-François Lyotard, who resembles the founder of a religion with respect to postmodernity in cultural sciences, insists that we are now in an age which declares the end of modern "grand narratives." He says that the present situation promotes mistrust of grand narratives, such as realizing freedom and equality, aiming for revolution and emancipation, or seeking consensus and legitimacy.[10] Postmodernism denies efficient totalization by systems and assimilation by consensus. It is based on the working of local and minor heterogeneity and the "paralogy" (i.e. anti-logical imagination) of differencification which is not mutually commensurated. In the background of postmodernism is mistrust of the ideals that have supported modern society, in particular the progressive thought of the enlightenment.

Regardless of whether the field is architecture, design, philosophy or the humanities, what is common to all forms of postmodern thought is that it incorporates criticism of modern functionalist reason. Modern society, which is extremely biased toward function, has colonized the search for the meaning of life which is an important human activity. The rise of postmodern thought indicates recognition of the significance of symbolic meanings, uncontaminated by function.

In modern society, symbolic meaning, unrelated to function, is a subjectivistic, personal and floating phenomenon. It has been significant in art and literature, but has been regarded as of secondary importance for the operation of society and was relegated from the public field to private life. Since the coming of the affluent society, however, meaning has started to assert itself in relation to human existence. This is reflected in the tendency to respect self-actualization, the value of life and personal decisions about lifestyle. These don not necessarily have correspondence with any entity, and are therefore related to the construction of identity by means of representation without transparency.

It may be an exaggeration to say that modernity has ignored the meaning of life, in particular the issue of representation which is not necessarily transparent. However, it is undeniable that modernity has at least functionalized this issue. A functionalized meaning is representation treated as a design to display utility, convenience and efficiency or as a symbol to maintain order. It is a meaning subordinate to function and not logic specific to itself. It is nothing but a meaning "colonialized" by function. One of the most important points in postmodernity is to insist that the aspect of symbolic meaning should be recognized as a public factor as important as structure and function. In short, it is to recover the signification that is not functionally contaminated.

There are no alternatives for modern society but to cross the border of *function primacy* because it has pursued modernity to an extreme. Modern society succeeded in deconstructing medieval society, in which the idea of structure had primacy and which maintained patterns by rules, through introducing the functionalist concept in addition to structure. The main activity principle in medieval society was to process things according to predetermined stereotyped patterns. It was a society in which rules (structure) dominated people in the name of God. To break through these limits, modern society introduced functionalist ideas to improve performance by control. By doing so, modern civilization invented a loop of structure and function as a device to construct a society. As fluctuations which do not fit the loop have started to occur frequently, however, new problems of the difference and meaning mechanism have arisen. The area of transfunctional and nonstructural symbolic meaning which surpasses function but is still at a nonstructural stage, has started to deviate from the modern stage of structure and function loop, and has caused postmodern fluctuations.[11]

Skepticism against the Enlightenment

Skepticism about modernity increased markedly in the 1980's. Its typical manifestation in contemporary thought is that on the one hand social philosophy of neoconservatism gained the strong persuasive power and on the other hand postmodernism became popular together with the enhanced movement of new age sciences making fluctuation and chaos its target. Although claims in neoconservatism and postmodernism basically contradict each other, they

1 Fluctuation of Modernity   115

strangely stood side by side in the 1980's. It is the very important point why it was possible. The both had the common aspect of skepticism against the modern thought of progressive enlightenment. At this point strange coexistence was possible. Moreover, as discussed in Introduction, the new age sciences shared skepticism about the modernism together with them in terms of reflexion to modern rational epistemology. In short, skepticism about modernism and reflexion on it are the major features in the philosophical and scientific thought of the 1980's. In this situation, the modern idea which had overwhelming influence was shaken greatly.

The social philosophy of conservatism is represented by the economist, Friedrich Hayek, and is developed by the philologist of ordinary language, John Austin. It raises doubts about the modern thought of progressive enlightenment that reason can control society intentionally and knowledge can be confirmed objectively.[12] It is in a sense a philosophy of anti-enlightenment.

Human society cannot be easily changed even if we plan to do so and also cannot be fully controlled intentionally. In society *spontaneous order* exists which is not set up consciously. For instance, market, language, ritual, mores and tradition belong to this order. This order was generated by the rules which people created as an unintended consequence of their performative action. Therefore, spontaneous order simply indicates the situation that action is repeatedly performed, and order must change if performative action changes. In short, order is dependent on performative action which reproduces it. Therefore, any attempts to induce objective and universal laws like natural laws cannot help but fail.

The characteristic of social theory of conservatism emphasizes the fact that action, which has been done not intentionally and consciously but performatively, generates rules or social order as a consequence. The basic claim of social philosophy of conservatism is *spontaneous order through performative action*.[13] According to Hayek, this kind of spontaneous order does not necessarily exclude intended change of a certain partial rule.[14] If conflict occurs on the rules to be followed, the rule which is followed performatively should be articulated intentionally, the question should be pointed at, and then the new rules should be set up intentionally. However, in this case, all the rules except ones which are in question should be presumed tacitly and performatively. In a word, the ground on which society is built must presume a tacit order which cannot be referred to rationally. The philosophy of conservatism regards this as the basis which sustains society. Modern philosophy of enlightenment has a critical difficulty in its basic presumption since it deals with intentional control ignoring the above issue as if it were possible.

The social philosophy of conservatism revived an anti-enlightenment standpoint by raising the question of performative affairs which could not be ascribed to the aporia between subjectivity and objectivity. This is one of the persuasive theories which attack the limit of control theory built by the modern age. In this background lies the trust in human forces of reality construction which are free from the idea of functional primacy.

2 Metamorphosis of Society

Transfunctional and Nonstructural

By pursuing modernism at its extreme we located ourselves in transfunctional and nonstructural phase which transcends the functional idea and is not haunted by structural idea like conventional patterns and rules. It is the field which meaning mechanism governs and this field does not follow the functional idea of management by control nor structural idea of domination by rule (the meaning herein described is not a meaning subordinated to function and structure, but what has the inherent logic of symbolic meaning itself). This is why the phenomena which cannot be absorbed by the framework of modern society are generated and fluctuation are displayed (see Figure 4.1).

Although there are functionalized and structured meanings, here we target a meaning before it appears in the society as a structural-functional form, and therefore, it should be called the *original meaning*. Following Ferdinand de Saussure, I make it a rule to ask the origin of meaning for difference, which has the independent logic that never follows function as control and is not governed by structure as rule. It comprises what can be called *power of meaning*.

From the standpoint of defining the descriptive concept of meaning as difference, the generating cause of meaning consists in *articulation of the world*. In other

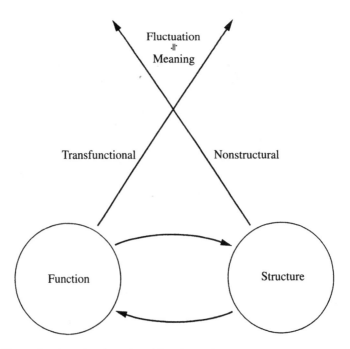

Fig. 4.1 Fluctuation from the viewpoint of function and structure

words, meaning is explored in *relation of life with the world*, and is generated by articulating the world. It cannot be confined by simple articulation of words. It comprises the articulation preceding words (not necessarily expressible by words, tacit and/or performative). What is articulated is difference. Herein, articulation means bringing any distinction into chaotic world and giving difference and identity to all the various things and events with distinction. We give meaning by articulation to the world, and the world has meaning when it is experienced as the mass of things and events which are articulated.[15]

If the way how life relates to itself with the world does have meaning, there must be will to power called *relating*. It is akin to Friedrich Nietzsche's the will to power. He criticizes in *Zur Genealogie der Moral* Herbert Spencer's idea that depicted modern society as organic functional body, and describes that highest grade activism could not be secured by the concepts of adjustment or adaptation. He argues that defining a human being by the ability of adaptation lacks the intrinsic nature of life, the will to power, and superiority of spontaneous and aggressive powers which can allow new interpretation of the world and give new direction. Eventually, adaptation to the environment cannot express the true power of life.[16] Meaning is the way which life relates to itself with the world, and therein the will to power is comprised. The requirement to social theory or social formation is to give its power forms.[17]

The reason of fluctuation of modernity consists in that meaning issued the declaration of independence, while it had never been given any primary position with being handled as something subjective and private. The true figure of fluctuation can be found in the self-assertion of meaning which cannot be comprised by functional and structural mechanism. What is important is to study fluctuation from the viewpoint of meaning and read symptoms of new order.

Metamorphosis as Metaphor

Realization of affluent society had changed people's mental structure. People are not as susceptible as before to such slogans as growth, progress, and development. They transformed themselves from those enhancing their performances by acting more efficiently and adapting themselves to environmental change to those realizing their human identity by presenting and editing meaning of their own life through creating differences of marked individuality.

This transformation may suggest the coming of a new era which might be said a transformation from adaptation to the environment to self-organization.[18] To change oneself according to environmental change is too heteronomous. Human beings have the ability to change themselves by their own forces regardless of environmental change.

Such symptoms are metaphorically represented by the pupal stage in metamorphosis of insect from larval to imago through pupa. This pupal stage is a period of dramatic change of constitution. The pupa is covered by a cocoon which intercepts influences from environment, and in appearance, it does not show any remarkable change. Within the pupa, however, an internal process of changing itself by its own mechanism is occurring, that is the scrapping of old constitution and building of new constitution progress simultaneously. Metamorphosis of pupa is an example of insects. However, could not it be said that self-organization similar to metamorphosis of insects occur in industrial society in the form of questioning again modern civilization? It may be considered an attempt transcending the idea of function primacy that modern civilization has been attaining.

Until present, the key word to conceptualize social change was growth and development and their counterpart concepts were decline and decay. These are the terms used to conceptualize changes as a mammalogical paradigm. For example, when we see human babies we can imagine their shapes and forms as they grow older. Babies grow by giving them adequate nutrition and knowledge. For this reason, the industrial society was oriented to growth and adaptation to environment. However, after human beings have managed to realize an affluent society, such thoughts began to show their limits. Essential metamorphosis appears silently but dramatically. To express such situation, insectological paradigm is more suitable than mammalogical paradigm represented by the concept of development or growth.[19]

This *metamorphosis* represents changes by scrapping old constitution and build new constitution by itself, by transforming itself to completely different one through establishing an new identity of itself, or in other words by self-organizing work. I consider that metamorphosis of pupa or age of self-organization is the changes actually occurring. Modern society is now beginning to play the story of metamorphosis.

Then, what is the goal of this story of metamorphosis? It is probably creation of a new civilization which gives only symptoms through the phenomena of dodging and slipping from the grip of modern idea. I think it can be called the *civilization of meaning*. It is to give importance of the first order to articulate new differences from the world and reedit conventional knowledge and culture.

Why self-organization can be a key word of the new age lies in the spirit which this word can bear. Till present, social change has been used as corresponding term to self-organization. I use this self-organization instead of social change with intention to emphasize that an individual human being changes society, but not that society changes itself. Society cannot be a subject of social change, but an individual human being is the very subject. I mean that society is at most an object word.[20]

The spirit which the term of social change sustained was orderly prosperity in the period of high economic growth. Contrary to this, the spirit which self-organization is to sustain is *vital stability* in the era of stable economic growth. Therefore, the transformation of key word from social change to self-organization means the conversion from order orientation under prosperity to vitality orientation under

2 Metamorphosis of Society

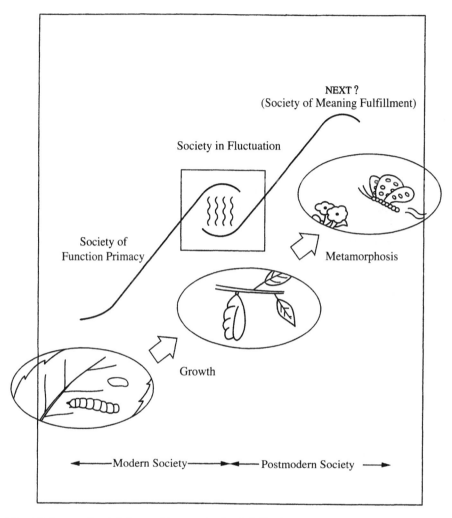

Fig. 4.2 Image of social change: Metamorphosis of civilization

stability. Because society is stable, vital power of each individual is required. When society was enjoying prosperity in the period like high economic growth, rather orderly behavior of each individual was required. The presumption of homo sociologicus bore this expectation. It reinforced the presumption of homo economicus who pursued his own interest, and presented the suitable image of people who supported the orderly prosperity. What can be associated from the spirit of the age of vital stability is not such an image that individuals are adapting to social change while society is growing and developing continuously, but, on the contrary, such an image that individuals challenge various attempts bravely and try to establish new action styles and orders while society is in a state of stagnation and stability.

The keyword conversion from social change to self-organization bears such the situation of age.

3 Identity and Self-Organization: Transformation of Self-Image

Another reason to cause a fraying around the edges in the modern reality is the advent of a world of electronic media by informatization, which collapsed the correspondence relation between entity and representation and induced the *deprivation of meaning*. Reality will become fragments of signs lacking the basic entity, unless it is guaranteed that representation of meaning is anchored at the definite existence. This is related to the *crisis of representation*, which features postmodernism or the loss of transparency of representation.

The collapse of *transparency of representation* or direct correspondence between representation and entity causes decentralization, multi-dimensionality and drifting not only of the self but of all identities as well, because identity which consists of creation and interpretation of representation becomes groundless, if it does not drop its anchor with a definite entity. When the representation is not a reflection of the entity, identity will (must) be constructed independently of the entity. Thus, in a postmodern society, situation appears that people have lost a stable place in which to anchor their consciousness and have to depend on a drifting identity.

Modern society sought human beings who do not ignore self evaluation and who make ceaseless efforts to attain goals. People were able to construct self-identity by relying on this standard model. At the coming of postindustrial and information societies, however, *grand narratives* such as emancipation, progress, enlightenment and universal truth lost reliability, and the baselessness and contingency of modern society were seen to cause such identities to fluctuate.

Drifting Self

Electric media revolution which is called the third information revolution, after the invention of language and printing technology, will result in a situation in which virtuality and reality are intermingled in every aspect of life. We have lost definite values to rely upon and are required to process meaningless information amid a flood of symbols which have lost the correspondence with entities. Under such circumstances, is it possible to establish a self-identity, or can identity itself exist?

Identity is linked with the concept of the sameness of self: ourselves as opposed to others, subjectivity, individuality and so on. What is common to these terms is the image of a unified self. In other words, identity has been used as a concept to show the way of existence of the self integrated through a certain standard of value.

3 Identity and Self-Organization: Transformation of Self-Image

As Erik Erikson put it, identity is our confidence in the process of ego development in the framework of a specific social reality, or is an answer to the question, "Who am I?"[21]

According to conventional modern thinking, the concept of the self refers to a subject which has a personal and preserving identity. To be a human being is to have a self or an internal identity that remains unchanged throughout life. For many years, it has been considered a tragedy for both individuals and society as a whole to lack a unified self or a definite feeling of identity. However, such a viewpoint is now dubious for the following reasons.

1. If we have a fixed identity in a rapidly changing society, we will risk disaster or a lack of adaptability. Therefore, we need to have a flexible identity.
2. Since society is becoming increasingly heterogeneous in terms of sense of values and lifestyles, a limited identity will restrict people's social interaction and the development of individuals.
3. In addition, since a limited identity is a reflection of a lack of social experience, people should be encouraged to play a variety of roles.

Such a viewpoint suggests that the self is always situational. A self will not be unified completely or preserved forever. While having the cores of personality and identity, everyone has a set of selves for different roles and spectators. In previous discussions of the situational self, however, the self has been regarded as situational only in a limited sense, having rarely been seen as being formed or reformed according to the situation. A self is a unified and preserving entity in a sense, and is generally regarded as being maintained throughout life as a continuous chain of memories, and having a coherent identity.

In the present diverse and fluid situation, it is difficult for us to have a unified and definite identity. We cannot find a stable place to which we regress ourselves, and are forced to live with a drifting identity. One of the causes of this situation is the coming of the consumer society, in which slogans to express individuality are for sale and we have been bombarded with ever-changing images of the self. The conventional self has been subjected to concentrated attack by images of the self offered to encourage consumption and has lost its substantial form. Most people have assimilated external identities into their apparently subjective selves and changed their own images.

As information media progress in the future, a *hyper-reality* that fits neither reality nor unreality in the conventional sense will repeatedly emerge and die off.[22] When multifarious fragmented signs generated by virtual reality and hyper-media start to proliferate, it will become impossible to maintain a definite self. Self-identity will become fluid. People will be at the mercy of fragmented signs whose meanings are disorganized by the flood of information. We will hardly be able to survive, if we obstinately cling to the establishment of a subjective self. It is easy to say that self-identity will fragment and disappear through the advancement of information society and consumerization. However, such an expression is dependent on the modern idea that fluctuation can be viewed only with negative connotations, and does not reflect positively on postmodernity. Fluctuating identity does not necessarily mean collapse of identity. Postmodernity will not take shape unless it reflects a new type of identity.

Hyper-Reality and Self-Actualization

The current advancement of information technology is intended to construct an institutional apparatus to enhance social control and efficiently transmit, accumulate and process symbols. Modern society has rationalized and improved the efficiency of processing materials and human resources. This thrust has now penetrated the realm of symbols. The resultant greater efficiency makes life easier in many ways. What used to consume time no longer does to such an extent. Options have increased for people. Through the videotext system, for example, people at home can shop and make reservations for hotels, transportation and theatres. People can transfer funds through banks any time from their homes, without being restricted by the business hours of banks.

Rising Importance of the Difference Motive

With the advancement of information technology, modern society will complete an unprecedented high-level and soft control system. If not only materials and personnel but also symbols are contaminated by functional rationality, social integration will lose its power. However, people are not so simple as to unconditionally accept such rationalization and control.

People nowadays, compared to those in the past, are less motivated by deficiency. For the functional mechanism to work effectively, people must be dominated by deficiency motives and stung with desires. Today, however, *difference motives*, such as self-actualization and the authenticity and quality of life, related to symbolic meanings rather than functions, are rising to add value to life.[23]

Most of the need classifications offered during the postwar period assumed deficiency motives. Typical of these is the hierarchical model of needs presented by Abraham Maslow.[24] This theory holds that the satisfaction of needs shifts from basic to higher level needs, or that higher level needs will not become apparent until those of the lower levels are satisfied. Physiological needs to eat or sleep come first, followed by needs for safety, belongingness, and approval. At the top is the need for self-actualization. Since the need for self-actualization has the highest level according to this theory, deficiency motives do not work in seeking the next stage. If there is a higher level deficiency need, the functional mechanism is effective. But, as the need for self-actualization is the highest level of human needs, deficiency motives become irrelevant. Although deficiency motives still exist, people are rather motivated by individualistic differences.

To seek differences is to realize a self different from the former self and/or others. The superficial embodiment of this is the coming of the consumer society

3 Identity and Self-Organization: Transformation of Self-Image

in which people express their personal selves using the sign-values of commodities. Such a motivation does not perhaps go so far as a genuine seeking for *self-actualization*, but nevertheless, the difference motive at least surpasses the deficiency motive. This suggests that people have become extremely sensitive to differences. Extreme sensitivity to differences means that symbolic meaning is held in greater esteem. A major act in pursuing and fulfilling meanings is to express one's self. For a meaning to emerge, moreover, a difference distinguishing it from other things must exist. Individuation and diversification are two terms which emphasize this difference. Under a difference motive, it is important to extract a variety of differences in one's self and interrelate them in order to express individuality.

Modern society has continued to disorganize the semantic space under the pressure of function primacy. With advances in information technology, an enormous volume of functional information to control materials and people will surge through society and will expand a blank world of lost meaning, where people feel like wanderers forcibly isolated not only from others but also from themselves. To recover the lost semantic space, therefore, people seek *another self* in pursuit of the meaning of life.[25]

Dominance of Simulacra

In the latter half of the 1970s, Jean Baudrillard expressed the view that, today, all systems are fluctuating in uncertainty. Reality is absorbed by hyper-reality or codes and simulations. The principle of simulation is replacing the old principle of reality to control us. Compliance with purpose has disappeared. Models generate us. Ideologies no longer exist. What exist are *simulacra* alone, generated by an operation of simulations.[26] In an advanced information society, reality will be absorbed in the hyper-reality generated by codes and simulations. Information (representation) which does not directly correspond to the entity is a sort of bubble and smacks of fiction. Such an aspect of information is a simulacrum, a term for all representations with no correspondence to the entity.

In the world of simulacra, pseudo-reality consisting of representation without transparency is dominant. Distinctions between original and copy and between reality and unreality become vague. The essentially fictitious is taken as reality. In extreme cases, reality is recognized only in fiction. This hyper-reality piles up fictitious realities to create multiple layers. The space composed of symbolic signs abstracts usefulness and functionality, where insane recognition of reality flies around. Consequently, concrete realities such as "what human beings should be" and "what life should be" are replaced with a "difference as image" unrelated to reality. Thus a movement is brought about to pursue a "difference as sign" or an image of a human being which does not exist anywhere.

This paradoxical world of hyper-reality is filled with the experience of *ilinks* (dizziness or the whirl of the brain), a play typified by Roger Caillois.[27] It is an eschatological aspect of contemporary controlled society. People existing there are no longer *Homo Sapiens* (intellectual animals) but *Homo Demens* (insane animals). To regard the Homo Demens image of the human being as unintelligent, incomprehensible or eventually controlled, as did Baudrillard, follows the viewpoint of modern rationalism. Baudrillard, who has an extremely nihilistic perception of contemporary society, is keen to describe its eschatological aspect. Nevertheless, the new space explored by high-tech media is indispensable for humanity's future and will be a frontier for next-generation industries. Nihilistic criticism of this fictitiousness does not yield fruit.

Even if the world of hyper-reality is paradoxical to the modern intelligence, it will make another reality indispensable for human life in the 21st century. It is more important to question what human beings will become or how society will be constructed in the future. That the self-image in postmodern society will be distracted by simulacra, as Baudrillard suggests, is doubtful. It is certain, however, that at least the subjective self which has been problematic in modern society will fluctuate to form another image of self.

Another Self

Simulacra with no distinction between reality and unreality will be formed to repeat infinite emergence and extinction. It will then become difficult to organize selves according to a specific value principle. Selves will no longer form distinctive shells.

As a case symbolizing the image of the self in postmodern society, it is interesting to cite the story of a person who experienced virtual reality using a remote control robot. The robot, which precisely models the upper part of the human body, is designed to reproduce exactly the motions of the operator's neck, hands and arms. Its eyes are a three-dimensional camera. When its hands grip an item, the resistance is conveyed to the operator. An operator sitting three meters from the robot gripped a small bar and inserted it into a hole, and tightened bolts, and picked up soft items and placed them in line. While playing in such a manner, the operator casually looked to his side and discovered a figure sitting in a chair and surrounded by a number of devices with cables hanging from its head and arms. It took several minutes for the operator to recognize that he himself was that figure. He said, "I had transformed myself into the robot. The real myself seen by the robot's eyes was strange enough. Seeing my figure from the eyes of a robot or another myself gave a shock to my identity." This is a story of a person who has become a robot in virtual reality and is shocked when he encounters himself in reality, or a story of a person who is surprised at experiencing *another self*. Schizophrenics sometimes say, "I cannot look away from myself even for a moment. If I look away, I will be dissected into pieces. I am always tense. Otherwise, other people will enter me and I will be lost." The story of the robot operator is similar to the loss of self experienced by schizophrenics. When we have a plurality of selves, we will live in a similar world.

If a virtual reality prevails, we may lose compatibility with the plurality of selves. Which is the real subject, the self who controls a plurality of selves, or the plurality of dissected selves? Whichever it is, the image of the self maintaining a firm subjectivity must dissipate. We may possibly believe that we are nothing but a figure circulating among a plurality of selves. The task of confirming the place to which we regress ourselves will become less important.

The characteristic image of the self in a society where *difference motives* are dominant is not the paranoid type but the schizoid type. To have the power of self-control is the condition for a paranoid type character not to become morbid, but the corresponding condition for a schizoid type character is not yet known. It may be the power of *self-editorship*, editing the chaotic state of fragmented differences and generating new meaning. The power of self-control must shift to the power of self-editorship. Without this shift, the result is paranoiac schizoid symptoms.

A typical example is "PC kids." It is not correct to refer to PC kids as autistic types. They are information citizens who experience *ilinks* by wandering from the display into the infinite world of the computer network. They do not expect efficiency from PC communications, but, on the contrary, unconsciously try to overturn the modern values of efficiency and convenience. Moreover, they have overturned meanings by dismantling the polarities of the framework of thought – such as fact and fiction, centre and periphery, intelligence and sensitivity, and work and play – established by modernity. Such behavior is schizoid, but absorption into it is paranoiac.

In modern society, many people feel anxious about what they should do, unless they are given goals or tasks to attain or accomplish. There are no predetermined goals and tasks in the actions of meaning fulfillment. What exists there is only a process of creating new meaning through differencification from orthodoxy or tradition. *Nomads*, who repeat trial-and-error processes in unknown fields, or people of the schizoid type, are more suited to such circumstances than those of the paranoid type or efficient or diligent people. To be preoccupied in meaning fulfillment (the pursuit of truth, good and beauty), however, means to be paranoiac. Therefore, people will not be able to thrive in the future unless they are double-minded people, paranoiac and schizoid at the same time. People will not be able to stick stubbornly to the establishment of a subjective self as before.

4 Self in Chaos

Self-identity will be chaotic until the modern self is dismantled and a new image of self is established. The chaotic self image may be perverse, distracting or morbid for conscientious people at the moment. Such confusion usually takes place in a period of transformation.

Perverse Self-Actualization

Fetish adherence to materials in consumption affects communication, reversing the normal order of preference between object and language. What Takeshi Ohira calls the *Monogatari* syndrome indicates this situation.[28] *Monogatari* is a Japanese word that normally means narratives. Since "mono" means commodities or materials and "gatari" means narrations, he uses Monogatari as a term to indicate the act of expressing selves through material commodities. The Monogatari syndrome is, therefore, related to the mental disease of people who seek self-actualization by means of commodities.

Typical Monogatari patients cannot explain their acquaintances well. Once the subject has been directed to clothing, decorations or other personal effects, however, they suddenly become able to describe people vividly. They are fluent when material objects are available to mediate discourse. In associating with other people, they use consumer goods or treat people as consumer goods to avoid collisions of animated feelings. They confirm their identities by what they wear. They can express or personalize themselves only by means of material objects.

The Monogatari syndrome is a mental disease which appeared in Japan during the bubble economy when consumer society was at its peak. Unlike a society in which production is given priority, the consumer society expedites not so much the acquisition of low-priced, good-quality products as the expression of our selves using material objects as signs, or representing our selves with consumer goods. This situation of the consumer society is convenient to promptly diversify values, personalize lifestyles and actualize selves. When actual definitions of diversification and individuation have not been established, it is natural that people want to establish them quickly and easily. Thus, the belief that material objects, signs and meanings are equal generates a self-actualization that relies on consumer goods.

Self-actualization relying on consumer goods often causes disturbance in personal communications. One illustration of the Monogatari syndrome is the story of a 25-year-old man working for an electrical equipment manufacturing company, who visited a doctor with symptoms of neurotic diarrhea. He could not understand what his problem was. The doctor asked him about his work and things in his life, but could not obtain definite answers. Once the topic changed to clothing, however, the Monogatari syndrome started. That business suits repress people's individuality was discussed. When his girlfriend came up in the conversation, he suddenly started a stream of Monogatari that was not understood except by experts in this field.

> I myself was deeply absorbed in fashion when I was a student, greatly affected by her. She was one of my classmates at senior high school. Her father was a manager in a trading company. She was certainly a daughter of a well-to-do family. She said, 'However fashionable you are, Poshboy cannot compete with Byblos.' It would have been allowed, if I had been a student. When I started to work for a company, I bought Armani suits, Coal Haan shoes and Nicole neckties. I had a Heuer watch, but I spent all my bonus pay to buy an Omega watch. I used an Ace attaché case for work and a Hunting World or Yoshida bag when I was off duty.[29]

4 Self in Chaos   127

He might intend to express tactfully himself with plenty of brand names such as Byblos and Poshboy which sound like alien words to ordinary people. A consumer society features increased consumption of products that are not guaranteed to be useful; consumers consume these goods to integrate themselves with the image and meaning given by the commodities. In the case of people with Monogatari syndrome, however, sign-values have become separated from commodities and symbolize individual persons. They incarnate themselves or have a self in society only through the existence of symbolized signs. Only through this pseudo-meaning is there any ground for existence and self-actualization. This may be acceptable, if people attain self-actualization in this way. If they fall into mental disease instead, however, it is meaningless and futile.

The final destination of the information society is a world of hyper-reality where even human beings change to signs. This world will be dominated by self-purposed signs or *simulacra* which constitute a society every time the necessity arises. Absolute values or the guarantees of fundamental existence will not be present in this world. It will become increasingly difficult to apply dualistic norms such as superior or inferior, good or bad, or true or false.

Contemporary Festival Space

Self-actualization has hitherto been seen in terms of bringing the subjective self close to the self expected by society, family, company and friends, in order to unify the self.[30] An age will possibly come, however, when people pursue *another self* in an area different from both the subjective self and the expected self. One phenomenon that predicts such a movement is the *Comic-market*, or what is normally called the *Comiket*, which is becoming increasingly popular among young people.

Comics are now one of the most powerful media in Japan.[31] In the world of comics are coterie magazines which parody original stories. Writers respectfully borrow characters from original stories and develop their own narratives. They extract favorite characters and elements from interesting animated cartoons and comics and generate new characters, relationships and plots. They gradually disorganize the original tales and lose their own stories as well.

Comiket is physical gatherings of people and materials for the exhibition, trading and direct sales of these coterie magazines. Comiket is not only a place for circulating such coterie magazines, but also a space where their contents are three-dimensional, or a space of hyper-reality. In this space, people, media and comics exist with identical weight.[32]

In Comiket, people do not use their real names but refer to one another with the names of characters in animated cartoons and comics or imaginary names which do not exist anywhere else. Many participants enjoy costume-play. Disguising themselves as characters in a cartoon or comic, they sell coterie magazines and act out specific performances. However, they do not pursue laughter or satire. For example, a person may hold a placard manifesting "Sanrizuka's downright fight" in one hand, and a coterie magazine from the Peach Girl series in the other. Why does he appear to be making a protest? He is not appealing to others at all. He is expressing his self outside real space by erasing his subjective and expected self, and has transformed to something alien by connecting himself to the placard and coterie magazine. In Comiket space, there are individual figures which disorganize the meaning, composed of morality, common sense and manners that support everyday life. However, this space is not chaotic. If it were chaotic, it could not have survived from 1975 until today. This space has succeeded in incorporating chaos as a type of order.

In Comiket, languages have been released from logic and have recovered their inherent poetic character. This space is exclusively composed of plays that have freed themselves from everyday life. Not only language but all categories of existence and signs are at play. All images are becoming a reality. From common and rationalistic viewpoints, perhaps nothing is more meaningless. However, such a view is not correct. Comiket space is meaningful, because it is meaningless. If signs are unified and controlled by the rules, semantic space will collapse. Meaning will never be unified. When it is unified, it will die. When languages and signs float without the entity, they recover the features of play and activate a semantic space.

In this way, Comiket exists as a hyper-reality where signs float without entities. Individual participants do not have an entity, either. Selves are created only in relation to floating signs. To acquire the evidence of existence, participants plunge a fragment of soul into the craziness and intoxication that envelope Comiket. This is a realization of *another self* in the area which has eliminated the modern self.

The case of Comics-markets or the contemporary festival space is very specific and not universal. However, symptoms of a new order are always to be found in specific and extraordinary phenomena. I think Comics-markets are displaying a power beyond the functionalist idea and predetermined routine structures. While modern selves are collapsing, a movement to pursue the ideal of another self is to be seen there.

5 Toward a Theory of Postmodern Identity

From Having to Being

Self-identity in the postmodern age is not based on *having*, but, rather, has become based on *being*. Such a transformation cannot be coped with using the idea of function primacy, but requires that of meaning fulfillment. Function primacy is effective for pursuing material abundance, but the present functional mechanism will lose its validity in the postmodern situation where the production and distribution of information and cultural resources have become a major source of value and the phase of identity is shifting from possession to existence. This is because *being* is related to a type of representation that does not necessarily reflect the entity and is concerned more with symbolic meanings, while *having* can be described in terms of function. Regarding the context of information, the problem is that whereas functional information reduces uncertainty and thereby controls the entity, meaning information, on the other hand, constitutes existence as a representation without transparency.

In *Nomads of the Present*, Alberto Melucci, discussing a new social movement in postmaterial society, expressed the increasing requirements for new freedom as a change from the "right to property" to the "right to existence."[33] In the background of social movements until the present have been requirements for economic rights and rights of citizenship. Although we are still in such an age, a new horizon toward democracy is being exploited by appeals to meaningful existence (life) in the fields of birth, death, disease and coexistence with the environment, which together form the basis of human life.

Rationalization and system control promoted in modern society have penetrated not only production and administration but also other areas which were formerly out of control. Emotional relations, sex, health, birth and death are all subject to control by medical or administrative organizations. In many cases, whether a person lives or dies depends on external factors beyond the individual's control. This can be seen in the moral issues surrounding cases of euthanasia, people being maintained by life-support machines, death due to overwork, troubles caused by the dosage and abuse of drugs, diseases related to pollution and troubles due to stress. The right to live is itself subject to control. Therefore, freedom of existence is an important subject.

New social movements include demands related to such problems. Most advocate environmental preservation, informed consent in medical treatment and opposition to nuclear power plants, but do not require sharing the gains of production. They do not rise up to demand distribution or redistribution of wealth. They are rarely routed through political parties or labor unions. Social movements appear at the citizen level centering on issues of existence and lifestyle.

Both the shift from the "freedom to have" to the "freedom to be" and from the "right to equality" to the "right to difference" are important factors that decisively determine what self-identity should be in the future. To guarantee the freedom to be, it is necessary, now more than ever, to recognize the "signifying process" of individuals and groups and make it autonomous and free from outside pressure, because significant existence is to express the self as it is by confirming and affirming it with meanings. If this process becomes the object of control or management, the freedom of existence will not be guaranteed.

Expression of meanings requires a difference that distinguishes it from others. It is important to confirm and express individuality by interrelating various differences. The modern functionalist idea enhances homogeneity and certainty by processing heterogeneity and uncertainties. It also encourages effective decision-making and actions toward goal-attainment and moreover tries to reduce differences as much as possible through standardization. By doing so, however, it often entrusts confirmation of the meaning of existence to external society and makes it an object of control.

As discussed in section two, meanings are sought in the relation of life or living with the world and generated through its articulation. If the way of relation of life to the world is a meaning, there exists a power that relates oneself to the world. Namely, meanings are stuffed with the power of life. The power of human beings cannot be expressed through adaptation to environments by means of functionalist ideas.

This reasoning can also be applied to the way self-identity should be. Today, society is highly differentiated into multiple functions diversifying the organizations to which people belong and upon which identity relies. Fragments of signs now devoid of meaning proliferate. Lifestyles are subject to the pressure of excessive choice. It is becoming difficult to state continuously and convincingly what we are. Under such circumstances, we will lose ourselves, if we have nothing but a flexible identity adapting ourselves to environmental changes.

As discussed above, in the postmodern situation where representations without transparency are dominant, we must actualize our selves by seeking *another self* through floating in society and editing the image of the self whenever necessary. However, the pastiche and schizoid character, specific to postmodernity, often leads to morbid phenomena of the fragmentation of identity and of homelessness. To continually confirm ourselves under drifting identities, we must maintain unification through fragmentation and coherence through change. To address such problems, the viewpoint of self-organization of identity is appropriate.

Self-Organization without a Master Plan

In contemporary complex society, it is not possible to seek the basis of identity in a specific model or collective body. Instead, it is necessary to have the internal ability to ceaselessly transform ourselves or the capability to redefine self-identity whenever necessary. This ability assumes self-reference or self-reflexiveness. The original discussion of this was included in George Mead's theory of the self.[34] These ideas involve grasping the self-identity not as a coherent and preserved entity but as an ever-changing and flowing reflexive process. However, Mead used reflexiveness only as a keyword for mind and development of the self. In this sense, his self-reflexion was subjectivistic and inevitably led to a discussion in which social norms and values were internalized in the self by individuals.[35] It is a socialization of the self and an image of human beings adapted to society by the self. For self-organization, it is not sufficient only to limit self-reflexion to the aspect of individuals adapting themselves to society.

Narrative Self

The essence of the *narrative self* is to grasp the reflexive process as a more active process of self-formation. It can also be understood as a process in which a variety of personal events is organized into a unified story by a plot. From the viewpoint of narrative self, Anthony Giddens described self-identity as follows.

> Self-identity is not a distinctive trait, or even a collection of traits, possessed by the individual. It is *the self as reflexively understood by the person in terms of her or his biography*. Identity here still presumes continuity across time and space: but self-identity is such continuity as interpreted reflexively by the agent.[36]

According to Giddens, self-identity is a "reflexive project of the self" consisting of biographical narratives which are subject to coherent and continuous revision. We agree that the narrative self makes it possible, by use of the plot, to bundle time as a historic feature and space as spread experience by systematically organizing a variety of episodes in life. Under the present circumstances, however, it is doubtful if the plot of a story of life itself really exists. The narrative self has fallen into the "dilemma that it must find a plot where it does not exist."[37]

Self-identity is not programmed by a plot, but rather organizes itself based on the episodes it has experienced in the developmental process. Although each episode in life has a meaning as an event, it is not organized in a narrative with a predetermined plot, but self-organizes the narrative itself together with other episodes. In this sense, identity-formation is a self-organization process without a master plan. This process assumes a paradoxical act of confirming the sameness by difference. In other words, the self is a self-referential process which continuously produces a new self (sameness) by generating and reacting to a nonself or the difference as a fluctuation inside itself.

Self through Nonself

The self continues self-organization by referring to its transformation during its life. A self as a definite, preserving and integrated entity does not exist. Yesterday's self can be today's nonself. Even if we admit that the sameness of the self exists at every moment, it is doubtful whether a self with continuity exists.

Takeshi Mikami expressed this form of existence of the self as, "I am I by not being I" and regarded this as the essence of the postmodern self.[38] "Not being I" is a heterogeneous existence for "the present I" or a fluctuation. This view of the self suggests that fluctuation generates a new self. Of course, most other selves generated as nonselves are controlled in order to maintain previous selves, or self-disorganization comes true when the new selves destroy the unified previous selves. This is equivalent to the dilemma of unification versus fragmentation discussed in the context of self-identity in the past. The essence of the postmodern self is, however, to confirm itself through a nonself it has generated by a difference motive. Therefore, unification versus fragmentation is not a dilemma, but a factor indispensable to establishing self-identity.

The fluctuation (fragmentation) of identity is a source of a new order (unification). To realize self-organization, however, the fragments as another self must maintain a relation with the previous self and form a new meaning. If fragmented selves remain meaningless in the dissipative state, this constitutes schizophrenia in the strict sense of the word. Self-organization of identity is ceaselessly establishing a new self by generating other selves within self and editing them. In this sense, the postmodern self is a project of self-organization of identity.

A typical model of the self in modern society lies in integration of the subjective self and socially expected self to actualize a self. However, when representations without transparency such as *simulacra* and hyper-reality start to proliferate in society through the coming of consumer society and the advancement of information technology, the decentralization and drifting of identity come out. One of the main characteristics of postmodernity lies in the fact that reality is constructed by representations which do not reflect the entity. When such a type of reality is dominant, the subjective self and the expected self which feature as the modern self loose their substantial meaning, and then people will pursue their self-actualization and generate another self in the area which surpasses the self in a modern sense, by editing fragmented signs whose meanings are broken up by the flood of information.

Self-identity in an age of postmodernity is identity that has a high degree of freedom and a flowing character that guarantee unification through fragmentation and coherence through change. It should be formulated as a self-organizing process without a master plan. The self is a process which continuously produces a new self by generating a nonself inside itself, or produces a self as nonself. This implies that self is nothing less than a paradoxical reproduction process of self–nonself. Namely, "I really become I by not being I."

Under the present conditions, it may well be that such a mode of identity seeking reflects the perverse self-actualization and distraction. These are disorders in an age of postmodern tendency, and self-identity will be chaotic until a new image of self is established. The important point, on which we must focus our attention, is not to regard these phenomena too easily as diseases of society.

The necessary condition of the self in a postmodern age is the editorship of differences which generates new meaning through editing fragmented and meaningless signs. As stated it is the power of self-editorship, contrasting with the power of self-control required of the modern self. We should recognize that the nurturing of this power will bring people a new will to life, and in its turn the creation of a new culture.

6 Reflexion Thought

Beyond Control and Fluctuation

In this chapter, I have discussed the social system and self-identity in postmodern times from the viewpoint of fluctuation and signification. Fluctuation and signification are important subjects in transplanting self-organization from the field of natural science to that of social science. In Introduction, I distinguished the cybernetic self-organization from the synergetic self-organization and characterized theory on the former as self-organization theory by *control schema* and that on the latter by *fluctuation schema*. In control schema, self-organization is discussed while focusing on structure and function and neglecting fluctuation and signification. In fluctuation schema in contrast, fluctuation phenomena jutting out of structure and function are focused on. By appropriating significance to this fluctuation, I attempted to find common factors between the theories of postmodernity and self-organization. The cybernetic self-organization based on control schema features modernity, while that based on fluctuation schema features postmodernity.

Above two standpoints on the self-organization theory are antagonistic to each other. Therefore, readers may be skeptical about discussing them in parallel. Certainly, such an attitude looks like a contradiction at a glance. As mentioned above, I have advocated the postmodern self-organization focusing on fluctuation and signification. However, this is not to deny the modern self-organization focusing on control schema.

Modernity and postmodernity constitute a continuous process. Therefore, postmodernity should be thought to have occurred to include modernity. Postmodernity has inherited the modern control schema as a gene. The working accumulated by modern enlightenment or progressivism does not vanish in the postmodern society, but is preserved as a method of social management in a relative form so that it does not maintain absolute superiority. The significance of cybernetic self-organization theory is to reformulate the conventional simple planning and conception of control in a more refined form. Nevertheless, it is not possible to discuss the whole of self-organization of society with the cybernetic self-organization alone.

If social changes are thought to have been caused by top-down control, it will be a conception to totally neglect the actual society. It should not be forgotten that synergy by the bottom-up performative action results in spontaneous order formation. For this reason, therefore, I incorporated the concept of meaning (currently fluctuation) in the loop between structure and function, which is mainly adopted by conventional social theory, and conceived a self-organization theory that argues changes with the hyper-loop of structure, function and meaning. It is a theoretical framework to grasp a self that becomes a non-self or to grasp changes to metamorphose to a different society by trying to be endlessly modern and unknowingly going through modernity.

As I discussed in Introduction, self-organization theory by control schema and that by fluctuation schema have "difficulty of petitio principii" by higher order control and "difficulty of randomness" by arbitrariness respectively. To overcome this difficulty, it is required to aim at self-reference. I presented a viewpoint to make it possible for both theories to open the horizon of common front by incorporating reflexion. The viewpoint of the hub of self-organization is not control or fluctuation but reflexion. In closing this chapter, therefore, I will discuss the possibility of social formation based on reflexion from the viewpoint of deconstruction of control thought.

Reflexion Thought

Theory of self-organization reads autonomy from fluctuation. If it is possible to design a new society, fluctuation is no more fluctuation. For this purpose, it is indispensable to build the anticontrol system. To say more, organization which has no control as its subject must be built up.

Although fluctuation is thought to be generated by dedifferentiation and differencification from the establishment, we have to inquire about the mechanism to transcribe the new differences into social structure. Namely, we have to formulate the mechanism where differences, which are newly articulated from the world, intervene in conventional system to acquire their own positions. For this purpose, reflexion thought is required which replaces the existing control thought.[39]

This thought forms the basis of reflexive movement of differences which return the newly articulated differences back to the existing system and acquire their own position in it. Namely, reflexion is a movement that will incorporate and transform new differences into structure. The dedifferentiation or differencification from the establishment could make itself significant only with the presumption of this reflexion. The fact that problem of fluctuation is in a topic means that things cannot go well any more only with control. Till now, modern society has pursued efficiency by consolidating apparatus of managerial social control. However, at present, it has been worked to the limit and arrived at the phase where control idea alone cannot administrate society. The only way is not to exclude fluctuation but to imagine a design of society where its vital power can be best used.

To establish reflexion thought, as the first step, it is effective to consider the *minimization of control*. When control is taken away from the social apparatus, fluctuation will appear and such existing entity as a control center will disappear. However, if the vital power of organization and society is generated by fluctuation, it must be supported. Too much control over people reproduces submissive role following person. We cannot expect such person any creative and revolutionary ideas. It is true that control can be a strong weapon when we attain the predetermined goal, but inversely can be fetters to explore the goals and challenge new possibilities.

On reflection, it is the modern idea to manage society with the control thought. It is rather a short period only extending to a few centuries in the human history (The control referred to here is distinguished from the medieval domination by rule). The effectiveness of control cannot help but become lower in the postmodern phase that is positioned as the re-injection of signification into society after the rationalization process of modern times. It is because meaning is to be fulfilled and not to be achieved like functional performance. Moreover, the end state like a goal cannot be set in meaning fulfillment. As control is impossible without given goal-value, so the problem of meaning has been expelled out of the public sphere and confined in the private sphere in the modern functional society. If only meaning is emancipated from the functional spell, the idea that meaning is the very basic issue of constitution of society is sufficiently possible. For this purpose, it is necessary to ask how anticontrol system can be possible.

The anticontrol system does not dissolve events into randomness or applause anarchism. As will be discussed in the next chapter, it should be formulated as a rhizomic system. As major principles of social formation, market, hierarchy (organization) and network have been presented so far. I think that rhizome should be added thereto. Rhizome is a movement body of differencification and a *generator of fluctuation* aiming at the rearrangement of existing values and institutions. Market is a system of exchange connoting negotiations with many and unspecified individuals. Hierarchy is a mechanism of action request based on authority. Network is an exchange mechanism based on the reciprocity of those concerned. In society, there is a mode of action that cannot be attributed to any of these three. It is an activity not reciprocal, not based on authority or not through negotiations with many and unspecified individuals. It will cause differencification from the established modes of action and the groping for alternative values. Hitherto, these activities have not been positioned as a principle of social formation, but regarded as a social movement or a movement oriented to an *alternative society*. As such activities become a source of social vitality, however, it should be added to the principles of social formation. If a rhizome exists, fluctuations are generated to make the society reflexive.

The reflexion thought urges a modification on self-organization based on control schema. As discussed in Chap. 2, self-organization of control schema has a three-stage control mechanism. The first is control embedded in social structure or structural control. This control entrusts the allocation of personnel and social resources to roles and role performance to law, norms or institutions, in order to ensure functional achievement. Structural control determines desirable action selection in advance under preset conditions. Action selection has been internalized in individuals to a considerable extent through socialization. The second is optimal control to input optimal personnel and resources to ensure functional achievement while premising a given social structure, or under a certain role arrangement and an allocation rule of personnel and social resources. What falls in this category is personnel rearrangement, reallocation of labor force or investment into public works, for example.

There is no room for reflexion to creep in the first or the second control. The structural control is a rigid and feedforward control. The optimal control aims at the best functional performance based on the allocation rule and existing roles. It is impossible to incorporate reflexion into such controls. Trying to do so will deprive the control of its validity. In the case of the third version or adaptive control, however, the story is different.

Adaptive control premises adaptation to environment as suggested by the term itself. However, this control is activated by changes not only in environment but also in needs and value of system members. By feeding back the conditions inside the system, this control requestions system's structure and function. This can be formulated as working to reflect the difference generated in the system on structural control. To emphasize this aspect, adaptive control may be renamed as *reflexive control*. This renaming produces a control schema that reflects the reflexion thought. Of course, as far as it is a control schema, there remains intentional intervention by a control center or its equivalent into the system and its change. Unlike the fluctuation schema, therefore, there is no viewpoint of order formation without a control center. However, reflexive control revises control schema in the sense that it can make fluctuation as differencification its object. At the same time, it relaxes the image of regimented society led from control schema and offers a meeting place for order formation from the top and that from the bottom. In the social management, this will offer a more realistic theory.

Let us consider a concrete scenario. Decentralization is now clamored, with programs executed to make local governments independent of the central government. In actuality, however, decentralization will not function appropriately, even if central government (control center) withdraws completely and delegates power to local governments. The central government may be indifferent to what local governments can do, but must intervene in other matters. How should the mode of division of labor be dealt with? The answer is that there are no other means than entrusting it to reflexive control.

As far as the synergy of differencification in society forms a new order, there are no problems. When order parameters drift without being concretely established, however, it is necessary to support parameter creation by exerting reflexive control. This is equivalent to support the creation of a new thing by midwifery rather than by control. Namely, in the case of reflexive control, activities change from control to support. The reflexion thought brings about support in place of control in social management.

Toward New Public Philosophy

What kind of perspective will the reflexion thought offer to public philosophy? The public philosophy has been a prime theme of modern society since civil revolution in the 17–18th centuries. The idea is, as is well known, to ask how social order can be formed with presumption of existence of free and equal individuals. This idea has been descended to the present days as democratic idea of freedom and equality. It is true that modern project has not realized this idea sufficiently. Upon more reflection, however, freedom and equality is the idea with which modern society was raised up through deconstructing the medieval societies. Is not it too simple to say to pursue them further more only because they have not yet been accomplished? I do not mean that we should abandon the idea of modern age, but mean that future society cannot be guided only by it. Indeed modernity may be an incomplete project. But cannot it be said that in the middle of completion, its deconstruction work has begun? In planning of new society, the more suitable public philosophy is required.

The idea of freedom and equality broke the Middle Age's idea of "domination of secular world by God." It promoted *modern as Godicide*. However, it was modernity that replaced God with institutional mechanism and substituted domination by God for control by institutional mechanism.[40] It can be said that realization of freedom and equality cannot help being an incomplete project with emerging control mechanism.

It looks rarely possible to construct the new public philosophy. However, a kind of trigger can be found. It must be a philosophy which would drive the thought and system of control to the background. Undoubtedly, it is not necessary to abandon them. At least, we have to give them positions enough to admit them as necessary evil. Namely, we have to pull them down from the principal role. In my view, it is the *support system* that can match meaning fulfillment and reflexion thought. Till now, whenever support is handled, it is generally done with making it subordinated to control idea. For example, if there is a person having an interesting idea, statesman or businessman often financially supports him. However, such support was limited to private one, but not institutionalized on a social scale and often given with thought that it should return as ideas or knowledge useful for enterprise or political party. Support of this sort is subordinated to control. It is goal-oriented and functional type of support. Not like that, first of all the support must come and then control will exist following the support. Namely, a public philosophy which can make support society instead of control society is required.

Though we will discuss about support and publicness in detail in the last chapter, there have been two types of publicness, when roughly classified. First is the administrative control type of publicness that limits private rights, as seen in the public works that aim at social welfare and improvement of social capital. This is the publicness as logic to justify the activities of authority. Second is what Habermas calls the civil (bourgeois) public sphere or the civil movement type of publicness. This is publicness as logic to transmit citizens' needs to the state, by forming political opinions through open discussions and social movements. The feature of this publicness is to raise public opinion against authority. However, at present, a new dimension of publicness which is not caught by the conventional framework has appeared. It is publicness based on support action exemplified by the activities of voluntary organization, NPO (nonprofit organization) and NGO (nongovernmental organization).

Support is a series of actions to maintain and/or improve the quality of others' actions, and finally empower them. In other words, it is essentially to give the suportee (other person) a power to exist or do things. The supporter does not aim at assistance or charity, but is motivated to find his own value in living and attain self-actualization as seen in volunteer and NPO activities. Support has, therefore, a private aspect (motive). However, this private nature assumes that the quality of others' actions is improved and the supportee is empowered. Therefore, this privateness is not the same as so called selfishness. Private self-actualization will in turn lead to cares and considerations for new supportee. In this sense, support activity has a possibility to open a new public space. Although it is inherently self-oriented, support is an act that involves the opportunity to link others, beyond private affairs. Here, we can find the possibility of new publicness. We should now recognize the importance of opening individual public space through support activities that are privately motivated by self-actualization, in addition to and more than the civil movement type of publicness and administrative control type of publicness that are based on an antagonism between public and private.

The project of modernity has institutionalized a control system. Industrial society has been maintaining close relationship with control as it is otherwise called controlled society. However, forecasting future of industrial society, control system will perhaps finish its historical role.

Part III
Development of the Self-Organization Theory: Deconstruction of the Society

Chapter 5
Beyond Network Theory

Network theory is a subject that should be discussed in relation to self-organization. Networks, whose concept orginated in the 19th century, are now in the limelight as information technology developed during the last 25 years, since they are now regarded as the third principle of social formation along with market and bureaucratic mechanisms beyond the fundamental structure of telecommunication. It is too optimistic, however, to render excessive expectation on networks. The network theory or networking theory includes an illusion that comes from excessive expectation. This chapter explains importance of the rhizome theory that stems from poststructuralism through critical discussions on the theory of network society, and proposes a rhizomic view of the system that makes the basis of self-organization. Uncritical admiration of network is to take sides with the promotion of functional rationalization. To find a new principle of social formation in networks, it is required to extract aspects that are unrelated to functional rationalization.

1 Admiration of Network?

Network is used in various forms in many fields. Therefore, there is no definition common to different fields beyond the abstract definition that network consists of nodes and links. In this regard, it is required to confirm the following historical developments: (1) network has been used mainly in the field of electrical circuits since the 19th century, (2) it has also been used for the problem of finding out minimum-cost path in transport network in operations research (OR) that developed after the World War II, and (3) the relations between small groups, organizations and states are expressed in sociology as networks in the trend of researches from sociometry to social network analysis through group dynamics, and structural analysis is being implemented therefore.[1] What is common to all the above research fields is that network is an object of mathematical analysis.

Types of Network

The concept of network has been used mainly in the field of mathematical science. There are no reasons, however, that networks should be used only for mathematical purposes. On the contrary, it is possible to use it in other fields as well, only if it is firmly defined. What should be noted is that "information network" or "network organization" has been used mostly as a concept that follows traditional customs, and networking has aimed at functional rationalization or improving the efficiency of collecting, transmitting and processing information.

Information network, to which importance is attached as a communication infrastructure is to increase the volume of information distribution and expand automatic information processing involving society at large, where standardized information is transmitted and processed. This is to decrease uncertainties in the system and improve the efficiency of decision-making. The effect of information network is to stretch a network of electronic communication (nerve network) in society and connect computers (brains) thereto, in order to realize a quick and speedy society.

Let us review the Point of Sale (POS) network, as an example. POS means the control of information at the point of sales by using a unit that reads the bar codes printed on the articles sold at stores to automatically manage sales and implement inventory control. Through a network that connects the head office and POS units at stores distributed in different areas, it is possible to total the sales in each area quickly and collect related information such as a list of best-selling goods. When POS units are used for the system of sale on credit, it is also possible to make inquiries regarding the credit of users with card readers attached to terminals and rationalize settlements by means automatic transfers. Network of this type enhance functional rationality and efficiency, and they have disseminated to the largest extent in actuality.

Network organization not only improves the rapidity and efficiency of decision-makings through the introduction of information processing technology, but also implements organizational innovation through learning and flexibly organizes relations among related enterprises. What is emphasized in this context is the formation of a loose coupling to break the rigidity of bureaucratic organization. Network organization generates a field that can connect heterogeneous information and viewpoints or make them interact with each other, and aims at exploitation of new markets and creation of business opportunities. Network organizations include the in-house PC communication network, any network to expedite cross-industrial exchanges and the local area network (LAN) that connects parent and subsidiary companies. These networks are used to develop niches for corporate innovation, correct inefficiency of vertically divided bureaucratic organizations and organically integrate dispersed workshops.

In contrast, *networking* which is touted to be responsible for creating an alternative society is a new principle of social formation that makes autonomous individuals connect with others freely and equally. This concept of networking originated in tandem with a new social movement that emerged in the latter half of the 1970s, in order to criticize industrial civilization and oppose controlled society in particular. What belongs to this type in a broad sense is new mutual-aid association that aims at solving various problems in life.

Networking is a method to organize voluntary civil movements with individuals as units. It aims at creating a moderate movement body in which individuals participate voluntarily, while maintaining the continuity with counter culture movement in the 1960s, but not organized under the leadership of a particular and professional activist, as it used to be in the old days. This type of movements began in the USA and included anti-nuclear movement in protest of nuclear weapons or power plants, ecology movement to protect the environment and nature, feminist movement that appealed women's self-reliance and rights, and consumer movements related to cooperative associations that demanded the right to independently purchase and sell their own products.

Regarding the networking movement, there are a number of different versions. Jessica Lipnack and Jeffrey Stamps, who are the pioneers of this movement, regarded it as the discovery of an "alternative America" and introduced various cases of networking. In order to describe that networking has decentralizing orientation unlike bureaucratic organizations, they proclaimed a statement of Transnational Network for Appropriate Alternative Technologies and Lifestyle (TRANET). According to them, network means a non-hierarchical system consisting of equal, independent and autonomous individuals; it does not rely on any part; it does not have a center; and it is composed of parts and links.[2] They also insisted that networking had removed a barrier that made the free and autonomous connection between individuals difficult without intervention by official organizations or groups in the past, and thus realized free and autonomous connection between individuals, with each as a unit.

However, such an idea is not really different from the conventional concept of good friends or a new phenomenon at all. As a specific feature of networks, it is said that they are a non-hierarchical system, which does not have a center or parts contributing to the whole, but a distributed autonomous system between parts. Even this way of thinking does not insist the originality of network concept, since markets are also a place where free and independent economic entities buy and sell goods and services.

Apprehensions of a Superpanopticon

To avoid misunderstanding, I would like to make it clear that I do not oppose networking, but only wish to point out that excessive expectation regarding networking would lead to an illusion. At the moment, network is a means to promote efficiency and enhancement of selectivity and lead to the completion of a modern project of functional rationalization. Ignoring of this point and over-admiring the fact that networks enable linkage between free and equal individuals will take sides with technocrats. Further advancement will be seen in the efficiency improvement and speeding-up of information and communication by means of media transmission, information highways and on-line systems.

Networks constitute a major system in an information society, which further improves efficiency as a principle of social formation that exactly fits functionalism. Concept of function intrinsically does not include hierarchical differentiation, but represents horizontal role differentiation. Therefore, networks are a mechanism that emerges when function is fully realized. In this sense, networks lead to the completion of modernity. Information technology has the power to convert hierarchical organizations into horizontal organizations. The networked society will further progress to a considerable extent in destroying the bureaucratic mechanism. Functional rationalization is equipped with such power.

As mentioned above, networks are mixed with a tendency to aim at rationalization and efficiency improvement of information transmission on one hand, and the formation of free and autonomous human relations on the other, both being called a network. This means that blind admiration of network constitutes a pretext to thoughtlessly promote the former type of network. Since computerization is not unavoidable in society, it is inevitable to build up the infrastructure to improve efficiency of information processing. With this likelihood, it is necessary to not become disoriented in admiring networks, but problematic points should be closely inspected. Otherwise, it will result in inputting privacy information voluntarily from a terminal in succession to subsequently take part in swelling a soft control society. As Mark Poster put it regarding the electronic society,

> Social security cards, drivers' licenses, credit cards, library cards and the like – the individuals must apply for them, have them ready at all times, use them continuously. Each transaction is recorded, encoded and added to the database. Individuals themselves in many cases fill out the forms; they are at once the source of information and the recorder of the information. Home networking constitutes the streamlined culmination of this phenomenon: the consumer, by ordering products through a modem connected to the producer's database, enters data about himself or herself directly in the producer's database in the very act of purchase.[3]

This database is an information society version of surveillance technology, which Michel Foucault discussed the function of panopticon of Jeremy Bentham in *Naissance de la prison*. Mark Poster calls it *superpanopticon*.[4] In a prison that is a symbolic case of panopticon, prison guards had to watch the behavior of prisoners in the cell by themselves. In contrast, superpanopticon is a guard-less watch system. Superpanopticon is a method to control the mass of people in an information society, where the surveillance apparatus of Foucault's discipline-training type that controls humans as individual bodies for a long period has transfigured to one that controls individuals with management of their history contained in a vast database under digital names. In order to participate in convenient and efficient transactions, people write their characteristics in a database to swell this abstract surveillance apparatus.

2 Rhizome Theory and Self-Organization

To construct a network acceptable as a new principle of social formation, without being satisfied with one as a functional rationalization apparatus for society and a superpanopticon, it is required to deconstruct the present network theory. As a procedure, I believe that the feature of *rhizome* contained in the network theory should be formulated from the viewpoint of self-organization.

The largest skepticism for network theory is whether the principle to change existing networks is included in the network theory. It is thought that the networking theory does not consciously have a viewpoint of self-organization for it to change itself and continuously proceed into metamorphosis. It is often defined that networks continuously change their relations. It is meaningless, however, only to define networks without theoretical formulation. For networks to always take in heterogeneous matters and change relations, a movement is required to add new differences thereto by participating in the creation of differences. This feature should be called rhizome rather than network.

Paradigm Shift in Society

I have reviewed the process where metamorphosis of modern civilization progresses with computerization as a catalyst.[5] The innovation of information technology and biotechnology will quickly advance from now on to expedite the deconstruction of modernity. Views on science, human beings and society will be reconsidered as a result. A major point thereof is a *paradigm shift from function primacy to meaning fulfillment*, under which the following four sub-shifts will take place (see Table 5.1).[6]

First, the motive of action shifts from deficiency motive to *difference motive*, or from the state motivated by deficiency feeling to one that is motivated by differences between multitudes of personalities. In modern society, the mode of action according to the means–end schema represented by production labor played a central role, which was a behavior governed by deficiency motive. To overcome the state of deficiency, it was recommended to behave more efficiently and rationally. As function primacy changed to meaning fulfillment, however, the action to efficiently

Table 5.1 Paradigm shifts in the society

Main shift	From function primacy to meaning fulfillment
First shift	From deficiency motive to difference motive
Second shift	From efficient persons to value-adding persons
Third shift	From control to support
Fourth shift	From social integration to social editing

attain the preset goal became no longer a matter of central concern, giving way to the action to fulfill meanings motivated by participating in the creation of differences. Computerization amplifies such a movement toward *differencification*.

Second, expected human resources shift from diligent persons featuring earnestness or efficient persons who tactfully deal with jobs to *value-additing persons* who are creative. Under the system of mass-production plant in the past, workers were required to act according to the clock-like workflow. Sabotage or tardiness and absence gave serious damage to production processes. Therefore, diligence was essential for production activities. Moreover, diligence was not everything for the production at plants. Without efficient job handling, earnest and diligent work alone did not raise productivity. Thus, the most reliable workers were those who efficiently attained the preset goal.

If the criterion of economic activities shifts to that centering on the creation of knowledge and added values, however, those who are only diligent or efficient will not be useful human resources. In the case of labor that does not suit the production at plants, such as product development, planning, designing and advertising, it is not sufficient only to diligently repeat or tactfully perform given procedures. It is important to explore and materialize what consumers want instead. In such a case, people cannot help but promote activities of idea exploring type, since the goal is not determined beforehand. This is a creative activity to generate new added values, and not productive activity of the conventional type. Generally speaking, success of a creative activity is not necessarily attained by diligent efforts alone, or by efficient collection of information through surveys of opinions and materials. Conversely, it is sometimes possible that an excellent idea occurs from a flash of insight during an arbitrary, unfocused thought process. In this context, those required are value-additive persons with knowledge and imagination.

Third, the system of social formation shifts from a control system to a *support system*. When activities center on the creation of added values, the control system loses its effectiveness. Creating added values is to generate new meanings or ideas. Control does not work effectively for such activities. A mechanism is required to expedite the creation of ideas and their materialization. The conception of support is indispensable for this purpose. The shift from control to support does not deny the former, but means retaining it as a necessary evil. The support system is not simply limited to economic activities, but it is a subject related to social formation as a whole. In a society where functional attainment is the pivot, *having* is a matter of concern, for which control is effective. In a society where meaning fulfillment is the pivot, in contrast, control withdraws into the background, since *being* is a matter of concern. Therefore, we need to inquire into what is signified by this *being*. As will be discussed in final chapter, however, control is the attainment of being in actuality and social movements have been transmuted into a symbolic challenge of being against control or a movement at the level of signification.

Fourth, in a society where difference motive is dominant, *social editing* to put individual differences together into a new meaning is more important than social integration by consensus formation. Consensus formation often consumes energy to summarize the greatest common opinions and ideas, while neglecting personal and distinctive ones. It is required now, however, to admit personal differences as far as possible and edit them to allow coexistence. In other words, it is required to unite differences while recognizing their autonomy and individuality, in place of the integration based on consensus formation. In past societies characterized by consensus formation, those who did not obey the consensus were either rejected or forced to accept it. In contrast, social editing focuses on creating new meanings, while admitting and interrelating the individual differences. Human relations will be edited in accordance with various policies. The ability of the editor will be evaluated based on how he or she utilizes individual differences. Editing human relations will spread throughout society, and people will compete with each other for handling the power of meaning creation.

The above sub-shifts are changes occurring interlocked with the transformation of a society centering on function into one that focuses on meaning. What governs these shifts is the rhizome that develops the dynamics of differencification and meaning fulfillment.

Movement Body for Differencification

The concept of rhizome was presented by poststructuralists Gilles Deleuze and Félix Guattari, who compared rhizome to a map.[7] Rhizome allows for an entry and exit from any point. It is always incomplete, multidimensional, and manifold, with one dimension deducted all the time. It is incomplete in the sense that one dimension is deducted, from which a new differencification emerges. Rhizome does not have a view of order such as a tree and its roots, and is a system always transfiguring into a different manifold through differencification. It does not have a hierarchical structure or a center, either, but is a chaos system that its elements interact with each other in complicatedly intermingled way. Any node on a rhizome can be connected to another node. Therefore, rhizome can be cut, disassembled, assembled, connected, and turned inside out at any dimension to accept changes all the time. As a result, rhizome can perform a kaleidoscopic movement.

In short, rhizome is an *anticontrol system*.[8] The essence of the rhizomic movement is to nullify and break the control mechanism. In a rhizome, the control mechanism exists as an object that can always be disassembled and changed. Of course, it does not break so easily. Attempts to break the control mechanism are often punished. To prepare for punishment, rhizome is equipped with a number of escape routes, like a map, that enable running away from any point.

Rhizome is a manifold without subject or object and a system to which dualism does not apply. There is no ontological dualism of here and there, or the dualism of right and wrong. Since rhizomes constitute a world that rejects dual opposition, they do not have the boundary that separates the inside from the outside. It is a system that cannot change itself affected by the environment. In other words, it is a *self-referential system* that does not have alternatives other than changing its character by itself for transfiguration.

Rhizome is originally a subterranean stem of a tree, such as a lotus root or a bulb. It is not a root, but a subterranean tree. Generally, trees are positively heliotropic to grow toward the sun. The goal of growth is predetermined. When a tree grows, its roots also grow to support it. This is called a tree-root system, which is a typical functional growth pattern. In contrast, rhizome does not have a predetermined goal of growth. The direction of growth is not determined in advance like in the case of lotus roots. If they encounter an obstacle, they grow into a different direction. Such growth of subterranean stems is a metaphor of differencification. In short, rhizome is a kaleidoscopic body of movement that does not fit the view of order such as a tree and its roots. It is a manifold lacking a center, ranking, or distinctions between subject and object and between order and chaos. In this way, rhizome is exactly a movement body that has deconstructed the conception of logically consistent order and an anticontrol system that incorporates fluctuations.

Kaleidoscopic System

One of the features of rhizome is the *principle of kaleidoscopic coupling*, which means that the relations between elements are based on arbitrariness and heterogeneity, or that a number of elements are not connected in accordance with inevitability. A system where elements are connected without inevitability is often an incoherent one.

In most of the present organizations including enterprises, status and roles are determined based on which constituent members are connected. It is thought that functional performance of organization is ensured only by doing so. However, rhizome is a system that denies it, assuming connections between its constituent members that are independent of status or role. Although it is a dominant view that society cannot be managed under such an incoherent principle, quite a few such connections already exist. It is arbitrary whom a person makes friends with or gets married. It is also rather arbitrary what enterprise he or she works for. Cross-industrial exchanges are now very popular to make different industries related, even though they are alien from exchanges according to normal conception. It is often the case, however, that creative activities are conducted through such exchanges. The kaleidoscopic connection of heterogeneous elements is a source of vitality. In addition, world of electronic media on the Internet features connection from an arbitrary terminal to another. This connection generates a feeling of vibrancy and expedites dynamic activities.

Hypertext World

The hypertext world in electronic media is also an example of rhizome, which has removed orders from the conventional document structure. Documents of hypertext do not require readers to read them in regular order from the beginning, but allows

2 Rhizome Theory and Self-Organization

to freely move back and forth between relevant places. The Hyper Card of Macintosh is a well known knowledge database that links different texts at user's disposal.

Let us take the example of a text on art. If you cannot make clear what you want there, you may warp your mind to immigrate into a text of history, for example, with the data collected in the art text kept in hand. You may then become interested in the view of universe and jump to the text thereof. You may then browse the texts of religion, astronomy and mythology led by your interest. In this process, you will be able to create a text customized for yourself (see Figure 5.1).

Such movement is completely different from the tree-shaped method to retrieve information from a conventional database. When you enter a database, the route

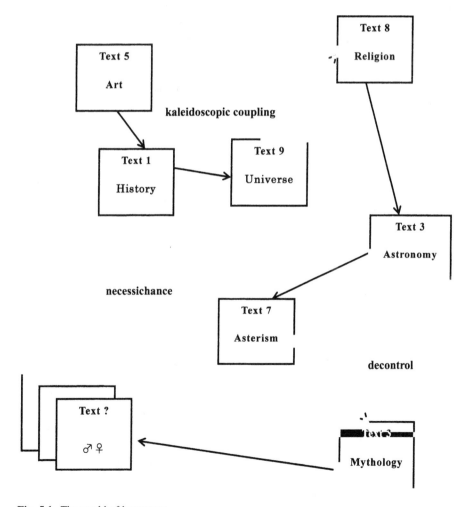

Fig. 5.1 The world of hyper text

branches into several directions at the entrance itself, from which you are supposed to select one. After that, you are required to repeatedly select one route at each node. You may select the text on history at the entrance, for example. You will then choose the ancient, medieval or modern age. If you select the modern age, you will be required to select Europe, Asia, America or the Middle East, etc. The procedure is uni-directional and sequential. In this sense, this retrieval is controlled. You cannot jump into the text of medieval India to obtain some materials from the text of modern French history and then return to the original text. If you want to move to a different text, you are required to return to the beginning and restart. In the hypertext world, there is no such control on the retrieval procedure, since it is a system that has what is called the *principle of decontrol*. It is free to jump from any text to another. The link between texts follows the *principle of kaleidoscopic coupling*. In this sense, it allows arbitrariness (chance). If you do not want to terminate retrieval, however, you have to be continuously linked to another text (necessity). The hypertext world is governed, therefore, by the principle of *necessichance*, which combines chance and necessity. Home pages on the Internet also have such a character. Decontrol, kaleidoscopic coupling and necessichance are the system characteristics that characterize rhizome.

Windows, which is currently the mainstream operating system (OS) for personal computers, has a similar structure to that of a hypertext. Two or more programs can be run simultaneously on one screen of Windows. You can draw figures and pictures in graphics, for example, which you can embed into a manuscript being created with a word processor. You can also embed a table summarizing the results obtained with a program for statistical calculation into the manuscript. In this manner, you can run multiple programs simultaneously, while browsing in between them, and eventually summarize what you want. You will feel dizzy, if you are not accustomed to such processing. A mechanism advances in the world of information for you to create value addition while browsing various fields. A tendency similar thereto can take place in human relations as well.

Extension/Discontinuation of Bus Routes

The extension/discontinuation of bus routes is also an example of rhizome. If we survey the history of bus routes, and we find that their opening, closing and extension/discontinuation are not logically coherent at all, while repeating rhizomic appearance and disappearance.

In its original stage, a bus route normally starts from a simple one, connecting one central point (often a major railway station) and another. Branching gradually takes place, however, with comparatively long routes or those reaching a dead end. As time goes by, this trend spreads in wide areas. A survey by Masaya Inada indicates that, after branching points have appeared or disappeared to some extent, bus operation (1) starts from one peripheral point to another, in addition to that serving the hub, with buses run, for example, on the route "Sakura Housing Complex – Aoba City Hall – Kakinoki Shopping Center" without passing the hub of transport in the city, or (2) circulate along loop lines within a radius of several kilometers in different areas, such as "Hikarigaoka Housing Complex – Tsukimi Primary School." This suggests the decentralization of bus routes.[9] The peripheral areas, which have been subordinate to the central point under the bus service system centering on a hub, acquire independence when peripheral point connecting bus routes are opened. The area enclosed by a loop line also establishes an independent life space.

To open a bus service route, it is required to obtain a license from relevant authorities. However, this procedure is not so complicated as that for railway routes. Bus companies open/close operation routes and increase/decrease the operation frequency based on the survey of the number of users implemented on a regular basis and sales of ordinary and season tickets. The factors considered by bus companies in this decision-making include the newly constructed schools, universities, hospitals, shopping centers and other public facilities that attract people along the routes; development of new towns and other housing sites; decrease in the number of passengers due to the popularization of private cars, traffic jams, construction of new roads; and petitions offered by residents in the area. Although the opening, closing and integration of routes are implemented based on rational calculations, the resultant changes in the route network is not coherent and repeat appearance and disappearance in complicated forms. If the population increases in an area, bus routes will be extended thereto. If a shopping center is opened, a bus stop will newly be installed. If more people gather to exert larger consumer power, routes will be extended accordingly. In the reverse situations, routes may be shortened or discontinued. The extension/discontinuation of bus routes exactly exhibits a rhizomic differencification.

Self-Referential Change

Rhizome is a self-referential system. It is a manifold that has various limits, magnitudes and dimensions, but not has the distinction between object and subject or measurable unification. Since it is a system to which dualism does not apply and a world that denies dual opposition, the paradox of self-reference does not emerge. It is a system that does not assume changing itself affected by the environment. Therefore, it has the *principle of spontaneous order* that cannot help but change itself by changing its character by itself.

In parallel with the performative action, the idea of the principle of spontaneous order is a central concept of social philosophy in Hayekian type of conservatism. The performative action means a tacit one that is not planned or rational, from which a number of social orders are spontaneously formed. An action form called performance comes up in conversation, to which the performative action is similar. It is an action performed by a casual idea or expression of desire, but not according to the allotted social status or roles. In society of human beings, order is often formed from such actions. Such a movement represents a rhizomic feature, though formation of spontaneous order from performative action is a form of self-organization. The language system is an appropriate example of this kind of order. When you speak, you are not conscious of the grammar word by word. While you maintain communication with others, new words are created and the grammar changes. When compared with that in the Heian era, the contemporary Japanese language system is much different both in vocabulary and grammar. It has changed though nobody intentionally did so. This means a "result-estimated" performative change of order, which has been brought about by a rhizomic movement of differential changes in words and the method of their utilization.

In short, rhizome is a movement body that changes its dimensions by itself through differencification. There is no stable structure, functional connection between elements, or even the conventional signification that is normally assumed. It is a world where lumps of difference exist around dimensions. Human beings often play in such a rhizomic manner. It is doubtful, therefore, whether they are acting coherently in unison. Although they may be behaving so superficially or officially, they are always acting for differencification in actuality. Rhizome theory is still highly abstract and is still at a stage of metaphor. It features the abandonment of efficiency, rationality and controllability in network theory. In other words, it formulates an anticontrol system as a metaphor, in which there are only ceaseless self-project and movement toward becoming.

Network recognizes a multi-dimensional connection of elements. It attaches importance to the horizontal connection, but not to the vertical connection by stereotyped bureaucratic method. However, it is premised on unification and maintenance of integration. Distinguished from network, rhizome denies unification and integration, as a movement body destined to continuous differencification. Since it is an incomplete movement body, rhizome performs *joint dislocation* when it encounters a network. It twines itself around the nodes of network, dislocates the existing joints, and replaces them to other nodes or makes them extend in other directions. Since rhizome assumes the action of those who are motivated by differencification, it does not rest in unification or integration. Even if it does so temporarily, it works to continuously change the connecting structure. To provide network with a character to change relations, it is essential to theorize such a rhizomic movement.

In my opinion, the point at which the rhizome intertwines with the network gives rise to a new principle of social formation. The basic principle implies new meaning generation by differencification for the rhizome and a loose integration of elements for the network. These two concepts repeat movements of integration and differencification, while entangling complicatedly with each other. The state where dynamic relation of tension between the force toward integration and that toward differencification is maintained would generate the realistic principle of social formation.

A question may be aroused that above is the same as the logic of opposition and integration assumed by conventional social theory. The schema of opposition and integration is to create new integration by lodging objection against the establishment. However, in the case of changes that cannot be reduced to the schema of opposition and integration or self-organization to change itself by its own mechanism in particular, a movement is required to reflect newly generated difference (meaning) to the existing system of differences. Such a viewpoint is not included in the conventional schema of opposition and integration.

Fluid Manifold

An interesting attempt to add the character of rhizome to network is seen in the *Theory of Network Organization* by Ken'ichi Imai and Ikuyo Kaneko. Since they did not refer to the discussion of rhizome, however, they did not consider its character consciously. The reason why their discussion is not streamlined is that it fluctuates between feature of rhizome as a fluid manifold and that of network as efficiency improvement of information transmission. Discussions on rhizome were evolved at some places, while network theory for efficiency improvement came to the fore at other places. In this manner, discussion on the two concepts vibrated as a pendulum swung right and left. As a result, the concept of network became equivocal and obscure.

Network theory by Imai and Kaneko is not on the information basis to promote functional rationalization of society, but it is for people to utilize and "create new connections and change relations," while performing the communication and making of new information.[10] For this purpose, "a dynamic view of information that is formed in the mutual relations of people with its meaning interpreted in the related context and continuously moves" is required, and importance is attached to the on-the-spot information that emerges on every occasion.[11] Networks are a "fluid manifold" that performs "formation of voluntary connection, redrawing the boundary with others and self-renewal," using the "on-the-spot information as a lever."

Human beings create information based on inter-relations. Conversely, a new relation is created by some information. There are no predetermined and functionally subdivided role relations, and an intersubjective meaning formation through communications creates a new relation. Therefore, networks are not composed of orderly relations, but always chaotic. Imai and Kaneko put it as follows.

> Since what we call a network lays stress on the subjectivity of members and diversified differences in between, various views of value and contexts coexist, and a state exists subsequently where they are opposed to each other. As networks do not have a mechanism to eliminate opposition by the control of hierarchical structure a priori, they are rather chaotic than orderly, which means that it is the essential quality of networks to place themselves in a chaotic state.[12]

This is exactly the same as the feature of rhizome insisted by Deleuze and Guattari, which represents a rhizomic network. It is not an action performed in the existing order, but is premised on the differencification movement trying meaning enrichment according to the situation on each occasion. As discussion progresses, however, it swings in the opposite direction. Since the theory of network organization deals with activities of industries and enterprises as a subject, it cannot help but be involved in the functional problem of attaining results and dealing with uncertainties, into which theory of information network for efficiency improvement creeps. If both aspects of efficiency and rhizome are successfully blended, there are no problems. However, they are sort of water and oil after all, to generate a state of uncomfortable coexistence. Imai and Kaneko put it,

> ... to address uncertainties, which are the most important problem at present age, a conception emerges to superimpose the advantages of market and organization. A positive stance is required not only to complement the disadvantages of market and organization, but also to superimpose their advantages. Network is nothing but a system to cope with uncertainty by combining market and organization.[13]

Both market and organization basically aim at dealing with uncertainties. According to Imai and Kaneko, although they have advantages and disadvantages, network are to superimpose their advantages tactfully and enhance the ability to cope with uncertainty. To reduce uncertainty is to improve the ability to control the environment and promote functional rationalization. If network are to enhance this ability, it will not be compatible with rhizome.

The *Theory of Network Organization* highly evaluates the POS network, since it constitutes a "micro-macro loop" that connects microscopic information to macroscopic one and feeds it back again to the microscopic level, thereby promoting self-organization. The POS networks adopted at convenience stores have an epoch-making significance. Customer behavior information is summarized on the spot when products are sold. If sales patterns in an area are different from those in other areas, information is interpreted to improve the display and stock of products accordingly. Convenience stores do not rely on average information, but take note on significant differences and analyze the information on qualitative scenes, in order to provide more efficient customer services. In short, the POS system is epoch-making in the sense that stores grasp diversified consumer needs quickly in a minutely thought-out manner, implement inventory control and product development based thereon and can perform bi-directional communications simultaneously with consumers and suppliers.[14]

This character of the POS system is advantage for enterprises to deploy efficient marketing, which is applicable to the control of purchasing behaviors in a soft manner. If the purpose is limited to economic activities to quickly respond to customer needs, it is a convenient and significant network. When it is expanded to cover administrative services or deal with credit information, however, problems on privacy and other matters will emerge. It gets out of the authors' intension, but the method of society management will become a POS like one that would lead to a hyper-control society, though a POS society is superficially convenient and comfortable.

The concept of network should strictly be distinguished from that of rhizome. Network is a mechanism to improve efficiency and promote rationalization of information processing and communication. In contrast, rhizome is a movement body to break control through differencification. It is required to distinguish one from the other and discuss the involved entanglement. If the two features are included in network, conceptual confusion will take place. Even if it is not the case, network concept is hackneyed from the engineering viewpoint and accompanies reading errors, even in case other images are to be roused.

Another Principle of Social Formation

Human beings have created plural principles of social formation. Rhizome will settle in society as a new version. As briefly discussed above, there have been three principles of social formation: market, hierarchy and network. Rhizome (subterranean stem) is the fourth principle of social formation that cannot be restored to the former three. Market, hierarchy and network are the principles of social formation in the framework of order constructed by modern society, while rhizome is an apparatus generating fluctuations at the *edge of chaos*, which contains order as well as chaos at the same time, and heralds the collapse of the order phase.

Network is the guaranteed principle of social formation in modern age, because the conception of function does not include vertical ranking that is seen in hierarchy. A major point of functionalist idea is to attain what cannot be done by a person through role assignment, which originally does not need hierarchical ranking in status. However, it has been the case that hierarchical and line authorities are substituted for the hitherto premature know-how on integration by networks. Regarding functional role assignment, roles are dispersed in a wide range, in that some are easy to perform and others are extremely difficult. Therefore, status has been prepared to reward people for the efforts to perform difficult roles.

A problem of network is that they exist as a current version of functional integration of society. Society is in a dynamic state to always include integration and disintegration between people. There is no complete integration. Even if network can make social integration, moderate, highly autonomous and significantly high in the degree of freedom, it is an apparatus for integration after all. Dynamics of society always includes factor for disintegration in opposition to normal factor of integration. This factor of disintegration, when it is ensured, is a source of social vitality too.

Now, we discuss the relation between four principles of social formation, by referring to relationship between two persons, for example. Let us assume a case wherein two persons, Mr. A and Mr. B, provide service peacefully to each other. When the benefit of Mr. B obtained from the service provided by Mr. A and that of Mr. A obtained from the service provided by Mr. B are both satisfactory, reciprocity holds between the two. When such reciprocity is ensured, two parties are integrated without a breach. If the reciprocity can be expanded from the two-person relation to that of multi-person relation, social integration will be realized. Primitive societies consisting of several hundred people are mostly united by such an integration method. This is a prototype of social formation by the principle of network.

Here arise two problems. One is whether such reciprocity can be ensured for modern nations, for example Japan, with more than tens of millions of people. Even if unspecified one-to-one connection has become easy by the information network, there may be a limit. The other is that it is impossible to maintain such utopian reciprocity. The world is not so lenient to ensure reciprocity for everybody. It is often the case that Mr. B is not satisfied with the service provided by Mr. A, when the reciprocity between the two is lost to generate a state of disintegration. If such a state emerges everywhere, social integration cannot work as expected. To avoid the state of disintegration, it is important to create a systematic mechanism to allow Mr. A to negotiate with unspecified person other than Mr. B. If Mr. A negotiates with unspecified person who have the service that can be provided by Mr. B and a satisfactory transaction is reached, the state of disintegration will be avoided. What has realized this system not through a one-to-one negotiation but as a mechanism is the market.

However, negotiation through a market is premised on free participation in principle. The market principle will not work successfully, therefore, if nobody else has the service that can be provided by Mr. B or when it is necessary to make it obligatory to receive the service from a third person. What has been contrived as a result is the hierarchy principle to impose a duty on person by authority for offering services. It is a duty of Japanese people to pay a tax according to the tax law. Bosses of an enterprise can require their subordinates to offer labor based on their authority. If Mr. B is a boss and Mr. A is a subordinate, Mr. B can do so for Mr. A.

A problem arises when above conditions on the provision of services do not hold. What will take place in such a situation? In principle, Mr. B must give up receiving the service to be provided by Mr. A. In short, Mr. B must go without receiving the service. This leads to a state of disintegration. It has been thought that a dispute will take place in such a situation as a complaint or opposition. However, it was a characteristic event of the age when having (rewards distribution) was a major concern in the material society. Although such a situation is seen even today, being or how to live has become an important subject in the advanced society that is shifting to a postmaterial society. When being (how to live) has become more important than having, Mr. A does not recognize the value of the services that Mr. B possesses, or changes the value of the services to orient to a different value. It is to try differencification by dissolution, cutting and turning-over of the existing institutionalized value.

Differencification is performed by volunteer, NPO and NGO activities as against the controlled administrative services. Differencification advocates: do not behave like an employee of a large enterprise, but promote businesses with fellows to which you can devote yourself by organizing a venture company. It encourages people to violate and evade the constraints imposed by a mere shell of regulations. In short, people are exhorted to activate a movement that challenges the existing order and expedites the formation of new values and meanings. This is equivalent to a rhizomic movement as a fluctuation generator.

For the modern civilization, rhizome is a movement body located on the edge of chaos, where systems are in an excited state to generate noise, fluctuations and cracks in social structure that is functionally specialized and differentiated. Noise and fluctuations are equivalent to mutation in biological evolution theory. However, it means new information emergence in social evolution. Such agency looks like accidental or random from the viewpoint of order. However, fluctuations at the edge of chaos lead to new order formation through its amplification. At the edge of chaos, microscopic aspect as individuals plays a more important role than macroscopic aspect such as the society and its organizations. The synergy between these microscopic elements performs new articulation of differences and creates meaning to form order. The roles and statuses allotted by social requests are dedifferentiated to make the actions free from dominance. At the edge of chaos, control becomes ineffective and authorities and system's whole are all nullified. Subordination of individuals to the whole is overturned, and the synergy between individuals leads to the formation of macroscopic order.

3 Anticontrol Type of Self-Organization: A Case Study of the Kobe Steelers Rugby Team

Rhizome develops a movement to enter through the cracks in institutionalized social structure to extract problems, disassemble them when necessary, and reassemble them from another viewpoint, which is comparable to the underground activities of resistance movements. They do not simply seek destruction, but generate chaos in different order, which suggests *anticontrol type of self-organization*.

Variations do not occur under a control system where the establishment is dominant or the pressure of regulation is too strong. Organizational transformation tends to occur when the validity of institutionalized rules, establishment and cultures has loosened and the pressure to control members has weakened. The condition necessary for organizational transformation is for reflexion reviewing the meaning of organization to vitalize through differencification from the existing institutional framework. To envisage a concrete image of rhizomic self-organization, we review the case of Kobe Steel's rugby team.

As rugby fans already know, the Kobe Steelers captured the All Japan Rugby Championship on January 15, 1995, which was the seventh consecutive honor, to rival the record established by the Kamaishi team of the Nippon Steel Corporation (Shin-Nittetsu). It is noteworthy that, in contrast to the Shin-Nittetsu Kamaishi team who stood at the top with constitution of conventional Japanese sporting world, the Kobe Steelers were crowned with glory with a completely different constitution, which was led by the originality of Mr. Seiji Hirao, the leader in the process to attain seven victories in succession. This rhizomic constitution is reflected in the terms "antisacrifice spirit," "systems are last," "creative destruction," "offbeat," "ad-lib rugby," "ever-changing team" and "abolition of the superintendent system." These terms typically embody the four features of synergetic self-organization addressed in Introduction, namely *fluctuations as a source of order, preference of creative individuals, acceptance of chaos* and *nonrecognition of a control center*. The Kobe Steelers always pushed away the obstacles in their path to rise to victory.

The team's strength lies in the metamorphosis and self-organization performed by itself through differencification and creative destruction.

Systems are Last

In the process of seven consecutive victories, the Kobe Steelers attached importance to the ideas *antisacrifice spirit* and *systems are last*. These are slogans to emphasize effort to play in a convincing manner and place priority on creative individuals, without requiring sacrifice for team members.

In the sporting world of Japan, sacrifice and devotion have emphatically been required for players. This spirit has been regarded as a virtue, with the tragic feeling contained therein predominantly accepted as a noble trait. Based on this tendency, there are group- and control-orientated conceptions for the team to attain a victory at the sacrifice of individuals. Seiji Hirao, who played the role of a leader in the seven-victory process, raised a head-on opposition to such a traditional conception and attempted to make the team another direction. In the personal messages on his home page on the Internet, he has stated,

> The Kobe Steelers seem to be a heterogeneous group among a number of sport teams in Japan. The exercising time is short. Members are not rigidly disciplined. The team does not have a dedicated leader, either. It is no exaggeration to say that the conception of its reinforcing policy is completely contrary to that adopted by other sport teams in Japan. . . . Any sport is originally a pleasure for individuals and offers a place where they can seek self-expression. Sports should not be suppressed by the tradition or group discipline. The pleasure of sports should be amplified by the group and work to accelerate the speed to attain self-realization.[15]

Rugby is essentially a team-play sport with 15 members on each side. In the background of the above expression, however, there is an idea that the ability of individuals should be reinforced more by organizing the team to completely exert the power of individuals. In this sense, rugby is an individual-play sport. Preference of individuals is definitely expressed in the opinion that sports are originally a pleasure for individuals and a place where individuals seek self-expression and self-realization, which must be accelerated by the group (team).

The primary purpose of a sport team is to win games over other teams. If the attainment of the goal by the team is prioritized, the self-insistence by the players will give way to the roles that are emphasized for the purpose of attaining the goal. However, the slogan of antisacrifice spirit contains the insistence that preference of individuals results in the enhanced competitive power of the team. In an interview regarding the problems in Japanese team-sports, Hirao replied,

> Sports are often practiced in Japan as a sort of education. In other countries in contrast, since there is individualism in the life of people, the notion that people participate in sports to acquire the spirit of cooperativeness seems to have come later. If Japanese people enter

a sport with the same feeling, they will definitely fail. In actuality, they failed in the past. Japanese people do not need to acquire spirit of cooperativeness any more. Everyday life is already full of cooperativeness. They have an idea of moral shared by people, which is seemingly based on the 'totalitarianism.' They need not carry coals to Newcastle. On the contrary, they are required to acquire individualism, to insist themselves, by participating in sports.[16]

He remarks that unlike in foreign countries where individualism exists first and people take part in sport to acquire the spirit of cooperativeness, team sports should be able to exert individualism or self-insistence in Japan, where the spirit of cooperativeness is emphasized excessively. This means that relation between individuals and the whole should be considered in the opposite direction in Japan and abroad. There are no values of being for the teams that do not hold without victimization of individuals. Leading individuals by forcing victimization does nothing but lowering the team power. Japanese people who have practiced control-oriented plays such as baseball cannot evaluate succor player Maradona's playing style, as characterized by "running alone," without using the phrase "personal power." Even a splendid step work that looks like personal power at a glance cannot be exhibited unless the personality of other members is fully exerted. Such a view did not exist in Japan.

Players were not confined in a framework, with individual personalities admitted and editorially organized to reinforce the power of the team. This is what made the Kobe Steelers completely different from the other teams. Referring to the phrase *systems are last* in an interview, Hirao pointed out the following disadvantages of Japanese system-oriented conception. It is often thought in Japan that rugby teams must be systematized to win games since each member is physically weak. Systematization implies multiplying, but not adding, the power of individual players. In actuality, however, systematization often undermines the power of individuals. Hirao explains this as follows.

It should be important for rugby teams to raise individuals first, by practicing plays based on individuals. Through this process, it may eventually be possible to evolve sign plays and integrate the individual movements and wills into one, in order to raise the total power of the team. Since every team tries the latter task first, however, it will be exhausted in the end.[17]

This is intention behind the phrase *systems are last*. Since the system is prioritized or capacity of the total is determined first, "population parameter (basic power)" does not increase at all. The secret of Kobe Steelers' strength is that team has know-how to raise, edit and organize the power of individuals. In short, raise the power of individuals and then combine players based thereon to create a team. It is a concept to organize a team regarding individual players first, but not considering organization as a prerequisite factor.[18]

In the Western style conception, placing priority on individuals is self-evident and is not a characteristic feature of self-organization in particular. As a matter of fact, Kobe Steelers introduced the western individualism, but did not end only by doing so. This team attempted a number of trials of self-organization under the slogan of creative destruction.

Team Building to Disprove the Common Notion

For organizations to attain self-innovation, it is not sufficient only to scrap unnecessary sectors through restructuring or promote reengineering to improve the functional efficiency of businesses. Self-purpose or autotelic innovation of structures and functions will end in the superficial innovation. What is essential is remeaning, or inquiring into the meaning of organization, based on which structures and functions should be changed.

Hirao started to captain the Kobe Steelers in 1988, the third year of his service at Kobe Steel, Ltd., when the glorious process began to rival the Shin-Nittetsu Kamaishi team to acquire seven consecutive victories, winning the All Japan Championship on January 15, 1989 for the first time. Upon taking the post of captain in 1988, he surprisingly executed a bold reshuffle of team members and converted the function of conventional positions to generate fluctuations in the team. More specifically, he assigned an inexperienced player to the stand-off position he had served until then, which was called the "control tower" of the team, and converted position playing the role of "control tower" from the stand-off a different position.

A rugby team consists of eight forwards (uniform numbers 1–8) and seven backs (9–15) as shown in Figure 5.2. The forwards form a scrum and jostle through the

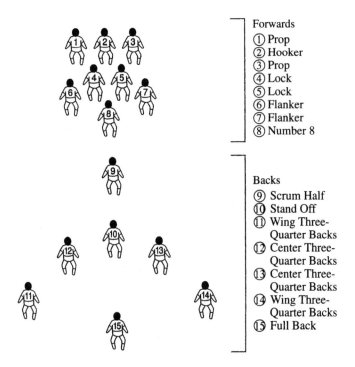

Fig. 5.2 The positions in the rugby football team

opponent players to take the ball. Since the play becomes combative, stout and powerful players are more advantageous as forwards. In contrast, the backs have an important role to receive the ball sent from forwards and effectively use it to acquire scores through passing the ball and running. Therefore, players fit for backs are those who are good in kicking and passing the ball, run fast and are quick in motion. Among the seven backs, the scrum half-back (9) positioned close to the forwards receives the ball from them and passes it to the stand-off (10) in back, who judges overall development of the play and determines instantaneously what he should do.

Hirao boldly converted members between different positions, because there was no ace in backs or efficient players. He shifted his position to the inside center (immediately behind the stand-off player who sends the ball to the wing or a score getter), where tries are easier. A problem was who should be nominated as the proxy of stand-off or the "control tower." For this position, Hirao appointed Hiroyuki Yabuki, who had experienced only a reserve scrum-half as a student of Meiji University, without particularly remarkable playing records. Yabuki was a fresh member who had joined Kobe Steel that very year and far from the status of a regular member. This appointment was equivalent to selecting a rank-and-file employee for the post of executive director in an enterprise organization.

Quite a few doubts and opposing opinions were raised against this appointment of the fresh member. There were some reserve members who were able to play the role of stand-off position. Yabuki was poor in kicking when he was a student. It is an absolute prerequisite for a stand-off player to have the ability not only for instantaneous judgment but also for passing and kicking the ball. This is a common sense at least in the rugby world. Depending on the situation, a stand-off player is required to effectively kick the ball or evade the attack of the opponent by implementing a touch kick to send the ball out of the field. Therefore, it was not conceivable in those days that a person who was not able to kick a ball adequately was nominated as stand-off player. Nevertheless, Hirao determined to assign the role to the inexperienced person having no particular skills. In short, Hirao attempted to break the stereotyped idea in the rugby world and reorganize the team attaching importance to passes. This resulted in an unexpected movement to perplex the defending formation of opponent team, from which the process toward seven consecutive victories started.

In the background of this conversion, there was another extraordinary intention to shake the conventional playing strategy. It was to convert the inside center into a hiding "control tower" for game making. In the past, Kobe Steelers deployed a strategy to adhere to a grapple, or a so-called mall, in which forwards jostle body lumps, which Hirao changed to one to carry the ball to remote places mainly by the pass work of the backs. In short, he brought a "ball game" to the fore in place of a grapple. Through such an unconventional practice (generation of fluctuation), Kobe Steelers created an innovative team (formation of new order).

Hirao implemented a new strategy to pass the ball to a place remote from the field of powerful competition at a time when it was not possible to win the game by sticking to the conventional strategies. In other words, he generated a fluctuation through such remeaning, broke the common idea and vitalized the team. This was not merely an action to make the generation of fluctuation a self-purpose, but it was invented from a review of meaning based on reflexion. This suggests that for self-organization to vitalize an organization, the generation of fluctuation through reflexion is extremely important. Remeaning is essential for fluctuations to create a new structure without simply destroying the existing one.

Offbeat and Ad-lib Rugby

Unlike baseball, rugby is a sport that features continued plays and kaleidoscopic changes in attacking and defending maneuvers. Although the positions were broadly divided into those of forwards and backs, it is not sufficient for players to devote themselves only to their positions. When compared with other sports, there are only limited rules for rugby. Therefore, it does not essentially end in a stereotyped pattern. However, a predetermined pattern has been esteemed in Japan.

The Kobe Steelers advocates a patternless rugby play as its special feature. The team is composed in such a way to fit each member, but not to frame players in a predetermined pattern, thereby aiming at the maximum exhibition of the player's ability. Thus, the team is ever changing and recommended to play an ad-lib rugby game.

In the rugby world in Japan, predetermined patterns have dominated in the playing strategy for a long time. Waseda University features the playing of "spread, approach and continuation" to effect "shaking," while Meiji University favors single-hearted "pushing" with a catchphrase of "move forward." Such patterns have supported the rugby world in Japan and created the tradition thereof. Nevertheless, such patterns or tradition cannot remain unchanged. As time goes by, patterns may change. If the physical or personal constitution of players changes, the playing patterns will naturally change. However, it was an unchanged practice in Japan to forcefully frame players in conventional patterns. The Kobe Steelers are an exception. In the process of winning the All Japan Championship seven times, its strategy continuously transfigured.

In the period from the first to the third victory when Hirao captained the team, it adopted a strategy to fight while deploying pass work mainly between backs. If the strategy to use scrums of human bullets with forwards is a grapple game in rugby, that with passing the ball between the backs will be a ball game in rugby. In place of conventional scrum-centered playing, Hirao established a strategy to pass the ball between backs and escape the power competition in a congregated skirmish. Thus, he opened a wind-hole in the rigid rugby circles in Japan restored the lost ball game features, by offering a concept of space and presenting a theory of "ball game and combat characteristics in rugby." Hirao's definition of rugby as "a game to carry the ball to deserted places" was proved to be closer to victory than the conventional theory accepted in those days that "rugby starts from a scrum and ends in a scrum."[19]

3 Anticontrol Type of Self-Organization: A Case Study of the Kobe Steelers Rugby Team

Hirao's favorite phrases are "a patternless rugby play" and "I want to change the team all the time." The first trial of these phrases was the rugby as a ball game fighting with passes. This unconventional practice (chaos) characterizes the changes in the strategy adopted one after another in the seven-victory process. In the year after the first victory, the team adopted a "short line strategy" to tactfully pass the ball among the backs standing at small intervals.

After the third victory, Ippei Onishi succeeded captain and shifted strategy to the reinforcement of grappling features, or rugby for the forwards to forcefully split the opponent team. The team pursued "tenaciousness and violence" to enhance the grappling rugby to the level of ball game rugby attained in the three-victory process. The team aimed at acquiring the National Intercity Non-Pro Rugby Championship for the fourth time. In the final game of this championship series, the team adopted an extremely simple strategy, which made the Sanyo Electric team, its formidable rival, feel a strong doubt that the Kobe Steelers would by no means resort to such a simple tactics. "The backs rescued the team from the pinch when Hirao was captain, while forwards do the same when Onishi has become captain. Such a scene symbolically represents changes in the Kobe Steelers."[20] In addition to the feature as a ball game, Kobe Steelers acquired enhanced grappling feature to perform self-organization to an unprecedented specific team, and was crowned with the championship three times in succession under the new captain.

Before the seventh victory, the captain changed to Takahiro Hosokawa in 1994. The strategies he proclaimed was "tough and speed" and an explosive rugby play to rush at a breath from a stable defending formation. This year, the team stuck to a power rugby play that it had denied for years. In the final game, the National Intercity Non-Pro Rugby Championship, at the beginning of the following year, Hirao, who played as a proxy captain, transformed himself into an aggressive stand-off and practiced a power rugby play by himself.

The features that characterize the seven-victory process of Kobe Steelers are the game play to quickly deploy the ball by effectively using spaces and the implementation of ad-lib rugby based on the judgment of individuals. As a result, its rugby kaleidoscopically changes according to the personalities of players without having a predetermined pattern. If some members change, playing method also changes. Strategy adopted in a year will never remain the same.

Such a character is the chief feature of the *edge of chaos*. It appears to be in a state of disorder at first glance, when the future is not foreseeable. Nevertheless, it is not totally a random state, either. It includes the power of phase-wise transition to generate a new pattern through the irregular interaction between small fluctuations. In this state, the emergence of new information is vitalized without dismantling the old order. The edge of chaos is a region where new information emergence and variation actively occur, systems are in an excited state, and fluctuations are frequently generated for self-organization. The Kobe Steelers attempted to positively capitalize on such chaos and used it to furnish a new team with the living power of self-organization.

Abolition of the Superintendent System

The philosophy behind the phrase *systems are last* is the concept that individuals exist before an organization does. Such philosophy brings about an attempt to depart from the control principle and is symbolized by the abolition of the superintendent system. In Japan, a number of sports including rugby are governed by conventional idea similar to those of physical training club, where individuals play for their teams or a tradition instead of esteeming their own participation. Therefore, exercise tends to be obligatory. In most cases, it is thought that a shorter way to victory is to manage the team under the leadership of a superintendent, exercise according to the menu prepared by the superintendent, and play following instructions by the superintendent. This kind of regimented sport is dominant in Japan.

A hazard associated with the organization management centering on control is that if the control exceeds its bounds, the independence of the members will be lost and this will stop the generation of new ideas or value additions. In sports, it means that team members tend not to exercise or participate in games based on their way of thinking. In Japan, there are few sports that esteem the independence of players, irrespective of whether they are amateurs or professionals. Rugby is no exception. The mainstream is those led by a superintendent both with student and company employee rugby teams.

In Kobe Steelers, the control principle once prevailed. In 1984, however, the captain Katsuhide Higashiyama at that time ceased the superintendent system and started one centering on the captain. The team has an off-season meeting where members elect a captain, who determines the policy of exercise and plays consulting with members. Regarding the abolition of superintendent system, Higashiyama says,

> For several years after I joined the team, we played the rugby of conventional style. Members took a day off only on the next day of a play. On other days, they repeated running with a ball. Even they had continued this pattern for a year, however, they were not able to win games. At last, the members started to complain 'why we should exercise so hard.' Then, they were suddenly awakened to realize that they themselves were the party who should determine what to do in a game. As a result, it was decided to do everything by themselves for a while. Thus, the superintendent system was suspended for a year, with the head coach remaining at its post.[21]

The superintendent or the coach is not allowed to enter the field during a rugby game, unlike in other sports. The game must be managed, therefore, based on the independent judgment of the captain and his players. This is the very meaning that we ourselves are the party who should determine what to do in a game. As the effect of abolishing superintendent system, the team advanced to the final game of the National Intercity Non-Pro Rugby Championship series next year for the first time since its founding. Under the conception of physical exercise club type, the superintendent is a control center often interfering in daily life of members. As the superintendent system was discontinued, therefore, the independence of members was enhanced, with the team transforming itself into one of the self-organization type with a catchphrase of creative destruction. Hirao succeeded in launching self-innovation programs one after another only because superintendent system had been abolished.

What should be noted, however, is that decontrol trend of Kobe Steelers continued even thereafter, in that the head coach was quitted in two years after the abolition of superintendent, which was followed by the discontinuation of coach system. As a result, the captain was burdened with whole responsibility for the team. This weakened the stance to coolly watch the team as a third party. Hirao, who became captain in 1998, recognized the necessity of a coach who would diagnose the team from the viewpoint of a third party and advise him on concrete strategies and tactics, thus requested Fumio Oyama, an old boy of the rugby club, to accept the post.

The abolition of superintendent system requires reviewing how the captain should be. Hirao, who experienced both the captain of Kobe Steelers and that of the All Japan Team (Japan) explains the difference as follows.

> Captains like me would like to be entrusted with everything. I would say, "Let me do things as I like. If we lose the game, I will quit this position of responsibility." Captain of Japan is more passive, somewhat like a middle-rung manager. This is not limited to rugby, but is common to any sport in Japan. I have enjoyed this position as much as I could. When seen from the historical viewpoint, however, its authority is extremely limited. The captain's sole responsibility involves how to transmit the intention of superiors. Therefore, the intentions of superintendent govern the captain's scope, number of job responsibilites, and degree of authority.[22]

This remark is to state that a team is not created satisfactorily unless the captain is assigned with authority to lead team members in the field. It is important for the *systems are last* philosophy to raise the ability of individual players. It is the basis of captaincy not to put players within a frame, but on editing and organizing their heterogeneous personalities. It is a role of the captain to put into practice his know-how on how to enhance individual skills.

In the announcement regarding new organization of Kobe Steelers in 1997, Hirao assumed the role of a general manager (GM), which superficially looked like a revival of superintendent system. It was a role to lead the team from a side closer to management, but not from a position in the field. Although the naming closely resembles a superintendent system, its contents are based on the spirit of *systems are last*. He pointed out this on his home page as follows: "There was a baseball team having a GM system. However, I had heard that it was not very successful. In my opinion, the role of GM is not to strengthen the 'control system,' but to expedite the 'creation of the environment that esteems the players' and, more importantly, to further promote the 'creation of a team autonomously managed by the players' as exemplified by the Kobe Steelers."[23] The Kobe Steelers permit self-control by individual players according to their ability and physical conditions. Exercise is limited to three days a week. By ensuring the time to make them think of rugby on non-exercise days, it is devised to augment their adherence to rugby and expedite the generation of intelligent contrivance.

The existence of individuals is a prerequisite for organizations to continuously perform self-innovation and acquire high-level organizational power. When this condition is satisfied, fluctuation is attempted in order to break any fixed pattern. It may temporarily bring about chaos in the organization. However, it is required to generate originality and contrivance through the cooperative action of members without rejecting the chaos, and minimize the control-minded intervention from the top. The independence of the members should be esteemed so as to create conditions to form new ideas and forms from inside. Only by doing so, self-organization competence emerges.

The efforts behind the seven consecutive victories of the Kobe Steelers have demonstrated that *fluctuations as a source of order*, *preference of creative individuals*, *acceptance of chaos,* and *nonrecognition of a control center* constitute the conditions for continuous self-innovation and self-organization. They also form a movement for new meaning and order creation that can work in opposition to control. In this sense, rhizome theory, which is based on differencification and reflexion, can become a strategy for deconstructing the control thought in modern times that often regresses to destroy of fluctuations.

Chapter 6
Toward a Support-based Social System

Modern society has made various control mechanisms strike root in the world. It is human efforts attempting to deconstruct God's dominance over the world that characterized the medieval society and retake an earthly world by the hands of human being, through such processes as expansion of bureaucratic mechanisms as a rationalization process of society, introduction of business administration to improve productivity and administrative intervention into markets. Introduction of such control mechanisms has contributed to the rise of democracy, but the increasing spread of control mechanisms has rendered industrial societies into similarly controlled ones.

Distortion of excessive control is now emerging concentrated and the limit of control is exposed everywhere. It is no longer possible to maintain a dynamic society with a management centering on control alone, as seen in the rigid administration, distorted and controlled education, and decreased private-sector vitality due to the permission/approval system. Nevertheless, such a control mechanism cannot be destroyed recklessly, or society will go out of control and make it impossible for us to maintain the life we are now enjoying. Until we deconstruct the excessive control and establish a new principle of social formation for a comfortable life, we have to be contented with some degree of control in society.

When the future of modern society is supposed, the control mechanism will inevitably terminate its historical mission. Although control does not vanish from this world, it shall at least withdraw from the front stage of society. What is required is how to construct a system that does not assume control. Human activities cannot be entirely controlled by people in higher positions, even though so attempted. Excessive control will create emasculated human beings and subsequently lead to the loss of social vitality. To establish a meaningful life and living conditions, a social structure is required to replace the control mechanisms.

The most promising social formation to replace control is a support system. To solve the social problems that have actualized in various forms, it is essential to undergo a structural change toward a support-based system. However, we have hardly accumulated scholarly knowledge on what would comprise a support system. Thus, we have to start discussions on support from scratch. This chapter discusses what support is from the viewpoint of decontrol, and the public philosophy that makes the basis of a support-based social system from the viewpoint of deconstructing the dualism between the public and the private.

1 Decontrol and Increasing Support Activities

In the 1980s, distortion of excessive control turned up concentrated and its review was promoted on a global scale. In the background of this movement, there was skepticism against the modern enlightenment thought that advocates the possibility of controlling society by reason and leading it toward a desirable state. What made the foundation of this skepticism is social philosophy of neoconservatism.

As discussed in Chap. 4, Friedrich Hayek who provided an ideological foundation to neoconservatism, or conservatism in a broad sense, propounded that customs, norms, institutions and other social orders are spontaneously created from the performative actions of people at their disposal, and we should make light of the fact that social orders are not rationally designed or controlled but are generated by the above action of human beings.[1] The advocacy of conservatism is not simply to preserve old and good tradition, but to re-evaluate the talented behaviors of ordinary people, or the spontaneous order formation through performative action, which modern rationalism has been apt to neglect, as it emphasizes planning and control thought too much.

"Deregulation" and "utilization of the private sector" in the 1980s reflected this social philosophy of neoconservatism, which prevailed in the USA and spread to the UK and Japan. The Reagan administration excluded goverment intervention as far as possible, advocating "a small government" to carry through the principle of free competition in markets, and promoted tax cut, review of welfare, and deregulation. Japan also promoted administrative reforms and deregulation, as proposed by the Second Provisional Commission on Administrative Reform, and privatized several public corporations.

The hypertrophy of social control (a large government) incurs an enormous amount of cost, which squeezes national budget to result in a deficit of the national treasury. Since the second half of the 1980s, societies of the former Soviet Union and East Europe fell into disorder to collapse the political regimes, which is attributed to the *failure of control*. This occurrence should be regarded, however, as a setback to the know-how or the control system to embody ideologies, rather than as a failure of the ideology of socialism.

Free nations followed suit to actualize the deregulation. However, the deregulation and adoption of free markets promoted in the 1980s did not necessarily bring about what had been desired. The Reagan administration had relaxed domestic control, but swelled international control to assume hegemony over the world with an enormous amount of war expenditure, as seen in the Strategic Defense Initiative (SDI). As a result, the USA revealed the deterioration of a nation's strength with

1 Decontrol and Increasing Support Activities   169

"twin deficit" in trade and budget, degrading to the status of a debtor nation and advent of protectionism. In Japan, deregulation was implemented for the corporate society, which did not directly lead to the improvement of people's life. Since Japan was not able to depart from the politics to protect the interest of stakeholders and local societies, efforts to relax control did not enrich the life of its people. This was because a new framework of social management was not proposed. It is not sufficient to simply lift regulations and retrospect to the market principle while relegating deregulation (decontrol) to a self-purpose. Problems of external (dis)economy that cannot be entrusted to the market principle will accumulate to seriously impede public services, particularly social security and welfare. What is now called for is construction of a decontrol system that can lead to the enrichment of life. Little will be attained, even if deregulation is promoted without such a system.

Under these circumstances, people have voluntarily promoted support activities since the mid-1980s to cope with the limit of administration on the supply of predominantly public services and goods. In the 1990s, in particular, volunteer activities by NPOs and NGOs gained momentum. The purpose of these organizations is to extend support activities by people based on their voluntary will in place of public administration in the fields of welfare, community development, environmental preservation, protection of human rights, international cooperation and so on.

The objectives of administrative activities for public interest are to promote "universally fair and square" principles, irrespective of whether the activities involve welfare services or environmental protection. However, they may not be able to adequately respond to the requirement of individuals who are distressed in particular problems. Even though public administration recognizes the necessity to extend support to those people specifically, it takes much time in the procedure to do so, and eventually the effort for support often misfired in actuality. It is often the case that necessary services are not provided due to long queues and complicated procedures, as far as people rely on public administration. Volunteer, NPO and NGO activities are not to criticize the ineffective public services impeded by managerial control procedures or appeal for smooth implementation of such services, but voluntarily promote their activities on their own accord.

Voluntary activities are to support others without pursuing profit-making, belonging to altruistic behavior according to the conventional concept. It is still a predominant view that society will not be formed or maintained with altruistic behavior as a prerequisite and the issue to adjust the disintegration and conflict resulted from egoistic behavior should be addressed. However, what we should take notice on is the fact that volunteer groups, NPOs and NGOs are rapidly increasing in both number and scale. Why do activities that look altruism grow so quickly? There is one possible motive that stands out amid the conventional dichotomy of egoism versus altruism.

In an age when *having* concern prevails to pursue material affluence, egoistic motives are predominant, and voluntary activities come to be regarded as typical altruism, or as the activities that are addressed by those who have withdrawn from the competition to acquire wealth or charity services extended to weak people by those who have acquired wealth. In this case, altruism is nothing but a residual of egoism. However, the situation becomes quite different in an age when material affluence is supported, and the concern of people has shifted to *being*, in which they are interested not in having, but in how to live or how to pursue self-actualization. What is in the background of volunteer activities is a motivation to seek self-identity, and not the acquisition of wealth, honor or power. In other words, it is an attempt to achieve self-actualization by supporting others. This is private but not egoistic, and looks like an altruistic activity.

The enthusiastic volunteer activities after the great Hanshin-Awaji earthquake in 1995 were symbolic events that told the arrival of the first year of volunteer movement. People became aware of the need to participate in public interest activities beyond those supported by missionaries and other western concerns. A number of volunteers rushed to the devastated areas from across the country to impress people all over Japan with the meaning of voluntary support activities by citizens. However, since most of the volunteers did not have the know-how on how to implement support activities or techniques were not established to adjust various activities, either, their goodwill was not fully demonstrated. As leaders assigned excessive loads to the volunteers, for example, complaints erupted among the volunteers. Moreover, discord was often seen between damage-stricken people and those who rushed to the site with dreams of volunteer activities without understanding the pain of the disaster victims. In promoting volunteer activities, it is important for leaders to grasp the competence of each member, judge whether he or she suits particular jobs, consider the time zone when the activities can be implemented, and organize easy and reasonable volunteer activities. Otherwise, those who are employed in companies or other organizations cannot freely participate in volunteer activities.

There are several problems including the above in volunteering activities. As Lester Salamon points out, attention must be paid to *voluntary failure* in addition to "market failure" and "government failure." Since volunteer activities do not pursue profit, they encounter a number of problems such as resource inadequacy, premature know-how on the management of organization, supply and demand gap in resources, paternalism, amateurism and other difficulties.[2] However, this does not mean that the significance of volunteering activities is impaired. Despite such problems, volunteer activities have continued to grow, with an increasing number of organizations and expanding scales. Under these circumstances, the Law to Promote Specified Nonprofit Activities, called the NPO law, was enacted in 1998. Voluntary activities are particularly significant in groping a new social order or publicness that can replace markets and the government.

Volunteer groups, NPOs and NGOs are new intermediate groups to mediate between individuals and society from the viewpoint of support. To realize highly sophisticated democracy, it is essential that such intermediate groups grow faultlessly. To this end, as well, it is important to discuss what support is and how it should be.

2 The Theory of Support

What are required in transforming a control-based society into a support-based one are to establish theories on (1) what support is, (2) how it should be provided, and (3) what kind of know-how it requires. A number of theories and techniques have been accumulated on the theme of control, and publications on management and administrative control are overflowing at bookstores and libraries. A Compendium of Laws is complete and judicial precedents are accumulated in quantities on the control of people. Nevertheless, books with know-how on support are hardly available at present. Although some books are published on the cases of support in relation to civil activities and recycle campaigns, there are no books on theories or know-how that systematized the concept and framework of support.[3]

What is Support?

There are terms similar to support, such as aid, help and assist. People routinely use terms related to support. In a number of fields similar terms are used, such as welfare support, official development assistance (ODA), learning support, care support, life support industries, decision-making support, diagnosis support system, business processing support and translation support. Many people tacitly understand that support is different from control. However, it is not quite clear how different these two terms are. Moreover, there are different types of support activities, such as support with goods (including money), support by some person and support with knowledge or information. Unlike these support forms with resources, there are mental and spiritual supports as well. Support is extended explicitly sometimes and implicitly at other times without the supportee being aware of it. Furthermore, cooperative relation can be considered to be a type of mutual support, if we dare say so. Even competition can be regarded as unintended support in the sense that it stimulates the competitor. Therefore, concept of support has a possibility to be included in all activities of human beings. This may make support appear to be an obscure concept. However, the term *support* is currently flooding in society as a matter of primary concern. This indicates the extent of the increase in society's demand for support. However, even among those who refer to support, there are many who use it only because it sounds good. Once the term has spread to such an extent and is abused sometimes, however, it should be reviewed correctly how support should be, or unnecessary confusion will take place. We define support first, therefore.

> Support is an approach of one actor (supporter) to the action of the other (supportee) who has an intention and a series of actions aiming at the maintenance and improvement of the quality of the other's action through an intervention in the action process with a spirit of care while understanding his/her intention, then finally arriving at the other's empowerment and the mutual realization between the both.[4]

Table 6.1 Composition elements of support

1. Approach to others
2. Understanding the intention of others
3. Maintenance and improvement of the quality of others' actions
4. Empowerment and mutual realization

As defined above, support requires an approach to the other as a prerequisite, and is meaningful only for a set of supporter and supportee. The essentials of support are the understanding of supportee's intention, maintenance and improvement of quality of other's action, and empowerment (acquisition of the power to do things) (see Table 6.1). Therefore, support is distinguished from conventional goal-seeking behavior to arbitrarily set a goal and efficiently attain it. It is required for the supporter to continuously feedback the information in what situation the supportee is and how the support action is perceived by supportee, and change action according to the intention of supportee. The intention of supportee must be cared, which is not possible without having the other's viewpoint, however. Support without care for supportee is not support in the true sense of the term.

The supporter can be an individual, organization or group. The supporter or the supportee need not necessarily be human beings. The supporter can be a personal computer or a wheelchair for the physically disabled. However, it is often the case that tools are fixed in regard to the understanding of supportee. Hammers are incorporated with the intention of supporter, for example, to drive a nail in a plate. However, hammers do not take action by themselves against the actor. In this sense, above definition of support does not apply to hammers. Since personal computers and transmission networks have a learning function, however, they are substantially superior to hammers in regard to the understanding of supportee. Therefore, the above definition of support applies thereto.

Those who extend support do not aim at simple charity or aid activities, but are motivated to establish a life worth living and self-actualization as a prerequisite. In this sense, support is a private behavior. However, this privateness is directed toward the improvement of the supportee's quality of action and elevation of the supportee's ability to do things, or empowerment of the supportee. Therefore, it is not what is called the egoistic behavior. Private self-actualization directly leads to extending care and consideration to others. In short, a *caring spirit* is critically important for providing support.

Care: Foundation of Support

Not to make support a narrow concept, it is important that its definition includes the need for the caring spirit, since care is the very origin of human existence. As Martin Heidegger puts it, care (Sorge) that represents the concern or consideration for other people or things forms the foundation of the existence of human beings. Care is a central concept that explains the existence of human beings in the world

2 The Theory of Support

who respond to meanings.[5] In other words, human beings respond to meaningful situations. The essence of human beings, which makes it possible to inquire and assess meanings, lies in the caring. Human beings have the ability to care about other people and things. By exerting this ability, we are involved in matters of concern and decide how we should deal with such concern. In this manner, we exist in the world by having concern and committing ourselves to other people and things. Concern and caring are fundamental concepts to express the existence of human beings.

The existence of human beings (Dasein) in the world (being-in-the-world) is characterized by their being concerned with either things and tools on their side or other human beings to whom they can commit themselves. According to Heidegger, there are two different modes in which such care can be shown.[6] The first is *instrumental care* (Besorgen), which concerns the things that are used in daily life, or involves taking care of things. The other is *solicitude* (Fürsorge) for human beings from the viewpoint of being with others or caring for others. Human beings essentially assume communal existence, or being with others; they commit themselves to communal existence with others either from the instrumental viewpoint or, more frequently, through actions showing consideration and care for others. The latter type of care, such as showing solicitude toward others, is the most important prerequisite for human existence and a condition that should be embodied by support.

Heidegger further classifies this care for others into two.[7] The first is the kind of care that accepts and makes efforts to remove the uneasiness and anxiety of others on their behalf. This implies accepting people's mental uneasiness and getting involved in its cause. The second type of care may not aim to remove the mental uneasiness but instead endeavors to present a model in order to help others realize what they want to be on their own, which is equivalent to the concept of support as discussed in this chapter. This kind of support effects the empowerment of others by forging ahead to help the supportee as much as possible without discontinuing the care.

The care to get involved on behalf of others, which includes efforts directed toward self-sacrifice, is sometimes necessary depending on the timing and circumstances, but it is hardly care in the true sense of the term. For instance, nurses who show excessive care for their patients occasionally suffer from the burnout syndrome as a result of over-nursing. Such care often results in paternalism and may lead to a dominance-dependence relation, since it tends to give rise to sentiments such as "I helped him" or "I acted as a substitute for her." This mirrors the supporter's feeling of superiority with respect to the supportee. However, genuine care does not fall into this pattern. In this type of care, the supportee becomes empowered to cope, and the supporter is glad to be able to provide this power. Thus, mutual realization is attained.

Support premises commitment to others like care and brings about self-actualization for supporter as seen in volunteer activities. As Erikson puts it, care is the source of vitality in life or in the grown-up period in particular.[8] In the sense that the supporter acquires vitality, care involves private interest (self-interest). To exert the power to care, it is required to be open for others and empower others. In this sense, care is oriented to others or altruistic. Therefore, care is a concept beyond the mere dualism of egoism and altruism.

Support consisting of care and empowerment of others is an altruistic behavior at a glance. It may be a predominant view, however, that society assuming altruistic activities is nothing but a castle-in-the-air or an idea of utopia. However, it may be shortsighted to think of support in this manner. Human beings interact with others not only through the *having concern* to have more or count profit and loss, but also through a life worth living, self-actualization and *being concern* for a larger degree. In other words, human beings are the existence aiming at not only having more but also self-actualization and an intelligent, aesthetic and ethical realization of life. As mentioned above, this tendency becomes stronger when material affluence is guaranteed. Care features that *egoism* (private interest) in being concern connects to *altruism* (public interest) in having concern without contradiction. Furthermore, privateness connects to publicness continuously to merge into one.

Support activities do not hold in egocentrism as they premise supportees. Supporter is required to monitor whether the state of supportee has been improved and review its own activities. In addition, it is essential that empowerment of supportee is realized. By doing so, the supporter attains self-actualization. In this manner, though support has private interest in self-actualization, it is action having an opportunity to connect with others while surpassing this self-actualization. Support activities provide an opportunity to achieve mutual self-realization as it assumes care for others, though stemming from individualism.

Support System

In order to make support actualized, the series of support actions should not be scattered but compose an integrated system. Support will not function efficiently if it composes a fixed system. Support must be able to change itself according to the changes in situation to which the supportee is subjected and affect the maintenance and improvement of the quality of supportee's action. Therefore, we define the system as follows.

> The support system consists of interrelated resources to enable support and a set of models (know-how elements) to utilize them, and constitute a self-organization system to flexibly change itself according to the changes in the situation of support.[9]

To implement support, it is required to have goods, information and other resources, and models (know-how elements) to effectively utilize these resources. In other words, the support system consists of various resources and models. Even if funds are available, support in the true sense cannot be expected unless the funds are interlinked with human resources or information, or know-how is provided. It is important for the support system to have models that interlink human, material and information resources for effective utilization of support. In the case of the

2 The Theory of Support

great Hanshin-Awaji earthquake, volunteers swarmed into devasted areas to swell confusion despite their goodwill. Although volunteer activities are the best example of support, their significance will be lost, if know-how on role assignment and procedures is not available for effective implementation of support.

The support system is not effective unless it can freely change itself according to the situation of the supportees. System composition must not be fixed, but be able to change flexibly. The control system is fixed relative to the relevant situation and places priority on rules and routines. In contrast, the support system should be able to organize its approach appropriately according to the understanding of supportee's intention (interpretation of meaning). For this purpose, it is important to implement *reflexive feedback*, but not the feedback for the supporter's own goal attainment. As support situation changes every moment, a fixed role action alone is not effective. New ideas and contrivances should be attempted continuously. This means that support system is in the nonequilibrium state where fluctuations always takes place rather than in the steady state. The self-organization theory agrees with the nature of support system in this sense, as its essential points are fluctuation and reflexion. In other words, support system requires self-organization theory with respect to the movement from control to reflexion and stable equilibrium to differencification.

In short, the necessary condition for support is to change the self from the standpoint of others. The supporter must change his or her actions according to the intention of the supportee, by feeding back (reflexion) in what situation the supportee is and how the support action is accepted. Supporter should not merely work with a desire to support or aid others, but should also correctly understand the requirements of the supportee.

The term *empowerment* included in the definition of support drew attention in the second half of the 1980s, mainly in the fields of social work and social care as a guideline to the program to improve living ability of physically disabled people. This was born by combining the traditional idea of mutual aid and self-help with antiracism, feminism and criticism of inequality and oppression. This concept started to be applied not only to the caring of physically handicapped people but also in a wider range including groups and communities.

According to Robert Adams, empowerment may be defined as a means, by which individuals, groups and/or communities become able to take control of their circumstances and achieve their goals, thereby being able to work toward helping themselves and others to maximize the quality of their lives.[10] The term empowerment adopted in the definition of support is one in such a broad sense, which includes not only the physically disabled as supportees, but also individuals, groups, organizations, communities and societies at large. Empowerment features that it does not entrust the maintenance and improvement of the quality of activities to experts, and a fact that supportees acquire knowledge and technology, thereby ensuring the ability to solve problems by themselves, or strengthening their own ability. The aim of empowerment is to establish a system that can strengthens the supportees' abilities and make it possible for people to gain strength in society.

Table 6.2 Conditions required for support

1. Do not bring supporter's intention to the fore.
2. Do not impose the supporter's intention to the supportee.
3. Duly take into account time and cost.
4. Do not impair supportee's self-reliance efforts.

Conditions Required for Support

Unlike conventional goal-oriented rational behavior, support maintains and improves the quality of supportee's actions and effects the supportee's empowerment, thereby attaining self-actualization of the supporter. Therefore, support is not egoistic but basically assumes care for others. From this viewpoint, several conditions are required for support (see Table 6.2).

First, the intention of supportee should have priority to others, in order to realize support. The purpose of supporter should not be in excess thereof. In other words, supporter's purpose or intention should not come to the fore.

Support has been extended to people in a number of cases. In the Renaissance period, Medici, a plutocrat from Firenze, Italy, extended his patronage activities and provided economic and spiritual protection to artists, artistic schools and activities. In the modern and present ages as well, politicians and businessmen offer financial support to those who have interesting ideas. However, such support is rather individual and not socially systematized in most cases, and controlling ideas tend to be preferentially addressed. Support has frequently been implemented for the reason that ideas or information useful to supporter will be obtained in return. As is often seen in the philanthropic activities conducted by enterprises, support aims at enhancing social reputation of the enterprises and is expected to bring profits eventually as a boomerang effect. In the period of economic bubble that lasted from the end of the 1980s to the beginning of the 1990s, enterprises competed with each other in promoting activities for social contribution, in the form of Mécénat campaigns and philanthropic movements, in which the intention of supporter side appeared in the front. These enterprises stop extending support without exception when economy grows dull, as the support is subjected to control conception. Support of this type belongs to the second class, as supporter's purpose surpasses the support action. Support from which supporter intends to enjoy a profit cannot be called support in the true sense of the word, unless the supporter takes no account of the outcome.

Second, support should be offered based on the requirement of supportee, and not be imposed on people. When the municipal office has constructed a facility for senior citizens, for example, it may urge elderly citizens' clubs to use it, in order to propagate that it is providing a useful service. Although this is apparently an administrative support measure, it is actually an unsolicited interference with the aged. Imposition is another name of control. To fulfill the responsibility of an economic power, Japan implemented official development assistance extensively to other Asian countries. Although Japan distributed an enormous amount of funds for this purpose, however, it could be called a imposition of aid, since Japan did not correctly provide the know-how to effectively utilize the funds. Therefore, it is important to check the feedback regarding the conditions of the recipient of the support.

Third, support should be offered at appropriate time and cost according to the requirement of supportee. If supporter contemplates the methods of support, postpones the schedule of support and spends too much money, support will not be implemented effectively. It is necessary for the supporter to perform cost-benefit analysis for efficient implementation according to the situation of the supportee. In other words, support must be efficient. Unlike the efficiency in attaining a goal in businesses, efficiency in support does not focus on the attainment of any gain by the actor (supporter), but is for others (supportees) to acquire benefit. Since this efficiency is not related to control by others, it is not contradictory to support.

Fourth, a system should not be formed for the supportee to rely on support and neglect self-help efforts. Excessive support that impedes self-reliance efforts must be avoided. If the supportee expects support and does not make efforts for a self-sustaining life, it is not a true form of support. Empowerment is included in the definition of support exactly for this reason. Support is successful only when supportees can do things by themselves. This includes problems related to whether support is appropriate, or to what extent it should be extended. Conversely, it also expresses the necessity of supportee's mental attitude. Support is meaningless if supportee does not make any efforts for self-reliance while expecting support from others.

Advanced countries provide food and medical aid to starvation-stricken developing countries in the name of humanism. If it exceeds the appropriate level, however, an aid-reliance constitution will be born to hamper the ability to do things by themselves (not empowered). It is pointed out that "indulgence" emerges as a result of excessive welfare services. Generally speaking, attention must be paid to the fact that support often spoils supportees and brings about a negative effect on them. Easygoing humanism obstructs support. Humanism appeals to the mind of people and charity activities are praiseworthy. However, humanism will never become the fundamental principle of society. Support should not be grounded on humanism or implemented as charity. A genuine support will not be provided from support activities represented by volunteer, Mécénat and philanthropic activities, unless they extricate themselves from the charity idea.

3 Some Cases of the Support

It would be useful to discuss various cases at this stage where a theoretical framework has not yet been established. Where and how support is implemented? This section addresses several cases. It is not meaningful, however, to introduce cases of support in an arbitrary manner. We focus, therefore, on self-organization included in the *support system* that was discussed in previous section.

One of the features of synergetic self-organization is *nonrecognition of a control center*. Self-organization that gives a positive meaning to fluctuation rejects a control center or its similar concept, namely authority, the wholeness of system, etc. This overturns the subordination of an individual unit to wholeness, which is a viewpoint to emphasize that macroscopic order is generated from synergy between elements. In other words, an anticontrol system that suits the self-organization theory and its concrete example is the support system.

Support as the Destruction of Control

Control system is effective to attain a given goal or maintain existing orders, but it does not suit the search for a new goal or activities to change a system. To break down rules that obstruct the enrichment of life, it is required not only to advocate deregulation but also to device a support strategy to emasculate control.

As a case to symbolize the destruction of control, there is a story to have supported a farmer group, in the Ohgata Mura village, Akita prefecture, which was once a topic in mass media and among people at the end of the 1980s. Farmers of this group did not use agricultural chemicals but used weed killers only once to produce rice (Akita Komachi) under new organic cultivation and shipped it to consumers in Tokyo as free-market rice detouring the agricultural cooperative. If consumers purchase rice directly from farmers, they will be charged with a violation of the Food Control Law. To stop the circulation of free-market rice in this case, the Food Agency guided carriers to refrain from delivering the rice and issued a notification to perform stringent control and on-the-spot inspection. But a number of consumers desire organically cultivated rice. To support the farmer group, thereupon, the Citizens' Group of Japan Recycle Movement set up the "Food National Trust Fund." Consumers were supposed to donate to the fund and received a certain amount of rice in return every month from the fund as "a gift through personal connection." Farmers are allowed to send rice free of charge to relatives and acquaintances as a seasonal greeting or token of gratitude, which could be supplied out of the purview of the planned distribution under the Food Control Law. Through this strategy aimed at the destruction of control, a support system was designed between farmers and consumers who wanted the contamination-free rice.

To maintain food control system, the Ministry of Agriculture, Forestry and Fisheries implements a rice import/export permission system, which forces Japanese people to buy expensive rice as a result. To undermine this system, an importer in Osaka devised a method to place fish on balls of Californian rice and import them as "sushi." This was to take advantage of the fact that processed rice such as pilaf was not controlled. It was discussed whether this was an import of rice or processed food. However, the insistence of importer was approved eventually. As this was a contrivance of an importer, it did not constitute support. If a third party other than those involved in the import business invented it, however, it would have been a full-fledged case of support. In a broad sense, it is a support action to undermine the Food Control Law, which is now a mere shell for the purpose of "food control."

The Food Control Law was enacted in the period of World War II to cope with the shortage of food, and maintained thereafter to ensure stable supply of the staple food for the nation. However, its initial significance has already been lost. It would be a wag-the-dog policy to regulate the production and distribution of rice and force customers to buy expensive rice in a new pretext of food security. As several attempts had been made to emasculate the timeworn Food Control Law, the administration was forced to revise it. This is suggestive in discussing deregulation. It is not sufficient to merely oppose control. Good attempts should be supported with suitable strategies. If know-how for support is accumulated not to be defeated by control, citizens will be able to acquire the power to change politics and society.

Support as Spontaneous Order Formation

A support system can be designed even when supporter and supportee are not separate entities. It is sometimes the case that an existing support system becomes self-organized as a new support system with a different purpose and target.

A television drama titled "University of Tokyo direct from a junior high school: senior high schools are no longer necessary," which was televised in the second half of the 1980s. This was baesd on the actual story of a boy who was skeptical about the controlled education, voluntarily quit senior high school and made efforts to advance to a university by sitting for the examination of university admittance qualification system (hereinafter referred to as "DAIKEN"), which he had casually come to know. The DAIKEN system was implemented after World War II to provide mainly working youths with a chance of receiving university education. Young boys and girls, who had not been able to take the senior high school course, took the examination of DAIKEN and were qualified for taking entrance examination of universities when they passed examinations in certain subjects. In the period of rapid economic growth, the DAIKEN became rather obsolete, since the ratio of the students going to senior high schools exceeded 90%. In the 1980s, however, those who took the DAIKEN examination rapidly increased.

In the 1980s, the deviation value based education, which was once a serious social problem, brought about an increase of "school dropouts," "bullying the weaker," "violence in schools" and "school phobia" to devastate schoolrooms. As a stopgap measure, a number of schools promoted controlled education to strengthen the regulations of uniforms, hair styles and personal belongings. Under such circumstances, the DAIKEN examination became a haven for the youths who were unable to adapt to the controlled education, and a return-match ground for senior high school dropouts to advance to universities. In the fiscal year of 1987, 80% of the successful candidates for the DAIKEN examination were those who had finished the junior high school course and dropouts from senior high schools, and 80% were aged 20 or less when the number of successful candidates were counted in terms of age. In addition, more and more young people started to positively use the DAIKEN as a strategy to receive university education. The aforementioned television drama primed the pump for this phenomenon.

In the wake of the televised drama, DAIKEN preparatory schools emerged, where an increasingly large number of those in the 15–16 age group attended. While noticing the changes in the status of DAIKEN examination, the Ministry of Education, Culture, Sports, Science and Technology reviewed the test subjects and methods as a means to diversify the opportunity for university education while maintaining the fundamental nature of DAIKEN. What is the most noteworthy is that youths who harbored doubts about the controlled education self-organized DAIKEN as a bypass for the university entrance examination. Schools and the society are also rather sympathetic toward DAIKEN students without having a feeling of discrimination. In this manner, the DIKEN itself changed its nature and underwent transformation. Self-organization to support system took place exactly in accordance with the principle of spontaneous order.

Support as Securing Freedom from Restrictions

In a support system, the supporter needs not necessarily be a human being, but can be a tool like a computer. Unlike conventional database, the hypertext discussed in the previous chapter is a system that provides support by secureing *unrestricted* information retrieval. Since the protocol to connect to networks is open for the Internet, unrestrictedness is secured for it to allow access from any computer and enable individuals to communicate with anybody in the world.

A hypertext is a knowledge database to allow free linkage between different texts according to occasional interest, since there are no predetermined utilization methods. We do not necessarily know in advance what we want to know. Usually, we trace a labyrinth of associations for that purpose. Such information retrieval has been made possibly by hypertext. It is not the world of database where data are related in advance, but a world where we relate data by ourselves and enrich our knowledge. The multi-media database represented by hypertext enables free editing of an enormous volume of knowledge. By using it, it is possible to create a database customized for an individual. This hypertext structure radically undermines the dendritic (tree-shaped) hierarchical structure, which typifies the conventional databases and texts, and enables unrestricted or free linkages between texts. In recent years, free linkages between Windows systems has enabled unrestricted browsing between word processors, statistic calculations, databases and electric mails freely.

3 Some Cases of the Support 181

The Internet is a telecommunication means that spurs this movement. It has no managers and its information is open in principle. It not only provides the benefit to improve the efficiency and convenience of telecommunications but also constitutes a medium to open the world as a *field*. As a matter of course, this openness has expedited the globalization of volunteer and NGO activities, international evolution of multi-national enterprises, and connected people of different races from across the world. The progress of such globalization has gradually and effectively melted the hierarchical structure that characterized the conventional texts and expanded the scope of unrestricted coupling.

Problems are arising, however. The non-manager system puts the activities on the Internet into a state of anarchy and entry of businesses is eroding the principle of freeware and openness of information. Although the Internet is a tool (support system) to ensure unrestricted links without a control center, it will soon lose its role as a tool for support if anarchical state and business principle erodes its original purpose.

Support as the Intake of Fluctuation

Support can take an economic form of budgetary arrangement that does not fit the conventional framework. Enterprises can no longer survive by producing goods alone, but they have to create added values. An intensive utilization of information led to the introduction of factory automation (FA) and office automation (OA). As a result, most of the production processes and office work were automated. Even if the production system were automated, it would be of no avail without products worth manufacturing that sell well for their added values. Before starting production, enterprises must create an idea that would realize added values.

Creation of added values is to create a new meaning or an idea people are deeply impressed with. For such an activity, neither control nor efficiency is effective. A mechanism is required to create a new idea and materialize it. Management and control are sufficient to efficiently manufacture predetermined products. These two intervening actions are not effective for adding value, since nothing other than endless differencification is effective to that purpose. Since value addition is merely seen as a byproduct of a process, it is important how we support creative activities. When creativity is expressed as a slogan, enterprises are required to transform themselves into decontrolled organizations thereby performing value addition. They must weigh not only the importance of efficiency but also prioritize on the creation of added values.

An accounting scholar says that a handsome amount of expenditure that juts out from the items in the financial statement is increasing in the finance of enterprises in recent years. The expenditure will eventually be allocated to some item under a plausible pretext, but it is often the money spent on "something interest" or on support. The scholar adds that there is a long-term positive correlation between the profit from the business of enterprises and the total expenditure that does not fit the balance sheet of the accounting system.[11] It is a support system design to systematize such side drops for support (equivalent to a fluctuation), for example. It is one of the measures conceivable from the accounting viewpoint to open new items in the balance sheet without forcefully confining the budget or expenditure for supporting the creation of added values or ideas in the conventional format.

In general terms, a mechanism should be created to incorporate fluctuations into organizations. In short, it is necessary to discuss how to implement support in order to facilitate and structuralize ideas that do not fit into the existing system. If an amount for that purpose is set in budget, it will constitute about 5% of the total. According to my hypothesis in Chap. 3, 80% of the actions of human beings are routine activities; about 15% are efficient and rational ones; and the rest (5%) comprise reflexive actions to extensively review and deliberate the meanings of the past. It is also required for organizations to allocate this 5% action as a reflexion sector. The work of this sector is to create a new difference through differencification from the existing experience and knowledge, return it to the existing system, and edit the resultant new meaning and knowledge. Creation of added values is a difficult task for the individuals who attempt to do so, which cannot be done easily. It is required, therefore, to at least attempt decontrol and establish a support system.

Intermediate Summary

In the above, four cases of support were discussed. The knowledge obtained therefrom includes four points with regard to support: (1) strategy aimed at destruction of control, (2) formation of spontaneous order, (3) securing freedom from restrictions, and (4) structurizing of fluctuation. Among these four points, what is the most important at present is the strategy aimed at destruction of control. Since the regulations are strong at present, relaxation from regulations makes an important point from various viewpoints. To actualize the slogan *from control to support*, it is conceivable to provide support to destroy unnecessary control first.

Nowadays, deregulation is a great social concern. It is not desirable, however, to make deregulation a self-purpose, or a regulation for deregulation is required. This will impair the genuine purpose of deregulation. Regulations assume some benefits. If deregulation becomes a self-purpose, therefore, conflicts will take place between parties with different interests on the order of deregulation, which would lead to a chaotic state. Regarding problematic regulations, it is important to devise a support strategy to emasculate such regulations and nullify the reason for their existence, like the Food National Trust Fund undermined the Food Control law.

It is also crucial to change the purpose of an existing system in order to usher in self-organization. The DAIKEN, organized originally to support working youths, was changed to a bypass route for those who had escaped from controlled education. This is a case noteworthy as a self-organization of support system. If the administration takes the initiative in changing a system, it is often the case that priority is placed on making guidelines with new rules, since it is exactly the job of administration. It will deserve the name of support more, if a support system is reconstructed spontaneously through the performative action of individuals.

Moreover, as seen in the cases of "hypertext" and "the Internet," it is an important subject to give secure unrestrictedness to information retrieval or communications that have been conducted rather inconveniently. Irrespective of whether such communication is implemented with tools, or human beings such as consultants or counselors, it is significant that unrestrictedness of subject performance is improved for suportees. It must be noted that this unrestrictedness does not simply mean convenience, but its essence is to enhance the freedom of activities.

Finally, it is also an important subject for support to structuralize the fluctuation (idea and action) that does not fit the existing conception or cannot be dealt with by the existing framework. For society to become dynamic and pursue high added values, fluctuations should be taken in beyond existing structural framework.

As human relations are complicated, so the problem of support is difficult to grasp. The subjects to be addressed from now on are to (1) further enrich the terminology support, (2) examine various cases of support to elaborate the theory of support, and (3) establish the social philosophy of support as a new principle of social formation. The subject (3) is related to the public philosophy that makes the basis of society as support system. For support to become a new principle of social formation in place of control, its contribution to public philosophy should be discussed.

4 Opening Publicness from Support

Replacing the idea of a control system with that of a support system opens up a new way of thinking in place of the conventional one that regarded public interest as opposed to private interest. In present society, most people are individualistic, which has led to the private–public conflict of interests. In such a scenario, it is essential to retain the existing *private* activities as a prerequisite and then find the opportunity to go beyond them into the *public* sphere. While volunteer and NPO activities allow their participants to pursue the private goal of self-actualization, they also promote interest and involvement in others, thereby making it possible to add publicness to private concerns.

Publicness normally refers to the *principle of the democratic formation of politico-economic order beyond selfishness*. Discussions on publicness hitherto can broadly be divided into two types. One is the civil publicness or the *civil movement type of publicness*. This is the publicness as the logic for citizens to form a public opinion on politics through open forums and social movements and to mediate civil desire to the nation state. A feature of this publicness is to raise public opinions while opposing public power. This type of publicness is typically represented by the public opinion seen in newspapers and televisions, civil movements for environmental preservation, anti-nuclear, peace and so on. The other is the *administrative control type of publicness*, which is seen in the social overhead capital improvement or public work for people's welfare. This is related to limiting private rights. What has been called "the work of political authorities" belong to this category. This is the publicness as the logic to legitimate the exertion of public power.

Who put a full-scale light on the problem of publicness for the first time was Hanna Arendt. She kept an eye on that poleis in ancient Greece were governed by the forums of free citizens, and proposed the concept of *public space as polis*. A polis is a space where communal activities are implemented with dialogue (discussion and lexis) as a medium and features that discussion was seen and heard by all citizens, and conveyed to the public as much as possible.[12] This nature of publicness is the origin of present-day information disclosure and accountability of enterprises, government, and other organizations, and the starting point of the publicness to build up public opinion through forums. In short, openness and formation of public opinion are the conditions of publicness.

The public space as a polis was invented with direct democracy of the poleis in ancient Greece as a model. A new version of this public space evolved to meet the conditions in modern society is *civil publicness* or bourgeois public sphere advocated by Jürgen Habermas. In *Structural Transformation of Public Sphere*, he regards that a space where forums are held is the foundation of civil publicness. The main point in his insistence is to be outside political power, evolve criticizing discussions against public power and press changes in political and economic orders to the state. This civil publicness was formed through the "literary public sphere" and the "political public sphere" that followed, which made their debut in the latter half of the 17th century and at the beginning of the 18th century.[13] Civil publicness is the original form of the *civil movement type of publicness* referred to above.

The concept of publicness is not limited to the formation of public opinion by citizens. Publicness includes the work and control by the government and local autonomous bodies. The activities by administration to provide and control goods and services that cannot effectively be supplied through markets are also public. They include activities related to defense, police, environmental hygiene, roads and parks. This is the publicness as the exercise of what is called the public power, which is equivalent to the *administrative control type of publicness*. In Japan, a characteristic equality holds between public and political authorities. In Japan where modernization progressed without experiencing civil revolution, civil society has not been established sufficiently unlike in Europe or the USA. For long years since the Meiji era, "public" has meant the bureaucratic authority system of the state crowned by the Emperor, and public interest has been the interest of the state. Democratization after World War II collapsed such a regime formally (at least so believed). In actuality, however, the administrative control type of publicness persistently prevails even at present.

4 Opening Publicness from Support   185

Declining Space of Publicness

In Japanese society after World War II, issue of publicness was evolved with above two types as an axis. In the second half of the 1960s and the 1970s, discussions on civil society and the public inspired a concern for publicness. In those days, theory of civil society was positively introduced, and social movements became active in opposition to the administrative control type of publicness exerted by the state or political authorities. Heated discussions were evolved on social revolution when anonymity and political indifference were prevalent in a mass society.

In the 1980s and the bubble economic period, however, people gradually lost interest in publicness, for the reason that individualism developed significantly due to the penetration of mass democracy and establishment of welfare state. As a result, privatism spread and privatization progressed from the 1980s to the period of bubble economy, when *the private* was eulogized for some time at a place separated from *the public*. As people buried themselves in the adherence to private life, social movements decayed or were forced to transmute. Individualism prevailed and the principle of market competition became predominant on the one hand, while a structure was created to entrust public affairs to political authorities unconditionally on the other. As a result, intermediate groups to mediate between individuals (private) and society (public) — neighborhood associations ("Chonaikai"), regional communities and voluntary associations—weakened.

Above situation applies not only to Japan but also to Europe and the USA for the most part. Habermas, who significantly influenced the discussion of publicness in the 1960s, deplored that the enrichment of welfare state and penetration of mass democracy collapsed the public sphere as a field of autonomous discussion and the civil publicness tended to disintegrate. In the 1980s, he started to use the term *autonomous publicness* in place of civil publicness in the past, aiming at recovering the power of "social integration" by inputting the impulse generated from the lifeworld in place of the "system integration" by the control media of currency and power. He seeks the possibility of a new publicness here and calls it the *autonomous and self-organized publicness*.[14] The autonomous publicness refers to the state where publicness is not generated to justify the political system with its own hand, or it is not the administrative control type of publicness. The autonomous publicness is the higher order intersubjectivity (consensus) self-organized from the discussion in the lifeworld.

The essential point of Habermas' autonomous publicness is to open publicness from the lifeworld. Although this viewpoint is important, a problem is that his publicness is captured by a "grand narrative" that seeks consensus formation and social integration, and still haunted by nostalgia for civil publicness in the 18th century. What he calls publicness follows the schema that publicness is intersubjectively meaning formation. It is anticipated that publicness is preceded by consensus formation with its procedural matter therefor left alone. Therefore, the discussion on autonomous publicness did not gather momentum or prevent people from losing interest in publicness in the 1980s. People eulogized the private at a place distant from the public sphere for long in a mass democracy and the welfare state.

In such circumstances, neoliberalism appeared in the 1990s by holding up the further pursuance of market principle that was once advocated by neoconservatism. Neoliberalism, which is on the extension line of social philosophy of neoconservatism, attempts to thoroughly promote deregulation and review welfare by the principle of market competition. Neoconservatism had an ideological aspect to insist that social disciplines, old and good families and communities be recovered. As one of its features, neoliberalism has wiped out this nostalgia for the past order. By cutting off this nostalgia, neoliberalism insists on a thorough market principle and globalism under the slogan of self-determination and self-responsibility.[15] Its completeness deserves the name of *market fundamentalism*.

However, applauding globalization and principle of market competition omnipotence spreads risk all over the world. Easy-going discussions on self-determination and self-responsibility contain *dynamics to close publicness*. The market fundamentalism that advocates the principle that the weak are victims of the strong dwarfs the problem of publicness to the naïve fairness of competition and a safety net for losers, though the advocacy of the safety net is not limited to that by neoliberalism. The market mechanism cannot deal with the problems of external (dis)economy, such as the distribution of public goods, pollution and environmental disruption that feature non-excludability and non-rivalness. The tendency to shelve such problems is equivalent to a manner pretending that there are no market failures, even though there are.

After the collapse of bubble economy and the vehemence of neoliberalism that professed globalization of the market omnipotence type, there emerged a tendency that should be called the *renaissance of publicness*.[16] A number of commentators started to insist on the reconsideration of civil society. This resuscitation of the discussion on publicness and civil society is based on a crisis consciousness against the dynamics to close publicness of neoliberalism. However, the paradigm of conventional publicness to assume the administrative control type of publicness that is authoritatively born by the state and the civil movement type of publicness in opposition thereto is no longer practical. Discussions are required to fill the *blank public space* dropped from the conventional paradigm. In conventional discussion on publicness, the public and the private are grasped dualistically to enlighten public sprit that cannot be reduced to selfishness. However, as individualism has penetrated into masses at large, publicness cannot be revived by simply appealing public spirit alone.

Under these circumstances, it is extremely difficult to reformulate publicness. However, it may be possible to find a clue to such a reformulation. It is to open an area where the control paradigm that has led modern society withdraws into the background. As a theoretical strategy for this purpose, I adopt the conception of support to replace control. Although support activities have a private nature, they premise otherness in the form of caring about others and, therefore, they have an opportunity to open a space for activities not captured by selfishness or the space for publicness.

4 Opening Publicness from Support

Opening the Public through Animating the Private

A feature of the conventional publicness was to deal with the public that was opposed to the private. Public affairs existed separately from private affairs. Participation in the issues beyond private affairs was to show public interest. Both the administrative control type of publicness and the civil movement type of publicness have a framework of the public in opposition to the private. As individualism has developed, however, people no longer feel a flavor of reality in the publicness that assumes the confrontation between the private and the public. This is all the more correct, since it has been advocated for more than 10 years in Japan that the preference on enterprises or the state be converted to that on individuals, in order to construct a society where people can really feel well-being. Enlightenment to hold publicness a high-handed attitude is not possible. This is reflected in that telecast public opinions do not form a new political or economic order but often become only a spectacle or a show.

What is now called for is to animate the private and open the public, or the viewpoint of *opening the public through animating the private*.[17] It is to find an opportunity to open the public in the private action, in place of publicness in opposition to the private. How is it possible, then? What is noteworthy is the fact that an area to be called the *voluntary support type of publicness* is spreading to replace the administrative control type of publicness and the civil movement type of publicness (see Figure 6.1). As private support activities, there are volunteer

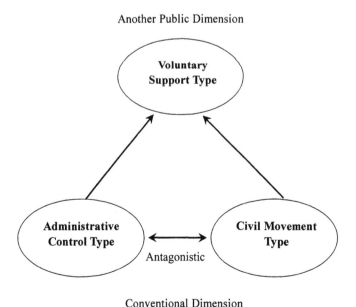

Fig. 6.1 New dimension of public space

group, NPO and NGO activities. These support activities are to provide highly public services by themselves without relying on government. Otherwise, it is often the case that these services are not provided when necessary. It is the basis of the voluntary support type of publicness to overcome the limit of administrative control type of publicness in the form of support activities by voluntary actions of individuals.

As discussed above, support is a series of actions aiming at the maintenance and improvement of the quality of others' action. Its essence is to empower others or make others acquire the power to do things or live. The supporter, who has a private motive to realize the worth of living or perform self-actualization, empowers others and improves quality of their actions, in order to satisfy his/her private motivation. In this case, private self-actualization and support of others are not separate, but form a perfect unity. What should be noticed is the importance that individuals open their own public space not only through publicness of the administrative control type and that of the civil movement type, but more than that through the support activities backed up by a private motive or self-actualization.

In Japan, people predominantly believe that publicness is the work executed by political authorities and the government. It is also widely accepted that public activities are for citizens to activate discussions in opposition to political authorities and present what the society should be. In any event, people have been enlightened that it is important to have not only interest in private affairs but also a public mind in thinking the formation of society. Although publicness to consider the nation state is still important, public activities performed by individuals should be evaluated more. In this sense, support activities represented by those of volunteers have the possibility to scoop up the publicness dropped from publicness of the administrative control type and that of the civil movement type.

There are several problems in volunteer activities. Optimism is dangerous (failure of volunteer). Despite these problems, however, volunteer activities are developing ceaselessly, while increasing their number and expanding their scale. There are currently no other means than volunteer activities to maintain the circuit to animate the private and open the public.

What is behind the volunteer activities is the motive to confirm one's identity. This means an existence of the will not to acquire wealth, honor or authority, but the will to finally attain self-actualization by supporting others, and acquiring the pleasure of oneself and power to live. It brings about activities that are private but not selfish and looks like altruism. The rally of the *will to volunteerism* is proved by the fact that the ratio of the people who pursue spiritual well-being rather than material well-being has been increasing since the 1990s.[18] The will to volunteerism reflects the orientation toward spiritual well-being.

It can be claimed that participation in volunteer activities is a full-fledged public action. To overcome the failure of government and that of market, it is important to open the public through animating the private. It is required for politics, government and civil movement to find publicness in the private action of individuals under the perspective conversion from control to support.

Toward a Practical Publicness

Publicness can be divided into two types: *practical publicness* and *discursive publicness*. Publicness opened from support activities constitutes a practical, not discursive, type of publicness. The discussion of publicness represented by Arendt and Habermas focuses on public opinion, debates and a discursive type of publicness. However, if there is publicness grounded on support, it will be that of the practical type. This means that performance of support itself includes publicness, or support includes performative publicness. Even if supporter is not conscious of publicness, support activity is related to performative publicness as a result. As the practical type of publicness, there were class struggles in the past. After class struggles declined, the practical type of publicness was succeeded to civil movements. This flow is cut at present. However, not only social movements, but also volunteer activities, NPO activities and other social participation movements can be the practical type of publicness, which means that action itself connects to publicness.

It is true that public space as discussion and public opinion of discursive type is important. However, what is necessary is to think two-level public space, i.e. the practical and the discursive levels. In recent years, practice has shrunk and discourse has swelled. There are too many people who play with discursive words, specious commentators and semiocrats. There are few intellectuals who actually practice. Practice and discourse should be balanced.

For publicness to be opened from support activities and subsequently for public space to be formed, these activities must penetrate into society as routines. To what extent it is realized makes a subject in opening a new publicness. It is well conceivable that the political and economic spaces where control media such as currency and power circulate swallow support activities from the idea of control. It is also possible for support to end only as an auxiliary concept after all to compensate for the inadequacy of the control by public power. The publicness in a new age may be opened by the recovery of the civil publicness (public opinions at salons, coffee houses and reading circles in the past) through the discussions at virtual communities and forums by rapidly progressing electronic media, rather than by the pubic space of the practical type of support activities.

In considering the above, it is important to position the public space as a small narrative rather than as a grand narrative. Publicness has been too grand a narrative. For publicness, the masses were required to hold a high-handed attitude to act "for the world and people" or "for the state," and, therefore, were apt to make ready to run away. More familiar publicness should be considered. For that purpose as well, people should have not only the discursive type of publicness but also an idea to incorporate publicness into routine activities. In a society where individualism has developed, involvement of people in publicness cannot be maintained, unless there is a public space that assumes the practice of individuals as a premise. It is important, therefore, to open the public space not only of the discursive type such as public opinions and debates, but also of the practical type including volunteer and NPO activities.

Support enables to form organizations that do not assume control and opens new publicness. It is an important subject to investigate its nature, but it should be preceded by practice of support. Public administration should change its focus from control to support and establish a division such as the people's life support section. This tendency is rising, but no such section has been established yet. If people are provided with the know-how and information on what they want to do at the support sector of municipal office, they will put more confidence in public administration. School education should abandon the control to constrain pupils by rules and deviation value of school records, but should concentrate on the support to expedite ability development and fostering. Enterprises should also transform themselves from the efficiency-oriented control organization to a support organization where it is easier to explore ideas and added values. Although control will not vanish from this world, it is impossible to find a clue to the solution for a number of problems Japan now encounters, unless the center of gravity of society shifts from control to support.

End Notes

Introduction Scope of the Self-Organization Theory

1. In the introduction to their report (Yovits et al., eds. 1962: ix), Marshall Yovits, an organizer of a symposium on self-organization in 1962, stated that the term "self-organization system" was used for the first time in a paper contributed by B. Farley and W. Clark to the 1954 conference.
2. Luhmann (1984, trans.: 5–11).
3. It may be possible to state that systems are self-organizational since they can change their structure through environmental adaptability, as actually reported by some analysts. However, since environment-adaptive changes had existed before we became conscious of self-organization (the theory of evolution in social organismic theory, for example), it is meaningless to cite the self-organization theory for this fact alone.
4. Russell's paradox is as follows. When we consider a set K ($X \in K$) of the sets X ($X \notin X$) that do not include itself as an element, the necessary and sufficient condition for the set K to be an element of the set of itself ($K \in K$) is that the set K is not an element of the set of itself ($K \notin K$). A contradiction can also be deduced that the necessary and sufficient condition for the set K not to be an element of itself is that the set K is an element of itself. In short, either way it is contradictory to say that the set K includes itself as an element or does not include itself as an element. When the self-organization system is described by the theory of sets, a similar paradox arises. This is because, despite the fact that a system is normally described as a set that does not include itself, the self-organization system shall be described as a set that includes itself as an element, since one of its characteristics is to change the self by itself.

   The limit of formal logic shown by Russell's paradox became decisive by the incompleteness theorem proved by Kurt Gödel. This theorem is not a paradox, as it has been proved. Logical analysis assumes that the truth or falsehood judgment is always possible for formal statements irrespective of empirical facts. Statements for which the true/false judgment is impossible shall not exist in the world of logic. Nevertheless, Gödel proved propositions for which this fact does not hold. More specifically, he used the axiom of natural numbers to verify that it is possible to make propositions (incompleteness theorem) for which the truth or falsehood cannot be proved within its system. Of course, if a new axiom is added to the original axiomatic system, the true/false judgment will be possible, whereas the new axiomatic system again generates propositions for which this judgment is impossible. Therefore, the incompleteness theorem is not shaken.

   The incompleteness theorem by Gödel means that it is possible to make cumbersome elements that cannot judge whether they are the self (the elements of the sets for which a true/false judgment is possible) or the nonself (not the elements of the set for which a true/false judgment is possible) out of the set of the self. In short, logic cannot verify itself and falls into the "contradiction of the nondetermination of self." In dealing with the self-organization system, it is essential to clarify the concept of the self. If an attempt is made to develop this process by formal logic, however, it will collide with the problem of the impossibility of self/nonself determination, which is similar to the incompleteness theorem by Gödel. In the self-organization world, a difficult problem lies in whether the self that recognizes itself is the self or the nonself. This problem is indeterminate from the viewpoint of formal logic.

In modern philosophical analysis, Russell's paradox has not yet been solved fundamentally. In their *Principia Mathematica* (Whitehead and Russell, 1910), Bertrand Russell and Alfred Whitehead, who tried to systematize symbolic logic, introduced a concept of logical hierarchy called the "type theory" to try to avoid paradoxes. However, this was a pragmatic compromise which only postponed the solution of essential problems. According to type theory, however, it is to roof over a roof of meta-conceptualization, such as meta-system against system and meta-meta-system against meta-system. As this meta-conceptualization withdraws infinitely, there are currently no means to close meta-conceptualization.

5 Varela (1979: 12–15).
6 See Kawamoto (1995). In his book, he developed his own views on the three generations of systems theory.
7 Tamito Yoshida (1990, chap. 11) used the term self-organization from a viewpoint which was completely different from that of this book. Based on the conception of information science, he advocated a version of self-organization of the language information and internal selection type. This refers to the "self-organization mediated by information" specific to human society, in order to distinguish it from Prigogine's "theory of dissipative structures," Haken's "synergetics," Varela's "autopoiesis," and other versions of "self-organization not mediated by information" in natural science. He made three attempts to clarify different versions of the self-organization of the language information and internal selection types.

The first was to cross the dichotomy of variation information versus storage (preservation) information and that of adoption (artificial selection) versus nonadoption (natural selection) obtained from the mechanism of variation, selection, and preservation in Darwin's theory of evolution to distinguish four phases, and to model the self-organizing process through four-phase circulation. The second was to classify the modes of self-organization into two types based on the dichotomy of self-organization with a given structure (relative first-order self-organization) and that with a changing structure (relative second-order self-organization). The third was to classify complex self-organization into eight types by crossing the four types by the dichotomies of individual/society and conservative/innovative, a traditional subject in sociology, and that of superiority/inferiority.

As seen above, Yoshida's self-organization theory bases its mechanism on the Darwinian type theory of evolution to describe self-organization by the dichotomies of the hierarchical nature of structure and traditional perspective of sociology. Yoshida's world of self-organization is a kaleidoscope having 16 versions of self-organization, each performing a four-phase circulating movement. This attitude widens the extension of self-organization to a degree which connotes self-organizational phenomena within its framework. In addition, as structural maintenance is also described so that it is within this framework, the range of self-organization dramatically expands. In addition, 32 versions of self-organization can exist if the dichotomy of preference structure and covariant structure, which is his cherished view, is added. Furthermore, 64 versions can exist if preference structures from motivational requisites and nonmotivational requisites are considered. In this manner, self-organization can be endlessly expanded.

Yoshida's theory smacks of a sort of belief that a superior theory is to logically connote all conceivable cases through different types. On the other hand, the intentions of the advocator are not transmitted on such aspects as why he develops a self-organization theory; what the reality suggested by self-organization is; and what significance it has on social recognition. Generally speaking, typing tends to deepen social recognition, as Max Weber did when he characterized the essence of the modern age. If a theory claims only the typing (theory) that

self-purports a logical connotation, it is not a theory in the true sense. A theory deserves its name only when it correctly reflects a recognition of reality. If the theories of Prigogine, Haken, and Varela are rejected on the grounds that they deal with self-organization which is not mediated by information, the reality aimed at by self-organization will be spoiled.
8 Ashby (1962).
9 See Maruyama (1963) and Foerster (1970, 1979).
10 See Geyer (1995). An instructive explanation is given by Ken'ichi Tominaga (1995: chap. 5) on the significance of the second cybernetics from the viewpoint of social systems theory.
11 Etzioni (1968: 31).
12 See Deutsch (1963: chap. 6).
13 See Buckley (1967: 58–66).
14 Ashby (1962).
15 See Nicolis and Prigogine (1977), Prigogine and Stengers (1984), Haken (1976, 1983), Varela (1979), and Maturana and Varela (1980).
16 Susumu Kuroishi (1991) tried to classify self-organization into cybernetic and synergetic versions.
17 The conventional view of science emphasizes the importance of formulating system behavior while focusing on the equilibrium state. Phenomena which deviated from the equilibrium state were called perturbations, deviances or noise, and were regarded as undesirable objects to be controlled. As studies on the nonequilibrium state progressed, however, researchers became conscious of the positive significance of fluctuations. In the bioholonics of biotechnology, for example, fluctuations are regarded as the "evidence of being alive." In thermodynamics as well, it has been confirmed that a new structure is formed from the amplification of fluctuations (a structure of convection is formed from random heat conduction, for example). In addition, $1/f$ fluctuations provide human beings with comfort. This has already been applied to electric fans and other electrical household appliances. It is also known that a certain degree of fluctuation must be given to brain cells in order to prevent aging.
18 Maturana and Varela (1980: 78–79).
19 Maturana and Varela (1980: 80).
20 Maturana and Varela (1980: 92).
21 Maturana and Varela (1980: 86).
22 Maturana and Varela (1980, xxvii).
23 Maturana and Varela (1980: 80–81).
24 Eigen-behavior is an action which converts the noise and perturbation in the environment into order and maintains the organization unchanged, or brings about an stationary state in the system (Vaz and Varela, 1978).
25 The "dynamics of recursion" and the "internal image" are two important concepts of autopoiesis. The dynamics of recursion is the process whereby a system undergoes a transition while still being affected by its condition immediately before, which Vaz and Varela explain by citing the immune network theory of Niels Jerne (Vaz and Varela, 1978). As shown by the action of the lymphatic tissue, when bacteria, toxins, or other antigens invade the human body, specific antibodies in the immune system react with, and counteract, these foreign substances, thereby preventing the outbreak of disease. In the conventional theory of the immune system, it was thought that antibodies would start their action after the entry of antigens or foreign substances, which are the nonself, into the human body from the outside. In contrast, Vaz and Varela believe that antibodies direct the activity of recognition to their own components and not to the outsides (antigens as foreign substances), while regarding the immune system as a network where components recognize each other. They state that the lymphatic system is not an image of antigen recognition by independent individual cell clones, but a series of alternate recognition events having different degrees of singularity and effectiveness, by encompassing the system as a whole; individual components, while recognizing each other or being recognized by others, are incorporated in the interactions between a number of other components; and what is important is the fact that the immune system functions by the feature of annular cause and effect or, more strictly, by the characteristics that are called recursion.

The foreign substances or antigens recognized by the lymphatic system are determined by the system organization and its recursive history in the past. In other words, the annular cause and effect network has formed an "inner image" by the dynamics of recursion, with antigens recognized based on their similarity to this inner image. Therefore, the organism responds to its inner image of the external elements, or the network responds to the "meaning" translated into a word that has been used by the network. Recognition is exerted not for the outside but for the inside.

26 Varela (1979: 32).
27 Luhmann (1984: chap. 4; 1988: chap. 2).
28 See Luhmann (1982: chap. 10) and Luhmann (1991).
29 Luhmann (1984: 83).
30 Yasuo Baba (1993).
31 Capra (1975), Watson (1973), Prigogine (1980), Nicolis and Prigogine (1977), and Haken (1976). As a movement from cultural science to a scientific basis to the idea of fluctuations, we should take note of poststructuralism and postmodern thought. However, I omit any explanation here in consideration of the context of the discussions. See Chap. 4 for the relation between these two ideas and fluctuations.
32 Jantsch (1980: 31).
33 Monad consists of elements that bear the existence of all things, which is discussed in *Monadology* by Gottfried Leibniz (1965). Unlike the material elements, these are simple entities that embody a true spiritual nature, spontaneously changing, reflecting each other, and connoting traces of the past and signs of the future as one of their features.
34 An easy-to-understand explanation is given in Gleick (1987: chap. 1).
35 Kuroishi (1991: 48–51).
36 Imada (2001: 44).
37 Blumer (1969: 63).
38 Conrad Waddington, a British biologist, regards such evolution as an "epigenetic process" (Waddington, 1975). The topics of evolution discussed as the main themes in social biology, including "evolutionarily stable strategies" and "ecological niches" in particular, are common to his ideas.
39 According to Imanishi, "the fundamental point of dispute is that geneticists advocate as a golden rule that mutation occurs at random, and therefore it does not have directivity, whereas I insist that this is never the case in practice since mutation, which has directivity from the beginning, is forced to occur as the necessity arises" (Imanishi, 1976: 20). He adds that "... the evolution theory does not close unless natural selection between individuals is considered when it is based on the random mutation, while it theoretically closes by itself even if the natural selection between individuals is not considered when it is based on the mutation having directivity" (Imanishi, 1976: 30).

Chapter 1 From Social Change to Self-Organization

1 See Bertalanffy (1968).
2 According to Bertalanffy (1968: 13–14), the 1945 paper in which he advocated general system theory (Bertalanffy, 1945) was not published in the catastrophe of World War II at the proofreading stage. Its outline is reproduced in Chap. 3 of his book (Bertalanffy, 1968). It is Anatol Rapoport and William Horvath (Rapoport and Horvath, 1959) who used the expression of "organized complexity."
3 Boulding (1953).
4 Wiener (1948).
5 Homeostasis means the working of organisms to keep their own order in a stable state in changing environment, such as the maintenance of body temperature and glucose level in

blood. It was systematized by Walter Cannon (1932), who remarked that homeostasis expresses the state where a system is stable while it is changing.
6 Wiener (1948: 162).
7 Wiener (1950: 15–16).
8 See Ashby (1956) and Shannon and Weaver (1949).
9 Parsons (1945).
10 Parsons (1945).
11 See Parsons (1951) and Parsons and Shils eds. (1951).
12 As the literature addressing the disputes on structural-functional analysis, or functional analysis in a broader sense, there are papers edited by Llewellyn Gross (1959) and Nicholas Demerath III and Richard Peterson eds. (1967) in the USA. Although no readings dealing with this theme have been edited in Japan, a reference list has been created by Akio Tanozaki ed. (1975) that enables taking a general view of the activity of the research of functionalism including critical work thereon. Also see Tominaga (1965).
13 Merton (1949, enlarged ed. 1968: 73–138).
14 Nagel (1956), Hempel (1959), and Cancian (1960).
15 Parsons (1970; 1975), Parsons and Tominaga (1979).
16 Merton (1949, enlarged ed. 1968: 136).
17 Radcliffe-Brown (1940).
18 Radcliffe-Brown (1952: 14).
19 Radcliffe-Brown (1952: 179).
20 Radcliffe-Brown (1952: 200).
21 Lévi-Strauss (1958, trans.: 279)
22 Lévi-Strauss (1949).
23 Boudon (1968) is a good example.
24 Parsons (1945).
25 Durkheim (1893, trans.: 273).
26 In applying the idea of cybernetics to general system of action, Parsons considered only typology based on the antagonistic relation between information and energy, while positioning information of relatively high degree as a control factor and energy of relatively high degree as a conditioning factor (Parsons, 1966: 28, Table 1). He did not sociologically develop the cybernetic control process, therefore, based on feedback mechanism.
27 Nadel (1957: 97).
28 Levy (1952: 56–57).
29 See Lange (1962: chap. 2–4).
30 Merton (1949, enlarged ed. 1968: 106).
31 Luhmann (1967).
32 The law of requisite variety is a version of Shannon's information theory (theorem 10) retermed by Ashby from the viewpoint of control theory. This law means that, for a control apparatus or a controller to succeed in controlling the object or the opponent, thereby ensuring an effective result (goal attainment), control apparatus or controller must have at least the same number of distinguishable actions or countermeasures (varieties) as those taken by the object. Variety means a number of characteristics to be distinguished for control apparatus or controller to take appropriate actions or countermeasures for the object. See Ashby (1956: chap. 7 and 11).
33 Luhmann (1967; 1972, trans.: Chap. 2, Sec. 1).
34 Luhmann (1967).
35 In applying Ashby's law of requisite variety to the social system theory, Luhmann did not use the concept of variety, but replaced it with complexity.
36 Yoshida (1974b).
37 Campbell (1965).
38 Luhmann (1964; 1967).
39 See Roger Nett (1953) for the pool of diversity.

40 In discussing the sociological figure suggested by modern systems science, Walter Buckley attracted it to the basic area of sociology and formulated the operation of adaptive system implemented with the environment in a similar manner to that of Luhmann. Namely, he considered the operation to map diversity of environment and constraint into organization as what corresponds to the reduction of environmental complexity. "When the internal organization of an adaptive system acquires features that permit it to discriminate, act upon, and respond to aspects of the environmental variety and its constraints, we say that the system mapped part of the environmental variety and constraints into its organization." (Buckley 1967: 63). He puts it that this mapping supports the evolution of an adaptive system.
41 Yoshida (1974b).
42 See Simon (1969: chap. 4) for the hierarchical composition.
43 See Mesarović et al. (1970: 43–49) and Takahara (1971).
44 Parsons (1966: 28).
45 Boulding (1970: chap. 1).
46 Deutsch (1963: chap. 6).

Chapter 2 Principles of Self-Organization and the Theory of Social Development

1 Parsons and Smelser (1956).
2 The formulation and improvement of structural-functional analysis have been promoted in Japan by Ken'ichi Tominaga, Naoki Komuro, Tamito Yoshida and other researchers. As for the logic of structural-functional analysis described in this chapter I have improved and reformulated based on their discussions in comparison with the theory of self-organization.
3 Ashby (1962).
4 Ashby (1962).
5 Ashby (1962).
6 Ashby (1962).
7 Ashby (1960: 98).
8 The activity change and structure change referred to here are not exclusive against each other, in that the latter inevitably accompanies the former. Therefore, there are two types of activity change. One does not accompanies structural change and the other. The activity change referred to here is the former, or activity modification that is possible under the ongoing structure. This distinction is necessary to conceptually classify the activity level and the structural level of system. According to the theory of change by Cancian discussed in Chap. 1, the former corresponds to change within system and the latter to change of the system.
9 The concept of equilibrium used here succeeds the one specific to structural-functional analysis that is defined as a state where the functional requisites of social system are appropriately gratified under a certain structure or a state where the force directed to structural change does not work. Therefore, equilibrium and structural stability are two expressions that represent one and the same state. Since such a concept of equilibrium lacks a clear-cut prescription on what is in balance with what, however, the contents of equilibrium tends to become ambiguous and causes misunderstanding. In the next chapter, I consider the equilibrium between functional requisites under a given structure and formulate the state of equilibrium of social system at a dimension different from that of structural stability and instability based on pluralism of functional requisites to be gratified by the social system. Therefore, I make the concept of equilibrium in the sense of structural-functional analysis valid only in this chapter. According to my view, equilibrium in the sense of structural-functional analysis is a concept on structural stability and instability, which is different in its nature from the concept on

convergence and divergence between different quantities generally used in mechanics and economics.
10 See Ashby (1962).
11 In sociology, structure and relation or pattern have not been clearly distinguished so far. Tamito Yoshida (1974a), for example, defined social structure as "a continuous and patternized relation... between the elements that constitute social system" and regarded relation of system elements and structure as identical. However, this does not distinguish social relation from social structure. According to my definition, structure is a characteristic to generate the relation or pattern. This represents a position that relation is generated by structure.
12 Social resources referred to here are the social objects that are useful for role performance to gratify functional requisites contributing to the goal-attainment of social system. Since the role performance has two aspects, i.e., contribution to the system and accompanied rewards acquisition, social resources are allocated as an instrument for role performance and distributed as rewards therefor.
13 Amitai Etzioni (1968: 31) states that human beings not only repeat and practice the ongoing processes to select and execute action, but also have the potential ability for control of controls. He also expresses his view that human beings regard the ability of control as an index to activeness.
14 To be correct, the partial order relation means that the following three rules holds between two arbitrary elements of a set. (1) $x \geq x$ (reflexivity), (2) if $x \geq y$ and $y \geq z$ then $x \geq z$ (transitivity) and (3) if $x \geq y$ and $y \geq x$, then $x = y$ (antisymmetry). The complete order relation (linear relation) is a relation where $x \geq y$ or $y \geq x$ holds (totalness) without exception in addition to the above three rules.
15 The concept of equilibrium used here is formally the same as that defined by Yoshida, i.e., "the state where gratifying level of any motivational requisite of the social system cannot hold without decreasing the gratifying levels of one or more of other motivational requisites, or the state where gratification of motivational requisites is Pareto optimized." However, its sociological implication is different. He thinks that equilibrium is to make "conditions of change disappear and be impossible" and deals with equilibrium and disequilibrium as a concept that means existence or non-existence of the "possibility" of change. As far as Pareto optimized state is defined as equilibrium, it is correct to understand that disequilibrium is the state where Pareto optimization has not been realized under a given condition (structure) or the state where attaining requisite gratification not inferior to that at present is possible under the partial ordered relation. Regarding the Pareto optimization as a case of optimization, a mathematical condition that *a solution set causes a partial relation* has an important meaning. It is difficult to understand, however, how this connects with the possibility or impossibility of structural change. Yoshida necessitated a concept of equilibrium to show "the limit of the possibility for realization of the hope under a given condition" as he wanted to theorize his strong interest in the state of oppression existing in himself, and distinguished it from the concept of admissibility that shows the state of gratification of requisites. This is to be duly evaluated. As far as equilibrium is defined by Pareto optimization, however, equilibrium and disequilibrium shall be interpreted according to Pareto conditions. In economics, subjective equilibrium as the maximization of utility or profit is distinguished from the market equilibrium as the balance between supply and demand. However, the concept of equilibrium itself is irrelevant to Pareto conditions. The equilibrium of social system referred to here is the same as the subjective equilibrium, but different with respect to the fact that objective function to be maximized is not a scalar but a vector. At this point, Pareto conditions are set. Therefore, the contents of equilibrium in the subjective equilibrium not only mean maximization but also contain the balance of multidimensional requisite gratifications at the same time. See Yoshida (1974a, 1974b) for his concept of equilibrium.
16 As a state of social tension that is not caused by a structural problem, panic, crises and other contingent states of emergency will be cited, for example. This can be regarded as a state

where the gratification of Pareto optimal requisites is disturbed by external disturbance input from the outside into social system or a state where the equilibrium of social system is disturbed. It is a problem of structural stability whether social system can recover equilibrium under the ongoing structure in this situation.
17. See Parsons (1951: 12) for the view to regard value as a symbolic element that is useful as a criterion for selection.
18. See Parsons (1966: chap. 2) for the discussions on a general system of action. Tominaga (1974) briefly explains in its note 15 that the subsystems of a general system of action are interdependent and interpenetrative.
19. Kei'ichi Sakuta (1972: 3–35) distinguished social system from cultural system, or the base of value, and personality system, or the base of needs, and discussed the significance to formulate it as an interrelation system of goal seeking behavior.
20. See Parsons (1951: 167–168).
21. Parsons (1951: 280–283).
22. The dichotomy, ascription vs. achievement and particularism vs. universalism, which is called "pattern variables," is a classification axis that characterizes the normative aspect of system structure. From the standpoint of this paper, it is understood as an axis to classify from what viewpoint personnel and resources are allocated to the role. The membership of territorial and blood relations represents the viewpoint of ascription and particularism, while knowledge and skill represent the viewpoint of achievement and universalism. As industrialization progresses, the framework of occupational role shifts from the former to the latter as proved by a number of cases in the history. For the discussions on pattern variables, see Parsons and Shils eds. (1951: 76–109).
23. Tsutomu Shiobara (1976: 124–125) introduced the states of congruence and incongruence in regard to the structure of social system. However, his definition is different from mine. According to his view, the congruent state of structure is a state where "requisites are gratified to a maximum" or the state of "equilibrium." Therefore, structural harmonization is equivalent to equilibrium of system. According to my definition, however, it means solving the conflict of social system at the structural level and expresses shifting to a structurally stable state of equilibrium.
24. Mayer (1972).
25. Yoshimichi Sato (2006) discussed the problem of intentional social change in relation to the micro–macro problem from the standpoint of rational choice theory. His issue was to investigate the reason why some intentional social changes succeed while others fail. He tried to investigate this work by game theory as a transition problem between micro–macro levels. This is an interesting trial to apply the unintended consequence of action to the theory of social planning. However, at present I do not directly refer to this subject.
26. In assessing the execution of plan from the viewpoint of policies, I referred to discussions by Tominaga (1977) that "social policies mean all actions by the official authority to intervene in the working of social system in order to raise the gratification level of functional requisites and social plan is the actions programmed in advance so that rationality and congruence of the means for actions are ensured." According to my view, however, the concept of policies is included as part of the concept of planning.
27. Lindblom (1968).
28. Mayer (1972: 117–121).
29. For the AGIL schema, see Parsons and Bales (1953) and Parsons and Smelser (1956). The former discusses the principle of logic that has created the AGIL schema and the latter addresses its application to economic phenomena.
30. See Parsons (1969: Part 4), for the discussions on the generalized symbolic media. Atsushi Naoi (1974) commented them in a simple and easy-to-understand form in relation to the internal boundary exchange process of AGIL. I referred to Zaltman and Duncan (1977) in regard to the term "strategy of change," but the trial to position the AGIL schema as a strategy of change is my idea.

Chapter 3 Signification and Reflexive System

1. Imada (1990).
2. See Imada (1985) for the relation between *zation-phenomena* and social change.
3. See Imada (1986: 214–221) for this significance and limits of meaning school. Setsuo Yamaguchi (1982) is suggestive as a discussion to have critically examined the insistence of meaning school. Kazuhisa Nishihara (1998) aims at dismantling and constructing the basis of sociological theory while relying on Alfred Schutz, which is instructive in order to confirm the horizon of phenomenological sociology.
4. Habermas and Luhmann (1971).
5. Yoshiyuki Sato (1986).
6. Among a number of functionalists, Luhmann may be only one researcher who has addressed the problem of *meaning* in social theory on a full-scale. However, he questions meaning with function to avoid ontological discussions on meaning. His scientific view is positivistic still remaining within the framework of modern science. In addition, his semantics is approximately equal to the function of information in systems science and infinitely approaches the problem of control. In the last analysis, his discussions connote meaning in control thought. This is nothing but a recasting of the problem raised by meaning school. According to my view, meaning school addresses reflexion of difference, which is at the limit of control thought and beyond Luhmann's semantics. For the idea of Luhmann on meaning, see Habermas and Luhmann (1971, Kap. 2).
7. Luhmann (1984, trans.: 63–66).
8. Giddens (1985), Hashizume (1985).
9. See Komuro (1966a, 1966b, 1974) and Yoshida (1964, 1974a).
10. Hashizume, Shida and Tsunematsu (1984).
11. As it is now dealt with in the field of natural science, the theory of self-organization can be treated with the scientific view of naturalism. Therefore, it is anticipated that a polemic be raised to the effect that it does not deny naturalism. However, the naturalism referred to here indicates subject–object separation in cognition of the Cartesian-Newtonian type and the scientific views of reductionism and determinism. Theory of self-organization in natural science raises an objection to such scientific views.
12. See Imada (1986: 13–18 and 126–137). The expression "connection of cognition to existence" recalls the epistemology and ontology in philosophy. Although these are the two largest fields in philosophy, relation in between is not necessarily clear. Epistemology is to question how knowledge is possible, while ontology is to question the essence of things (being). As the latter tends to fall in metaphysics, dialog does not hold well between the two.

    My view is that it is science to cross-links epistemology and ontology and its procedure is the scientific method. Science should be involved both in theory and experience. However, the former is a problem of cognition and the latter a problem of existence. Science is the work to connect cognition with experience and therefore can be expressed as connection of cognition to existence. In regard to experience as existence, however, the view of positivism is greatly different from that of interpretatism. The former considers existence with sense data such as occupational status and education level, i.e., measurement feasibility. In contrast, the latter considers the issue, for example, how the Protestant ethic and the spirit of capitalism in the West and "Iki (chic)" in Japanese culture complete their existences. Although one thinks existence simply and the other follows a complicated procedure therefor, both refer to the issue how to complete existence. If science is defined as connection of cognition to existence, however, it is possible to regard that both positivism and interpretatism perform work of the same category as science.
13. Yosuke Koto (1986) remarks that it is not sufficient only to discuss his views of action and society, in order to critically succeed and go over Parson's structural-functionalism. The most important point hitherto missed in the criticism against Parsons is attention to

the scientific view. At the bottom of Parson's researches, there is a coherent scientific view or analytical realism to integrate idealism and positivism established at the early stage. This scientific view is a trial of integration, really specific to Parsons and the postwar age, to recast the outstanding features of positivism and realism and forcefully integrate the two. After all, however, this analytical realism was only standing at the position of naturalism. Parsons no longer used this term after World War II, presumably because the scientific view of hypothesico-deductive type stemmed from physics had become popular to make it no longer necessary to clarify his own position with a specific term, as pointed out by Koto.

14 For example, this is similar to obtaining a variant of hypothesico–interpretative–understanding by rotating cognition plane alone and that of hypothesico–deductive–verification by rotating existence plane alone. It is also possible to rotate both planes simultaneously to obtain a variant of hypothesico–interpretative–verification. The triangle of methodology constitutes the basic structure to prescribe what such transformative reason should be and proves the sterility of questioning which method is superior.
15 Weber (1921–22: trans.: Part I, 9–11).
16 See Imada (1986: 242).
17 The following has been summarized based on Imada (1986: chap. 7).
18 Hashizume (1985: 66).
19 Ochiai (1987: 13).
20 Hashizume (1985: 55).
21 Hashizume (1985: 66–67).

Chapter 4 Self-Organization and Postmodernity

1 Nowadays, rationality means mainly the systematic procedure to contrive an effective means for goal attainment or purposive rationality. However, the concept of rationality by Weber widely ranges from the ethos (value ethics) supporting modern civilization to historical philosophy.
2 See Mannheim (1940: 51–60). Imada (2001: 50–57) discusses modernity as a rationalization process in relation to the concept of rationality by Weber and Mannheim.
3 For function primacy, see Imada (1994: 91–93) and for control-performance schema, see Imada (1986: 238–241).
4 Imada (1987: 4).
5 Imada (2001: 140).
6 Deleuze et Guattari (1972, 1980), Derrida (1967, 1972).
7 The term "deconstruction" has been used mainly as the discourse of philosophy or the critique of literacy. It should not be limited in such a small range, however. It can be positioned as a work to re-question the society, or a work to disclose, dismantle and reconstruct the structure established in modern times. See Derrida (1972) for deconstruction.
8 Smart (1991).
9 Jencks (1977).
10 Lyotard (1979).
11 This process is staging postmodern scenarios. At the moment, however, postmodernity features nothing but pastiche and schizoid tendencies.
12 See Hayek (1973) and Austin (1960).
13 See the discussion by Hitoshi Ochiai for social philosophy of conservatism. According to him, immutable foundation of conservatism is the tradition performatively formed and prejudiced views that cannot rationally be referred to and the authority that cannot individually be ascribed to. The thought of Hayek and Austin is in the same category as this notion and is a new expression of conservatism in the modern times (Ochiai, 1987: 13–14). For the

spontaneous order advocated by Hayek, systematic discussion by Itaru Shimazu (1985) is suggestive. In addition, the notions of conventional situation generated by performance and generation of order through tacit states of affairs which cannot be described rationally can be traced back to later Wittgenstein who came to advocate the language game theory.
14 Hayek (1973: 45–46, 115–118).
15 Regarding this point, Akira Tokuyasu (1990) expresses a similar view in relation to the construction of meaning. He says, "... construction of meaning can be thought as created in the form of articulation of the world.... We give a meaning to the world by action of articulation. Conversely, the world has a meaning when it is experienced as a set of articulated affairs and phenomenon."
16 See Nietzsche (1887, trans.: 79). According to Yoshiyasu Inoue (1989), Nietzsche, together with Weber, required the aristocratism of spirit that endures uncertainty, and rang an alarm bell against the bias toward the reduction of uncertainty harbored by modernism.
17 Let us consider a concrete example. Christopher Alexander, a postmodern architect, compiled the power of various meanings and attempted to make it a concrete form of architecture. His attempt is considerably different from the method of shaping form of efficiency, convenience and exclusion of waste premised by functionalism (modernism). An arrangement of architectures designed by him in Japan is that of Higashino High School, Iruma City, Saitama Prefecture, which is an incarnation of the ideal school image he compiled by listening to the opinions of pupils, teachers, clerks, servants, PTA members and others related to school education. The completed arrangement of school buildings is largely different from ordinary ones. First of all, a homeroom passage is at the center of school. On both sides of the passage, several schoolrooms are arranged. Each schoolroom is in an independent house. There are no corridors between different schoolrooms. Pupils walk to a different schoolroom after a class has finished. They have to use umbrellas on rainy days. In this manner, inefficiency is accepted in order to weigh the importance of touching nature. The homeroom passage and schoolrooms are connected with a sunroom attached outside. The homeroom passage constitutes a sort of street, in that pupils walking thereon can play or talk with those in schoolrooms. It embodies the concept of veranda-like porch ("Engawa") that has been lost in Japan. At an eminence, there is a dining room that commands a fine view. The dining room is sectioned into small partitions in which friends can enjoy taking lunch together.

In short, the design of these school buildings completely denies the way of modernist thinking as "form follows function" or "beauty is in function." Compiling the image (meaning) of school resulted in a design that is inefficient and irrational from the viewpoint of modern conception. It does not have a functional structure, but is close to an amorphous and kaleidoscopic form. It exactly deserves the naming of a molding in the non-functional meaning world, having no definite style or structure and taking no account of efficiency. It is a representation of humaneness that has been neglected.
18 A number of researchers in Japan addressed the self-organization from the viewpoint of social science from the latter half of the 1980s to the beginning of the 1990s. They include Takatoshi Imada (1986), Osamu Sudo (1988), Toshiyuki Masamura (1989), Atsuhito Eguchi (1990), Tamito Yoshida (1990), Yoshiyuki Sato (1991) and Seigo Obata (1991).
19 Imada (1989).
20 Imada (1986: 176).
21 Erikson (1950; 1964).
22 According to Jean Baudrillard who used it first, the term hyper-reality is the whole of signs that do not accompany entity. The world of hyper-reality is that of a fiction dominated by *simulacra* that are generated by codes and simulation. He maintains that an illusion to believe that hyper-reality is reality prevails in the present society. See Baudrillard (1975). The hyper-reality will be discussed immediately below.
23 Imada (1987: 30–33).
24 Maslow (1954, 2nd ed. 1970).
25 Imada (1994: 143–156).

26 Baudrillard (1975, trans.: Introduction).
27 Caillois (1958).
28 Ohira (1990).
29 Ohira (1990: 28–29).
30 According to the sociologist Mead, the self is composed of "I" and "Me". "I" can be called a subjective self and expresses what is often called subjectivity. In contrast, "Me" is an expected self which has taken in others' eyes or social requests. In individual persons, "I" and "Me" interact to compose a self. This is a model to explain how society penetrates individuals, determines their behavior and becomes a psychological part of the self.

Self-identity is integration of the subjective self and the expected self to actualize a self. This can be regarded as a typical model of self-identity in modern society. In a traditional society where the modern individual has not been established, the subjective self and the expected self are not distinguished from each other because the image of the self is not selected by the individual but is determined by his/her status in the community. The establishment of a modern subjective self has been emphasized in relation to individualism. This has separated two types of self (I/Me). However, the expected self in modern society was an ideal and hardly attainable image, such as that of heroes or the ideal images of people offered by society. The subjective self, therefore, could not help but approach the expected self for self-actualization. Self-actualization was an always-postponed process of becoming close to the expected self. Cf. Mead (1934) and Imada (1994: 150–152).
31 The market for comics in Japan is one billion volumes, or ten per person, each year. They were monopolized by boys and girls in the past, but have now been expanded to embrace middle-aged salaried workers.
32 The first *Comic-market* was held in December 1975, which reportedly was attended by 32 interest groups and about 600 people. Since then, the Comic-market has been held annually at different locations as the numbers of participants have increased. Six hundred interest groups and 9,000 people participated in the market of comics held in December 1988. *Comiket* 38, held August 17 and 18, 1990, was reportedly attended by 16,000 interest groups and 150,000 people.
33 Melucci (1989: 177–179).
34 See Mead (1934).
35 Imada (1987: 206–207).
36 Giddens (1991: 53).
37 Mikami (1993: 75).
38 Mikami (1993: 124).
39 Imada (1989).
40 Imada (1987: 190–194).

Chapter 5 Beyond Network Theory

1 Sociometry is a technique developed by Jacob Moreno to measure and analyze the network structure in groups and implements investigation with the psychological relation such as the selection and rejection of human relations. Based on sociometry, group dynamics were developed to address the issue of group pressure, group cohesion and leadership, and social network analysis, which includes competition and cooperation between enterprises, control and collaboration in a local society, and coalition and opposition between states.
2 Lipnack and Stamps (1982: Chap. 10).
3 Poster (1990: 93).
4 Poster further develops the discussion by Foucault and expresses the fact that the modern formation of power is transformed and elevated using the electronic media as a superpanopticon.

End Notes

5 Imada (1987; 1988; 1994; 2001).
6 See Imada (1994: Chap. 2), where five social shifts are cited, including the shift "from network to rhizome." However, this shift is treated separately here, since it has a character related to the other four and an abstract level that is different from the others.
7 Deleuze et Guattari (1980: Introduction).
8 Imada (1987: 196–198).
9 See Inada (1990: Chap. 4 and 5).
10 Imai and Kaneko (1988: 33).
11 Imai and Kaneko (1988: 51–54).
12 Imai and Kaneko (1988: 203).
13 Imai and Kaneko (1988: 155).
14 Imai and Kaneko (1988: 79–86).
15 Quoted from "Kobe Steel Rugby Club Steelers," the first story of "Nadahama Romance," from Hirao's personal home page, at http://plaza6.mbn.or.jp/~hirao10/ (as of 1998). This website has since been closed down.
16 Mainichi-shinbun Osaka-honsha Undo-bu ed.(1996: 256–257).
17 Mainichi-shinbun Osaka-honsha Undo-bu ed.(1996: 266).
18 The ideas symbolized by "antisacrifice spirit" and "systems are last" provide a number of suggestions to the formation of Japanese organizations, which are characterized by groupism. Salaried workers in Japan, who are often called a "company-first person" or a "company animals," have sacrificed themselves to contribute to their companies. The most important reason for the generation of such strain is the "enclosure" of employees in the organizations by enterprises under the Japanese management. Through this enclosure, the Japanese enterprises have established a mechanism that does not take into account the rationality of individual employees (Imada, 1993). The Japanese management, symbolized by the three sacred treasures, or seniority system, life-long employment and enterprise labor unions, was a reasonable system for utilizing human resources under the labor force situation prevalent in Japan after the World War II. Although it has been excellent in pursuing the rationality of the enterprise organization as a whole, it has victimized the pursuance of the employees' rationality. In this way, the Japanese management system thoroughly pursues the rationality of the organization, but often disregards that of the employees. The remarkable economic power of Japan was established at the expense of this sacrifice. As a result of such enclosure, group thinking emerges and critical thinking is paralyzed. It also brings about a mutual reliance in decision-making, lock-step mentality, dependence on inner groups, and other similar characteristics, and create a state wherein know-how is not developed to strengthen individual abilities or build up individual-oriented groups or organizations. While considering the restructuring of Japanese organizations, it is required to create organizations that will support individual self-realization so that the ability of individuals will be fully exhibited based on the ideas of "antisacrifice spirit" and "systems are last."
19 Nagata (1997: 34).
20 Nagata (1997: 173).
21 Nagata (1997: 178–179).
22 Nagata (1997: 186).
23 Quoted from "Kobe Steel Rugby Club Steelers," on Hirao's personal home page, at http://plaza6.mbn.or.jp/~hirao10/ (as of 1998). As formerly mentioned, this website has already been closed down.

Chapter 6 Toward a Support-based Social System

1 See Hayek (1973).
2 Salamon (1995: 44–48).

3 It has been attempted to make support an object of science mainly in relation to decision-making in the fields of science and technology, as represented by the decision support system (DDS) and the expert system to attempt the realization of support on computer software. However, neither one intends the general framework, or the theory of action and social system, which is dealt with in this paper. Discussions by Kobashi (1988) is instructive as a case where support is addressed from the standpoint of cognitive science.
4 For this definition of support, see Imada (2001: 287–288). Also refer to Kobashi and Iijima (1997) and Shien Kisoron Kenkyu-kai ed. (2000) for a similar conception.
5 Heidegger (1935, trans.: 53).
6 See Heidegger (1935, trans.: Chap. 3 and 4).
7 Heidegger (1935, trans.: 114–115).
8 According to Erikson, care is a power to be acquired in life or in the adulthood in particular. If we fail to do so, life will fall in stagnation and languishment. Care is not the consideration for others, but an indispensable power for self-actualization.
9 See Imada (1997).
10 Adams (1996: 5).
11 This is knowledge obtained and digested from the discussion with Professor Muneya Sato, an accounting scholar, for which responsibility rests with me.
12 Arendt (1958: 50). She divides the activities of human beings into three: "work," "labor" and "action," and define that "work" and "labor" are economic activities, while participation in action which is distinguished from the former two is the engagement in publicness. "Action" is an intersubjective communication through the "discussion" performed by free citizens. The life sphere as *Oikos* is a private area where current economic activities are dominant, while *Polis* is a public area composed of discussion and communal activities.
13 The literary public sphere reflected publicness based on the discussions on culture and art that occurred at coffee houses in the UK, salons in France and reading circles in Germany, from the latter half of the 17th century to the 18th century. Regardless of their social status, everybody was able to participate in the discussions at these places or at coffee shops in particular, where people had only to pay for a cup of coffee and had discussions on culture and art. Such public spaces were formed as a place where political opinions were created in opposition to the state authority in the process when the civil society separated from the state. However, there is a limit in the formation of political opinions by literary public sphere. As the economy of capitalism expands, therefore, the themes for discussions became tinged with politics. Regarding publicness as a function to intervene between the civil desire and the state by public opinions, therefore, Habermas called it the political public sphere, while distinguishing it from the literary public sphere. This was the origin of civil publicness.
14 Habermas (1985, trans.: 364–365).
15 The core claims of neoliberalism are 1) thorough pursuit of the market principle by deregulation, 2) reduction in public expenditure for social welfare services, 3) privatization of state-owned public corporations and 4) emphasis on self-determination and self-responsibility in place of public interest and communities.
16 When neoliberalism, which advocated the collapse of the bubble economy and globalization with market omnipotence, was at its highest point in the latter half of the 1990s, some researchers harbored a crisis of conscience against this tendency and began to address the issue of publicness at the same time, without being aware of how the two were linked. The term "renaissance of publicness" is a reference to this phenomenon. In the early 21st century, this approach to the theory of publicness yielded fruit. A series of such movements have formed a rapidly swelling trend, which can be called a public philosophy movement. For a special issue on publicness, see the *Japanese Sociological Review* (Japan Sociological Society, 2000), ten volumes by Sasaki and Kim eds. (2001-2002) on the public philosophy, Yamaguchi et al. eds. (2003), Sato et al. eds. (2003), Shionoya, Suzumura and Goto eds. (2004), Soranaka et al. eds. (2004), Yamawaki (2004), and so on. Moreover, Tadashi Kobayashi and other interested persons, including Yamawaki and myself, have set up a network on public

philosophy (http://homepage2.nifty.com/public-philosophy/network.htm) with active online discussions.
17 Since I became interested in contemporary development of public philosophy, I have consistently insisted on the importance to animate the private to open the public (Imada, 1999; 2001; 2006). This stance was named as opening the public through animating the private by Tae-Chan Kim who understood my intention.
18 The public opinion poll on people's life, which has been implemented by the Prime Minister's Office (currently the Cabinet Office) every year since 1958 asks 10,000 people on which they place priority in life, material well-being or spiritual well-being. The rating was higher with material well-being than spiritual well-being before 1976; almost the same from 1976 to 1979; and went into reverse in 1980 and 1981. The difference in number between the advocators of material well-being and those of spiritual well-being has expanded gradually until today, though there have been some fluctuations. See the report of the Naikaku-fu Seifu Koho Shitsu (2003).

Bibliography

Adams, Robert, 1996, *Social Work and Empowerment*, London: Macmillan Press.
Arendt, Hannah, 1958, *The Human Condition*, Chicago: University of Chicago Press.
Ashby, W. Ross, 1956, *An Introduction to Cybernetics*, London: Chapman & Hall.
Ashby, W. Ross, 1960, 2nd ed. rev., *Design for a Brain: The Origin of Adaptive Behavior*, London: Chapman & Hall.
Ashby, W. Ross, 1962, "Principles of the Self-Organizing System," in Heinz von Foerster and George W. Zopf, Jr. (eds.), *Principles of Self-Organization: Transactions of the University of Illinois Symposium on Self-Organization*, Oxford: Pergamon Press, pp. 255–278.
Austin, John L., 1960, *How to Do Things with Words*, Oxford: Oxford University Press.
Baba, Yasuo, 1993, "Luhmann to Jiko-Soshikisei (Luhmann and Self-Organization)," in Yoshiyuki Sato and Nasu Hisashi (eds.), *Kiki to Saisei no Shakai Riron (Social Theory of Crisis and Revitalization)*, Tokyo: Maruju-sha, pp. 253–268.
Baudrillard, Jean, 1975, *L'Échange symbolique et la mort*, Paris: Gallimard. (Grant, Iain trans., 1993, *Symbolic Exchange and Death*, London: Sage).
Bertalanffy, Ludwig von, 1945, "Zu einer allgemeinen Systemlehre," *Deutsche Zeitschrift für Philosophie*, 18 (3/4). (unpublished)
Bertalanffy, Ludwig von, 1968, *General System Theory: Foundations, Development, Applications*, New York: George Braziller.
Blumer, Herbert, 1969, *Symbolic Interactionism: Perspective and Method*, Englewood Cliffs, N.J.: Prentice-Hall.
Boudon, Raymond, 1968, *A quoi sert la notion de "Structure"?: essai sur la signification de la notion de structure dans les sciences humaines*, Paris: Gallimard. (Vaughan, Michalina trans., 1971, *The Uses of Structuralism*, London: Heinemann.)
Boulding, Kenneth E., 1953, "General Systems Theory: The Skeleton of Science," *Management Science*, 2, pp. 197–208, reprinted in Kenneth E. Boulding, 1968, *Beyond Economics, Essays on Society, Religion, and Ethics*, Ann Arbor: University of Michigan Press.
Boulding, Kenneth E., 1970, *A Primer on Social Dynamics: History as Dialectics and Development*, New York: Free Press.
Buckley, Walter., 1967, *Sociology and Modern Systems Theory*, Englewood Cliffs, N.J.: Prentice-Hall.
Caillois, Roger, 1958, 1967 éd. rev., *Les jeux et les hommes: le masque et le veritige*, Paris: Gallimard. (Barash, Meyer trans., 1961, *Man, Play, and Games*, New York: Free Press.)
Campbell, Donald T., 1965, "Variation and Selective Retention in Sociocultural Evolution," in Herbert H. Barringer, George I. Blanksten, and Raymond W. Mack (eds.), *Social Change in Developing Areas: A Reinterpretation of Evolutionary Theory*, Cambridge, Mass.: Schenkman, pp. 19–49.

Cancian, Francesca M., 1960, "A Functional Analysis of Change," *American Sociological Review*, 25, pp. 818–827.
Cannon, Walter B., 1932, *The Wisdom of the Body*, New York: W.W. Norton.
Capra, Fritjof, 1975, 1982 rev. ed., *The Tao of Physics: An Explorations of the Parallels between Modern Physics and Eastern Mysticism*, London: Murray Pollinger.
Deleuze, Gilles et Félix Guattari, 1972, *L'Anti-Œdipe: capitalisme et schizophrénie*, Paris: Editions de Minuit. (Hurley, Robert, Mark Seem, and Helen R. Lane trans., 1983, *Anti-Oedipus: Capitalism and Schizophrenia*, Minneapolis: University of Minnesota Press.)
Deleuze, Gilles et Félix Guattari, 1980, *Mille plateaux: capitalisme et schizophrénie*, Paris: Editions de Minuit. (Massumi, Brian trans., 1988, *A Thousand Plateaus: Capitalism and Schizophrenia*, London: Athlone Press.)
Demerath III, Nicholas J. and Richard A. Peterson (eds.), 1967, *System, Change, and Conflict: A Reader on Contemporary Sociological Theory and the Debate over Functionalism*, New York: Free Press.
Derrida, Jacques, 1967, *L'Écriture et la différence,* Paris: Editions de Seuil. (Bass, Alan trans., 1978, *Writing and Difference*, Chicago: University of Chicago Press.)
Derrida, Jacques, 1972, *Positions*, Paris: Editions de Minuit. (Bass, Alan trans., 1981, *Positions*, Chicago: University of Chicago Press.)
Deutsch, Karl W., 1963, *The Nerves of Government: Models of Political Communication and Control*, London: Free Press of Glencoe.
Durkheim, Émile, 1893, *De la division du travail social: etude sur l'organisation des societes superieures*, Paris: Felix Alcan. (Halls, W. D. trans., 1984, *The Division of Labour in Society*, Basingstoke: Macmillan.)
Eguchi, Atsuhito, 1990, "Ho Shisutemu no Jiko-Soshikisei (Self-Organization of Law System)," *Kyudai Hogaku* (Kyudai Law Review), 60, pp. 1–104.
Erikson, Erik H., 1950, 1963 2nd ed., *Childhood and Society*, New York: W. W. Norton.
Erikson, Erik H., 1964, *Insight and Responsibility: Lectures on the Ethical Implications of Psychoanalytic Insight*, New York: W. W. Norton.
Etzioni, Amitai, 1968, *The Active Society: A Theory of Societal and Political Processes*, New York: Free Press.
Foerster, Heinz Von, 1970, "Cybernetics of Cybernetics", Paper delivered at *1970 Annual Meeting of the American Society for Cybernetics*.
Foerster, Heinz Von, 1979, "Cybernetics of Cybernetics," in Klaus Krippendorff (ed.), *Communication and Control in Society*, New York: Gordon and Breach, pp. 5–8.
Geyer, Felix, 1995, "The Challenge of Sociocybernetics," *Kybernetes*, 24 (4), pp. 6–32.
Giddens, Anthony, 1985, *The Constitution of Society: Outline of the Theory of Structuration*, Cambridge: Polity Press.
Giddens, Anthony, 1991, *Modernity and Self-Identity: Self and Society in the Late Modern Age*, Stanford: Stanford University Press.
Gleick, James, 1987, *Chaos: Making a New Science*, New York: Viking.
Gross, Llewellyn (ed.), 1959, *Symposium on Sociological Theory*, New York: Harper & Row.
Habermas, Jürgen, 1981, *Theorie des kommunikativen Handelns*, 2Bde., Frankfurt am Main: Suhrkamp. (McCarthy, Thomas trans., 1984–1987, 2 vols., *The Theory of Communicative Action*, Boston: Beacon Press.)
Habermas, Jürgen, 1985, *Der philosophische Diskurs der Moderne*, Frankfurt am Main: Suhrkamp. (Lawrence, Frederick trans., 1987, *The Philosophical Discourse of Modernity: Twelve Lectures*, Cambridge, Mass.: MIT Press.)
Habermas, Jürgen und Niklas Luhmann, 1971, *Theorie der Gesellschaft oder Sozialtechnologie: Was leistet die Systemforschung?*, Frankfurt am Main: Suhrkamp.
Haken, Herman, 1976 (1978: 2nd ed.), *Synergetics: An Introduction, Nonequilibrium Phase Transitions and Self-Organization in Physics, Chemistry and Biology*, Berlin: Springer Verlag.

Haken, Herman, 1983, *Advanced Synergetics: Instability Hierarchies of Self-Organizing Systems and Devices*, Berlin: Springer Verlag.

Hashizume, Daisaburo, 1985, *Gengo Gemu to Shakai Riron: Wittgenstein, Hart, Luhmann* (Language Game and Social Theory: Wittgenstein, Hart and Luhmann), Tokyo: Keiso Shobo.

Hashizume, Daisaburo, Kiyoshi Shida and Naoyuki Tsunematsu, 1984, "Kiki ni tatsu Kozo-Kino Riron: Waga Kuni ni okeru Tenkai to sono Mondaiten (Structural-functional Analysis at a Crisis: Its Development and Problems in Japan)," *Shakaigaku Hyoron* (Japanese Sociological Review), 35 (1), pp. 2–18.

Hayek, Friedrich A. von, 1973, *Law, Legislation and Liberty, vol. 1: Rules and Order*, Chicago: Chicago University Press.

Heidegger, Martin, 1935, *Sein und Zeit*, Unveränderte 4. Aufl., Halle: Max Niemeyer. (Stambaugh, Joan trans., 1996, *Being and Time*, Albany: State University of New York Press.)

Hempel, Carl. G., 1959, "The Logic of Functional Analysis," in Llewellyn Gross (ed.), *Symposium on Sociological Theory*, New York: Harper & Row, pp. 271–307.

Imada, Takatoshi, 1985, "Henka no Seiki to 'Zeshon' Gensho (Century of Change and 'Zation' Phenomena)," in Nagai Yonosuke (ed.), *Niju Seiki no Isan* (Inheritances of the Twentieth Century), Tokyo: Bungei Shunju, pp. 495–499.

Imada, Takatoshi, 1986, *Jiko-Soshikisei: Shakai Riron no Fukkatsu* (Self-Organity: Revitalization of Social Theory), Tokyo: Sobun-sha.

Imada, Takatoshi, 1987, *Modan no Datsukochiku: Sangyo Shakai no Yukue* (Deconstruction of the Modern: Future of Industrial Society), Tokyo: Chuo Koron-sha.

Imada, Takatoshi, 1988, "Jiko-Soshiki suru Joho Shakai (The Self-Organizing of Information Society)," *Soshiki Kagaku* (Organizational Science), 22 (3), pp. 60–75.

Imada, Takatoshi, 1989, "Rifurekushon Shiso: Kindai no Choshutsu (Reflexion Thought: Beyond Modernity)," *Gendai Shakaigaku* (Contemporary Sociology), 14 (1), pp. 5–22.

Imada, Takatoshi, 1990, "Shakai Riron ni okeru Gengoronteki/Imironteki Tenkan (Linguistic and Semantic Turn in Social Theory)," *Riron to Hoho* (Sociological Theory and Methods), 5 (2), pp. 105–108.

Imada, Takatoshi, 1993, "Nihonteki Keiei no Tenki (Turning Point of the Japanese Management System)," *Soshiki Kagaku* (Organizational Science), 27 (1), pp. 4–14.

Imada, Takatoshi, 1994, *Konton no Chikara* (The Power of Chaos), Tokyo: Kodan-sha.

Imada, Takatoshi, 1997, "Kanri kara Shien e: Shakai Shisutemu no Kozo Tenkan wo mezashite (From Control to Support: Toward Structural Transformation of Social System)," *Soshiki Kagaku* (Organizational Science), 30 (3), pp. 4–15.

Imada, Takatoshi, 1999, "New Dimension of Public Space in Japan," Paper presented at the *Beijing Forum on Public Philosophy: The Public Space and Public–Private Issues in Asia*, Chinese Academy of Social Sciences, Beijing, May 15–17.

Imada, Takatoshi, 2001, *Imi no Bunmeigaku Josetsu: Sono Saki no Kindai* (A Discourse on the Civilization of Meaning: Modernity and Beyond), Tokyo: University of Tokyo Press.

Imada, Takatoshi, 2006, "New Dimension of Public Space," *International Journal of Public Affairs*, 2, Research Center on Public Affairs for Sustainable Welfare Society (Chiba University), pp. 73–87.

Imai, Ken'ichi and Kaneko Ikuyo, 1988, *Nettowaku Soshikiron* (Theory of Network Organization), Tokyo: Iwanami Shoten.

Imanishi, Kinji, 1976, *Shinka towa Nani ka* (What is Evolution?), Tokyo: Kodan-sha Academic P.E.

Inada, Masaya, 1990, *Imi no Mekanizumu ni kansuru Kenkyu: Shugo Hyosho no Seisei to Shometsu wo toshite* (Research on the Mechanism of Meaning: Through Generation and Extinction of Collective Representation), Master's Thesis submitted to the Graduate School of Decision Science and Technology, Tokyo Institute of Technology.

Inoue, Yoshiyasu, 1989, "Itosezaru-Kekkaron ni miru Fukakujitsusei no Shogu (On the Treatment of Uncertainty in the Theory of Unintended Results)," *Riron to Hoho* (Sociological Theory and Methods), 4 (1), pp. 117–132.

Jantsch, Erich, 1980, *The Self-Organizing Universe: Scientific and Human Implications of the Emerging Paradigm of Evolution*, London: Pergamon Press.
Japan Sociological Society, 2000, *Shakaigaku Hyoron* (Japanese Sociological Review), 50 (4).
Jencks, Charles A., 1977, *The Language of Post-Modern Architecture*, London: Academy Editions.
Kawamoto, Hideo, 1995, *Otopoiesisu: Daisan Sedai Sisutemu* (Autopoiesis: The Third Generation of Systems Theory), Tokyo: Seido-sha.
Kobashi, Yasuaki, 1988, *Kettei wo Shiensuru, Ninchi Kagaku Sensho 18* (Supporting the Decision, Selections on Cognitive Science 18), Tokyo: University of Tokyo Press.
Kobashi, Yasuaki and Jun'ichi Iijima, 1997, "Shien no Teigi to Shienron no Hitsuyosei (Definition of 'Support' and Call for the Theoretical Research)," *Soshiki Kagaku* (Organizational Science), 30 (3), pp. 16–23.
Komuro, Naoki, 1966a, "Kozo-Kino Bunseki to Kinko Bunseki: Parsons Wakugumi no Hatteneki Saikosei e mukatte (Structural-Functional Analysis and Equilibrium Analysis: Toward Developmental Reconstitution of Pasonian Framework), *Shakaigaku Hyoron* (Japanese Sociological Review), 16 (4), pp. 77–103.
Komuro, Naoki, 1966b, "Shakaigaku no Ippan Riron Kochiku no Kokoromi, Jo/Ge (Trial of the Construction of General Theory of Sociology, I and II) *Shiso* (Thought), 508, pp. 1–20; 510, pp. 98–111.
Komuro, Naoki, 1974, "Kozo-Kino Bunseki no Ronri to Hoho (Logic and Method of Structural-Functional Analysis) in Kazuo Aoi (ed.), *Riron Shakaigaku, Shakaigaku Koza 1* (Theoretical Sociology, Sociology Lectures 1), Tokyo: University of Tokyo Press, pp. 15–80.
Koto, Yosuke, 1986, "Parsons kara Habermas e (From Parsons to Habermas), *Gendai Shakaigaku* (Contemporary Sociology), 12 (1), pp. 24–33.
Kuroishi, Susumu, 1991, *Sisutemu Shakaigakiu: Okisa no Chi* (Systems Sociology: Knowledge of the Size), Tokyo: Harvest-sha.
Lange, Oscar, 1962, *Całości i sozwój w świetle cybernetyki*, Warszawa: PWN. (Lepa, Eugeniusz trans., 1965, *Wholes and Parts: A General Theory of System Behaviour*, Oxford: Pergamon.)
Leibniz, Gottfried W., 1965, *Monadology and Other Philosophical Essays*, translated by Paul Schrecker and Anne Martin Schrecker, Indianapolis: Bobbs-Merrill.
Lévi-Strauss, Claude, 1949, 1967 2nd ed., *Les structures élémentaires de la parenté*, Paris: Mouton. (Bell, James H. and John R. von Sturmer trans., 1969, *The Elementary Structures of Kinship*, Boston: Beacon Press.)
Lévi-Strauss, Claude, 1958, *Anthropologie structurale*, Paris: Plon. (Jacobson, Claire and Brooke G. Schoepf trans., 1963, *Structural Anthropology*, New York: Basic Books.)
Levy, Marion J. Jr., 1952, *The Structure of Society*, Princeton, N.J.: Princeton University. Press.
Lindblom, Charles E., 1968, *The Policy-Making Process*, Englewood Cliffs, N.J.: Prentice-Hall.
Lipnack, Jessica and Jeffrey Stamps, 1982, *Networking: The First Report and Directory*, New York: Run Bernstein Agency.
Luhmann, Niklas, 1964, "Funktionale Methode und Systemtheorie," *Soziale Welt*, 15, SS. 1–25.
Luhmann, Niklas, 1967, "Soziologie als Theorie sozialer System," *Kölner Zeitschrift für Soziologie und Sozialpsycologie*, 19, SS. 615–644.
Luhmann, Niklas, 1972, *Rechtssoziologie*, 2 Bde., Reinbek bei Hamburg: Rowohlt. (King, Elizabeth and Martin Albrow trans., 1985, *A Sociological Theory of Law*, London; Routledge & Kegan Paul.)
Luhmann, Niklas, 1982, *The Differentiation of Society*, translated by Stephen Holmes and Charles Larmore, New York: Columbia University Press.
Luhmann, Niklas, 1984, *Soziale Systeme: Grundriß einer allgemeinen Theorie*, Frankfurt am Main: Suhrkamp. (Bednarz, John Jr. with Dirk Baecker trans., 1995, *Social Systems*, Stanford, Calif.: Stanford University Press.)
Luhmann, Niklas, 1988, *Die Wirtschaft der Gesellschaft*, Frankfurt am Main: Suhrkamp.
Luhmann, Niklas, 1991, "Shakai Sisutemuron no Genzai (Present State of the Social System Theory)," in Kawakami Rin'itsu (ed.), *Shakai Sisutemuron to Ho no Rekishi to Gendai (Social Systems Theory, History of Law, and Contemporary Age)*, Tokyo: Mirai-sha, pp. 243–274.

Lyotard, Jean-François, 1979, *La condition postmoderne: rapport sur le savoir*, Paris: Editions de Minuit. (Bennington, Geoff and Brian Massumi trans., 1984, *The Postmodern Condition: A Report on Knowledge*, Minneapolis: University of Minnesota Press.)

Mainichi-shinbun Osaka-honsha Undo-bu (ed.), 1996, *Otokotachi no Chosen: Kobe Seiko Rugby Club* (The Guys Challenge: Kobe Steel Rugby Football Club), Tokyo: Sekaibunka-sha.

Mannheim, Karl, 1940, *Man and Society in an Age of Reconstruction: Studies in Modern Social Structure*, London: Routledge & Kegan Paul.

Maruyama, Magoroh, 1963, "The Second Cybernetics: Deviation-Amplifying Mutual Causal Processes," *American Scientist*, 51, pp. 164–179.

Masamura, Toshiyuki, 1989, "Komyunikeshon niyoru Jikososikika ('Self-Organization' through Communication)," *Shakaigaku Hyoron* (Japanese Sociological Review), 40 (2), pp. 5–20.

Maslow, Abraham H., 1954, 1970 2nd ed., *Motivation and Personality*, New York: Harper & Row.

Maturana, Humberto R. and Francisco J. Varela, 1980, *Autopoiesis and Cognition: The Realization of the Living*, Dordrecht, Holland: D. Reidel Publishing Co.

Mayer, Robert R., 1972, *Social Planning and Social Change*, Englewood Cliffs, N.J.: Prentice-Hall.

Mead, George H., 1934, *Mind, Self and Society: From the Standpoint of a Social Behaviorist*, Edited and with an Introduction by Charles W. Morris, Chicago: University of Chicago Press.

Melucci, Alberto, 1989, *Nomads of the Present: Social Movements and Individual Needs in Contemporary Society*, London: Hutchinson Radius.

Merton, Robert K., 1949, 1968 enlarged ed., *Social Theory and Social Structure*, New York: Free Press.

Mesarović, Mihajlo D., D. Macko and Yasuhiko Takahara, 1970, *Theory of Hierarchical, Multilevel, Systems*, New York: Academic Press.

Mikami, Takeshi, 1993, *Posuto Kindai no Shakaigaku* (Sociology of Postmodernity), Kyoto: Sekai Riso-sha.

Nadel, Siegfried F., 1957, *The Theory of Social Structure*, London: Cohen & West.

Nagata, Hiromitsu, 1997, *Hirao Seiji: Ridashippu no Tessoku* (Hirao Seiji: Cardinal Rule of Leadership), Tokyo: Mikasa Shobo.

Nagel, Ernest, 1956, "A Formalization of Functionalism: With Special Reference to its Application in the Social Science," in Ernest Nagel, *Logic without Metaphysics: and Other Essays in the Philosophy of Science*, Glencoe, Ill.: Free Press, pp. 247–283.

Naikaku-fu Seifu Koho Shitsu (Government Public Relations Division of the Cabinet Office), 2003, *Kokumin Seikatsu ni kansuru Yoron Chosa* (Public Opinion Poll on People's Life).

Naoi, Atsushi, 1974, "Shakai Taikei no Kozo to Katei (Structure and Process of Social System)," in Kazuo Aoi (ed.), *Riron Shakaigaku, Shakaigaku Koza 1* (Theoretical Sociology, Sociology Lectures 1), Tokyo: University of Tokyo Press, pp. 137–188.

Nett, Roger, 1953, "Conformity-Deviation and the Social Control Concept," in Walter Buckley (ed.), 1968, *Modern Systems Research for the Behavioral Scientist*, Chicago: Aldine, pp. 409–414.

Nicolis, Gregoire and Ilya Prigogine, 1977, *Self-Organization in Nonequilibrium Systems: From Dissipative Structures to Order through Fluctuations*, New York: John Wiley & Sons.

Nietzsche, Friedrich W., 1887, *Zur Genealogie der Moral: Eine Streitschrift*, Leipzig: Leipzig Verlag von C. G. Naumann. (Kaufmann, Walter trans., 1969, *On the Genealogy of Morals; Ecce Homo*, New York: Vintage Books.)

Nishihara, Kazuhisa, 1998, *Imi no Shakaigaku: Genshogakuteki Shakaigaku no Boken* (Sociology of Meaning: The Adventure of Phenomenological Sociology), Tokyo: Kobun-do.

Obata, Seigo, 1991, *Gengo Koi toshiteno Hanketsu: Hoteki Jikososhikisei Riron* (Judgment as Speech-Act: A Theory of Legal Self-Organization), Kyoto: Syowa-do.

Ochiai, Hitoshi, 1987, *Hoshushugi no Shakai Riron: Hayek, Hart, Austin* (Social Theory of Conservatism: Hayek, Hart and Austin), Tokyo: Keiso Shobo.

Ohira, Takeshi, 1990, *Yutakasa no Seisin Byori* (Mental Disease in Affluent Life), Tokyo: Iwanami Shoten.
Parsons, Talcott, 1945, "The Present Position and Prospects of Systematic Theory in Sociology," in Talcott Parsons, 1954, *Essays in Sociological Theory* (rev. ed.), New York: Free Press, pp. 212–237.
Parsons, Talcott, 1951, *The Social System*, New York: Free Press.
Parsons, Talcott, 1966, *Societies: Evolutionary and Comparative Perspectives*, Englewood Cliffs, N.J.: Prentice-Hall.
Parsons, Talcott, 1969, *Politics and Social Structure*, New York: Free Press.
Parsons, Talcott, 1970, "Some Problems of General Theory in Sociology," in John C. Mc-Kinney and Edward A. Tiryakian (eds.), *Theoretical Sociology: Perspectives and Developments*, New York: Appleton-Century-Crofts, pp. 27–68.
Parsons, Talcott, 1975, "The Present Status of 'Structural-Functional' Theory in Sociology," in Lewis A. Coser (ed.), *The Idea of Social Structure: Papers in Honor of Robert K. Merton*, New York: Harcourt Brace Jovanovich, pp. 67–83.
Parsons, Talcott and Robert F. Bales, 1953, "The Dimensions of Action-Space," in Talcott Parsons, Robert F. Bales and Edward A. Shils, *Working Papers in the Theory of Action*, New York: Free Press, pp. 63–109.
Parsons, Talcott and Edward A. Shils (eds.), 1951, *Toward a General Theory of Action*, Cambridge, Mass.: Harvard University Press.
Parsons, Talcott and Neil J. Smelser, 1956, *Economy and Society: A study in the Integration of Economic and Social Theory*, Glencoe, Ill.: Free Press.
Parsons, Talcott and Ken'ichi Tominaga, 1979, "Taidan: Shakai Sisutemu Riron no Keisei (Dialogue: Formation of Social Systems Theory)," *Shiso (Thought)*, 657, pp. 1–26.
Poster, Mark, 1990, *The Mode of Information: Poststructuralism and Social Context*, Cambridge: Polity Press.
Prigogine, Ilya, 1980, *From Being to Becoming: Time and Complexity in the Physical Sciences*, San Francisco: W. H. Freeman & Co.
Prigogine, Ilya and Isabelle Stengers, 1984, *Order out of Chaos: Man's New Dialogue with Nature*, New York: Bantam Books.
Radcliffe-Brown, Alfred R., 1940, "On Social Structure," in Radcliffe-Brown, 1952, Chap. 10.
Radcliffe-Brown, Alfred R., 1952, *Structure and Function in Primitive Society: Essays and Addresses*, London: Cohen and West.
Rapoport, Anatol and William J. Horvath, 1959, "Thoughts on Organization Theory and a Review of Two Conferences," *General Systems: Yearbook of the Society for Systems Research*, 4, pp. 87–93.
Sakuta, Kei'ichi, 1972, *Kachi no Shakaigaku* (Sociology of Value), Tokyo: Iwanami Shoten.
Salamon, Lester M., 1995, *Partner in Public Service: Government-Nonprofit Relation in the Modern Welfare State*, Baltimore: Johns Hopkins University Press.
Sasaki, Takeshi and Tae-Chang Kim (eds.), 2001–2002, *Kokyo Tetsugaku, 10 Kan* (Public Philosophy, 10 Vols.), Tokyo: University of Tokyo Press.
Sato, Yoshimichi, 1998, 2006 Eng. ed., *Intentional Social Change: A Rational Choice Theory*, Melbourne: Trans Pacific Press.
Sato, Yoshiyuki, 1986, *Weber kara Habermas e: Asoshieshon no Chihei* (From Weber to Habermas: Horizon of Association), Tokyo: Sekai Shoin.
Sato, Yoshiyuki, 1991, *Seikatsu Sekai to Taiwa no Riron* (The Theory of Lifeworld and Dialogue), Tokyo: Bunsin-do.
Sato, Yoshiyuki et al. (eds.), 2003, *Shimin Shakai to Hihanteki Kokyousei* (Civil Society and Critical Publicness), Tokyo: Bunshin-do.
Shannon, Claude E. and Warren W. Weaver, 1949, *The Mathematical Theory of Communication*, Urbana: The University of Illinois Press.
Shien Kisoron Kenkyu-kai (ed.), 2000, *Shiengaku: Kanri Shakai wo Koete* (Supportology: Beyond Controlled Society), Osaka: Toho Shuppan.

Shimazu, Itaru, 1985, *Jiseiteki Chitsujo: F. A. Hayek no Ho Riron to sono Kiso* (Spontaneous Order: F. A. Hayek's Theory of Law and its Foundations), Tokyo: Bokutaku-sha.

Shiobara, Tsutomu, 1976, *Soshiki to Undo no Riron: Mujun Baikai Katei no Shakaigaku* (Theory of Organization and Movement: Sociology of the Intermediating Process of Contradiction), Tokyo: Shin'yo-sha.

Shionoya, Yuichi, Kotaro Suzumura and Reiko Goto (eds.), 2004, *Fukushi no Kokyo Tetsugaku* (Public Philosophy of Welfare), Tokyo: University of Tokyo Press.

Simon, Herbert A., 1969, *The Sciences of the Artificial*, Cambridge: MIT Press.

Smart, Bary, 1992, *Modern Conditions, Postmodern Controversies*, London: Routledge.

Soranaka, Seiji et al. (eds.), 2004, *Shakai Undo to iu Kokyo Kukan: Riron to Hoho no Furontia* (Social Movements in Public Space: Identity, Modernity and Contentious Politics), Tokyo: Seibun-do.

Sudo, Osamu, 1988, *Noizu to Keizai Chitsujo: Shihonshugi no Jiko-Sosikika* (Noise and Economic Order: Self-Organization of Capitalism), Tokyo: Nihon Hyoron-sha.

Takahara, Yasuhiko, 1971, "Haiaraki Sisutemu (Hierarchy System)," in Akira Nomoto and Toshiro Terano (eds.), *Sisutemu Riron, Sisutemu Kogaku Koza 1* (System Theory, System Engineering Lectures 1), Tokyo: Nikkan Kogyo Shinbun-sha, pp. 91–144.

Tanozaki, Akio (ed.), 1975, *Parsons no Shakai Riron* (Parsons' Social Theory), Tokyo: Seishin Shobo.

Tokuyasu, Akira, 1990, "Shakai Imiron no Kanousei (Possibility of the Social Semantic Theory)," *Riron to Hoho* (Sociological Theory and Methods), 5 (1), pp. 43–56.

Tominaga, Ken'ichi, 1965, *Shakai Hendo no Riron: Keizai Shakaigakuteki Kenkyu* (Theory of Social Change: A Study from the Perspective of Economic Sociology), Tokyo: Iwanami Shoten.

Tominaga, Ken'ichi, 1974, "Shakai Taikei Bunseki no Koironteki Kiso (Action Theoretic Foundations of Social Systems Analysis)" in Kazuo Aoi (ed.), *Riron Shakaigaku, Shakaigaku Koza 1* (Theoretical Sociology, Sociology Lectures 1), Tokyo: University of Tokyo Press, pp. 81–136.

Tominaga, Ken'ichi, 1977, "Shakai Keikaku no Rironteki Kiso (Theoretical Foundations of Social Planning)," Keizai Kikaku-cho Kokumin Seikatsu Seisaku-ka (Economic Welfare Bureau of the Economic Planning Agency) (ed.), *Sogo Shakai Seisaku wo Motomete* (In Search for the Comprehensive Social Policy: The Logic to Welfare Society), Tokyo: Okura-sho Printing Office, pp. 124–147.

Tominaga, Ken'ichi, 1995, *Koi to Shakai Sisutemu no Riron: Kozo-Kino-Hendo Riron wo mezashite* (Theory of Action and Social System: Toward a Structural-Functional-Change Theory), Tokyo: University of Tokyo Press.

Varela, Francisco J., 1979, *Principles of Biological Autonomy*, New York: North Holland.

Vaz, Nelson M. and Francisco J. Varela, 1978, "Self and Non-Sense: An Organism-Centered Approach to Immunology," *Medical Hypothesis*, 4, pp. 231–267.

Waddington, Conrad H., 1975, *The Evolution of an Evolutionist*, Edinburgh: Edinburgh University Press.

Watson, Lyall, 1973, *Supernature: The Natural History of the Supernatural*, London: Hodder & Stoughton.

Weber, Max, 1921–22, *Wirtschaft und Gesellschaft*, Tübingen: J.C.B. Mohr. (Rtoh, Guenther and Claus Wittich (ed.), 1968, *Economy and Society: An Outline of Interpretive Sociology, 2 vols*, New York: Bedminster Press.)

Whitehead, Alfred N. and Bertrand Russell, 1910, *Principia Mathematica, 3 vols*, Cambridge: Cambridge University Press.

Wiener, Nobert, 1948, 1961 2nd ed., *Cybernetics: Or, Control and Communication in the Animal and the Machine*, Cambridge, Mass.: MIT Press.

Wiener, Nobert, 1950, *The Human Use of Human Beings: Cybernetics and Society*, Boston: Houghton Mifflin.

Yamaguchi, Setsuro, 1982, *Shakai to Imi* (Society and Meaning) Tokyo: Keiso Shobo.

Yamaguchi, Yasushi et al. (eds.), 2003, *Atarashii Kokyosei: Sono Furontia* (New Publicness: Its Frontier) Tokyo: Yuhikaku.

Yamawaki, Naoshi, 2004, *Kokyo Tetsugaku towa Nanika* (What is Public Philosophy?), Tokyo: Chikuma Shobo.

Yoshida, Tamito, 1964, "Kodo Kagaku ni okeru 'Kino' Renkan no Moderu (Model of Functional Relevance in Behavioral Science)," *Shiso* (Thought), 482, pp. 36–50. (Included in Yoshida, 1990, Chap. 4)

Yoshida, Tamito, 1974a, "Shakai Taikei no Ippan Hendo Riron (A General Theory of Change of Social Systems)," in Kazuo Aoi (ed.), *Riron Shakaigaku, Shakaigaku Koza 1* (Theoretical Sociology, Sociology Lectures 1), Tokyo: University of Tokyo Press, pp. 189–238. (Included in Yoshida, 1990, Chap. 7)

Yoshida, Tamito, 1974b, "Shakai Shisutemuron ni okeru Joho-Shigen Shori Paradaimu no Koso (A Vision of Information-Resources Processing Paradigm in the Theory of Social Systems)," *Gendai Shakaigaku* (Contemporary Sociology), 1 (1), pp. 7–27. (Included in Yoshida, 1990, Chap. 6)

Yoshida, Tamito, 1990, *Joho to Jiko-Soshikisei no Riron* (Theory of Information and Self-Organity), Tokyo: University of Tokyo Press.

Yovits, Marshall C., George T. Jacobi and Gordon D. Goldstein (eds.), 1962, *Self-Organizing Systems 1962*, Washington D.C.: Spartan Books.

Zaltman, Gerald and Robert Duncan, 1977, *Strategies for Planned Change*, New York: Wiley.

Author Index

a
Adams, Robert 175, 204
Alexander, Christopher 201
Arendt, Hanna 184, 189, 204
Arrow, Kenneth 88
Ashby, Ross 7, 9, 11, 13–14, 36, 43, 56–57, 59, 86, 193, 195–197
Austin, John 105, 115, 200

b
Baba, Yasuo 20, 194
Bales, Robert 76, 198
Baudrillard, Jean 123–124, 201
Bentham, Jeremy 144
Bertalanffy, Ludwig von 8, 34–36, 194
Blumer, Herbert 28, 194
Boudon, Raymond 195
Boulding, Kenneth 34–35, 50–51, 194, 196
Buckley, Walter 12, 193, 196

c
Caillois, Roger 123, 202
Campbell, Donald 195
Cancian, Francesca 38, 51, 195–196
Cannon, Walter 8, 37, 195
Capra, Fritjof 21, 194
Comte, Auguste 40
Cooly, Charles 28

d
Darwin, Charles 29, 45, 192
Deleuze, Gilles 20, 147, 153, 200, 203
Demerath III, Nicholas 195

Derrida, Jacques 113, 200
Descartes, René 21
Deutsch, Karl 12, 52, 193, 196
Dilthey, Wilhelm 90
Duncan, Robert 198
Durkheim, Emile 37, 40–41, 44, 96, 195

e
Eguchi, Atsuhito 201
Erikson, Erik 121, 173, 201, 204
Etzioni, Amitai 12, 193, 197

f
Foerster, von 11, 12, 193
Foucault, Michel 144, 202
Freud, Sigmund 37

g
Gadamar, Hans-Georg 90
Galileo, Galirei 94
Geyer, Felix 11, 12, 193
Giddens, Anthony 87, 131, 199, 202
Gleick, James 194
Gödel, Kurt 6, 89, 191
Goto, Reiko 204
Gross, Llewellyn 195
Guattari, Félix 20, 147, 153, 200, 203

h
Habermas, Jürgen 85, 86–87, 137, 184–185, 189, 199, 204
Haken, Herman 4, 8, 15, 21, 192–194

215

: Author Index

Hart, Herbert 105
Hashizume, Daisaburo 87–88, 104–106, 199–200
Hayek, Friedrich 105, 115, 151, 168, 200–201, 203
Heidegger, Martin 90, 172–173, 204
Hempel, Carl 38, 195
Hirao, Seiji 157–165, 203
Horvath, William 194
Hosokawa, Takahiro 163
Husserl, Edmund 90

i
Iijima, Jun'ichi 204
Imada, Takatoshi 194, 199, 200–205
Imai, Ken'ichi 153–154, 203
Imanishi, Kinji 29, 194
Inada, Masaya 150, 203
Inoue, Yoshiyasu 201

j
Jantsch, Erich 22, 194
Japan Sociological Society 204
Jencks, Charles 113, 200
Jerne, Niels 193

k
Kaneko, Ikuyo 153–154, 203
Kawamoto, Hideo 8, 192
Kim, Tae-Chan 204–205
Kobashi, Yasuaki 204
Kobayashi, Masaya 204
Komuro, Naoki 88, 196, 199
Koto, Yosuke 199, 200
Kuhn, Thomas 36–37
Kuroishi, Susumu 27, 193–194

l
Lange, Oscar 42, 195
Leibniz, Gottfried 194
Lévi-Strauss, Claude 40–41, 62, 113, 195
Levy, Marion 42, 195
Lindblom, Charles 76, 198
Lipnack, Jessica 143, 202
Luhmann, Niklas 5–6, 12, 19–20, 42–45, 85–87, 191, 194–196, 199
Lyotard, Jean-François 113, 200

m
Mainichi-shinbun Osaka-honsha Undo-bu 203
Malinowski, Bronislaw 37
Mannheim, Karl 110, 200
Maruyama, Magoroh 11, 193
Masamura, Toshiyuki 201
Maslow, Abraham 122, 201
Maturana, Humberto 7, 15–18, 20, 193
Mayer, Robert 72, 76–77, 198
Mead, George 28, 130, 202
Melucci, Alberto 129, 202
Merton, Robert 38, 195
Mesarović, Mihajlo 196
Mikami, Takeshi 131, 202
Montesquieu, Charles 40

n
Nadel, Siegfried 42, 195
Nagata, Hiromitsu 203
Nagel, Ernest 38, 195
Naikaku-fu Seifu Koho Shitsu 205
Naoi, Atsushi 198
Nett, Roger 195
Newton, Isaac 21, 35, 94
Nicolis, Gregoire 193–194
Nietzsche, Friedrich 117, 201
Nishihara, Kazuhisa 199

o
Obata, Seigo 201
Ochiai, Hitoshi 105, 200
Ohira, Takeshi 126, 202
Onishi, Ippei 163
Oyama, Fumio 165

p
Pareto, Vilfredo 36, 65–66, 197
Parsons, Talcott 12–13, 16–17, 19, 36–39, 41–45, 48, 54, 69, 76, 88, 96, 98, 195–196, 198–200
Peterson, Richard 195
Popper, Karl 45
Poster, Mark 144, 203
Prigogine, Ilya 8, 15, 21, 192–194

r
Radcliffe-Brown, Alfred 37, 39–42, 44, 195
Rapoport, Anatol 35, 194
Russell, Bertrand 6, 89, 191–192

Author Index

s

Sakuta, Kei'ichi 198
Salamon, Lester 170, 203
Sasaki, Takeshi 204
Sato, Muneya 204
Sato, Yoshimichi 198
Sato, Yoshiyuki 86, 199, 201, 204
Saussure, Ferdinand de 116
Schutz, Alfred 96, 199
Shannon, Claude 36, 43, 195
Shida, Kiyoshi 88, 199
Shien-kisoron Kenkyu-kai 204
Shils, Edward 195, 198
Shimazu, Itaru 200
Shiobara, Tsutomu 198
Shionoya, Yuichi 204
Simon, Herbert 196
Smart, Barry 113, 200
Smelser, Neil 196, 198
Soranaka, Seiji 204
Spencer, Herbert 40, 45, 117
Stamps, Jeffrey 143, 202
Stengers, Isabelle 193
Sudo, Osamu 201
Sumner, William 45
Suzumura, Kotaro 204

t

Takahara, Yasuhiko 196
Tanozaki, Akio 195
Tokuyasu, Akira 201

Tominaga, Ken'ichi 38, 88, 193, 195–196, 198
Tsunematsu, Naoyuki 88, 199

v

Varela, Francisco 7, 15–18, 20, 192–194
Vaz, Nelson 193

w

Waddington, Conrad 194
Ward, Lester 45
Watson, Lyall 21, 194
Weaver, Warren 36
Weber, Max 37, 90, 93, 96, 98, 109–110, 192, 200–201
Whitehead, Alfred 192
Wiener, Nobert 4, 11, 35–36, 194–195
Wittgenstein, Ludwig 87, 104, 106, 201

y

Yabuki, Hiroyuki 161
Yamaguchi, Setsuo 199
Yamaguchi, Yasushi 204
Yamawaki, Naoshi 204
Yoshida, Tamito 44–45, 88, 192, 195–197, 199, 201
Yovits, Marshall 191

z

Zaltman, Gerald 198

Subject Index

a
action
   conventional 107
   frame of reference 37
   performative 107
   rational 98–99, 107
   reflexive 98–99, 107
   spiral movement of 97
adaptation 11
added values 181–182
AGIL schema 54–55, 64, 198
allocation
   personnel 62
   resource 62
   rule 62–63
altruism 174
anticontrol
   paradigm 15
   system 135, 147
antisacrifice spirit 158, 203
articulation, of the world 116
autopoiesis 7–9, 15–21
   features of 16

b
being 128, 170
   concern 174
boundary-generating 9
butterfly effect 25

c
care 172–174
   instrumental 173
   for others 173
caring spirit 172

catastrophe theory 95
category mistake 19
change
   cognitive schema for 73–75
   control of 73, 78
   implementation and control of 75–76
   planning of 73–74, 77
   social 84, 118–119
   strategy of 76–77
change through implosion 1
chaos 24–25
   edge of 155–157, 163
coffee houses 204
cognition, connection of – to existence 91, 199
Comic-market 127–128, 202
complex spiral movement 97, 101–104
(neo)conservatism 105, 114–115, 168, 185
consumer society 121
contradiction of self-indeterminacy 6
control 2, 9–13
   adaptive 11, 13, 46, 51–52, 60, 63, 69–70, 77
   center 25–26, 178
   de- 150
   failure of 168
   feedback 10
   feedforward 10
   hierarchy of 46–50
   higher-order 27
   minimization of 134
   of controls 12
   optimal (optimum) 13, 46, 51–52, 60, 63
   –performance schema 110
   reflexive 28, 136
   schema 4–5
   structural 13, 49–50, 62–63

creative individuals   2, 23–24
cybernetics   4, 9, 20–21, 35–36, 43
   first order   11
   second order   12

d
deconstruction   113
dedifferentiation   134
democracy   110
deregulation   182
development
   economic   53–54
   social   53–55, 66, 71
   system   59
   vector   66–67
difference   97
differencification   7–8, 19, 29, 86, 97, 106, 113, 125, 134, 146–148, 151, 153–154
disenchantment   109
diversification   112

e
egoism   174
eigen-behavior   18
empowerment   172, 175
equilibrium
   analysis   26
   concept of   64, 196–197
   of social system   65
   theory   22–23
evolutionary change, logic of   45

f
factor theory   36
feedback
   as consciousness   12
   mechanism   50
   of consciousness   52
   second   13
fluctuation(s)   2, 21–24, 29, 90, 111, 134–135, 156, 193
   amplification of   2
   critical   15
   of modernity   117
   order through   21–22
   schema   4–5
   science   21
   social implication of   29
Food Control Law   178

freedom
   to be   129
   to have   129
function   100
   concept of   38
   primacy   110–112, 114, 123, 128, 200
functional
   achievement   53–54
   analysis   38–39, 44
   differentiation   20
   requisite   55, 88
   validity   65
functional-structural analysis   43
functionalism   19, 41, 84, 95–96, 100
   decline of   88–89
   essence of   88
functionalist architecture   111

g
general system theory   34–35, 194

h
having   128
   concern   169, 174
hierarchy   135, 156
homeostasis   16–17, 194
Homo Demens   124
hyper-reality   121, 123–124, 127, 132
hypertext world   148–150

i
identity   120–121
   fluctuation (fragmentation) of   131
   self-   125
incompleteness theorem   191
individuation   112
information
   emergent   15
   gathering   74
   processing   51
institutionalization   61
internal image   18, 193
interpretative science   90–91

j
joint dislocation   152

k
kaleidoscopic coupling   148–150

Subject Index

l
language game 104–108
law of requisite variety 19, 43, 195
lifeworld 86

m
market 135, 156
  fundamentalism 186
meaning(s) 85, 100, 102, 113, 134–135, 199
  as differencification 103
  civilization of 118
  deprivation of 120
  descriptive concept of 97
  explanative concept of 97
  expression of 129
  functionalized 114
  original 116
  power of 116
  –reflexion 103
  –reflexion schema 98
  school 84–85, 87, 96
mechanistic theory 34
metamorphosis 8, 117–118
method
  hypothesico–deductive 91–93
  meaning–interpretative 91–93
  observatory–inductive 91–93
  scientific 91
methodology, triangle of 91–93
modernity 109–110
Monogatari syndrome 126
morphogenesis 13
motive(s)
  deficiency 122, 145
  difference 122, 125, 145

n
narrative(s), grand 120
necessichance 150
needs 66
neoliberalism 186
  core claims of 204
network 135, 141–144, 152–155
  information 142
  organization 142
  Point of Sales (POS) 142, 154
networking 142–143
new age sciences 114
NGO 169–170
NPO 169–170

o
ontogeny 18, 20
order 21–22
  spontaneous 115, 151
orderly prosperity 2
organismic theory 34
organization 56–58

p
paradigm shift from function primacy to meaning fulfillment 145
Pareto optimal 65–66
part–whole schema 6
pattern variables 198
PC kids 125
persons
  diligent 146
  value-additing 146
planning, social 72–73
postmodern
  architecture 113
  phase 134
  society 124–125
postmodernity 112
poststructuralism 113
power
  of self-editorship 125
  will to 117
process
  deterministic and mechanical 50
  developmental 51
  purposive 51
  random 50
progressive enlightenment 115
public
  opening the 187, 205
  philosophy 136–138
  space 186
  space as polis 184
publicness 137, 183
  administrative control type of 184
  autonomous and self-organized 185
  civil 184
  civil movement type of 183–184
  discursive type of 189
  dynamics to close 186
  practical type of 189
  renaissance of 186, 204
  voluntary support type of 187

r
rationality 109
  functionalist 110

reason, transformative 93–94
recursion, dynamics of 18, 193
reduction of complexity 43–44, 86
reflexion 89, 96–97, 133
  thought 134–136
reflexive
  competence 108
  feedback 175
  system 97
regulation 46–49
representation, crisis of 120
resource(s)
  allocation 62
  social 197
rhizome 135, 145, 147–148, 150–156
  theory 20
right to
  existence 129
  property 129
role 62
  arrangement 62–63
  expectation 68
rule, arbitrariness of 106
Russell's paradox 191

s
self 28–29, 130, 202
  another 124–125, 128, 131
  enlarged 13–14, 29
  narrative 130
  postmodern 131
self concept, enlargement of 13, 58
self-actualization 122, 126
self-identity 130–132
  in the postmodern age 128
self-organization 1–3, 8–9, 90, 117–118
  anticontrol type of 157
  approaches to 26–27
  cybernetic 26, 133
  difficulties of 27
  feature of 57
  features of synergetic 23
  horizon of 30
  layer 46–49, 55, 59–61, 66–70
  mediated by information 192
  synergetic 15, 24, 26, 98, 133
  without a master plan 130–132
self-organizing 6–9
self-reference 5–7, 27
  paradox of 7, 14
  schema 5, 7
  scientific view of 90
self-referential system 147, 151

self-reflexion 27–30, 130
signification 112, 113
simulacra 123–124, 127, 132
social
  editing 146–147
  integration 146–147
social system(s) 43, 51, 63
  theory 19, 24, 36–39
  theory of functionalism 26
sociometry 202
structural
  conflict 69
  harmonization 70–71
  incongruence 69
  information 44
  instability 65
  tension 65
structural-functional analysis 36–39, 42–44,
    55, 58, 64, 76, 88–89, 195–196
structuralism 40, 44, 100
structurally indispensable requisite 69
structurally stable
  equilibrium 63
  system 60
structure(s) 100, 197
  as model 40
  as reality 40
  concept of 39, 44
  conflict of allocation 69
  conflict of role 69
  design 75
  self-referentiality of 97–98
  social 39–41, 45, 48, 61–62
superintendent system, abolition of the 164
superpanopticon 144, 202
support 137, 171–172
  as spontaneous Order
      formation 179–180
  as the destruction of control 178–179
  as the intake of fluctuation 181–182
  as the securing freedom from
      restrictedness 180–181
  conditions required for 176
  essentials of 172
  from control to 182
  system 146, 174–175
symptom 90
synergetics 4–5, 21
  principal point of 15
system(s) 2, 17, 33–34, 42, 57, 86
  analysis 36
  are last 2, 24, 158–159, 164–165
  change of the 38
  change within 38

Subject Index

   cognition   36
   control   146
   problems   72
   realization of the   17
   spiral movement of   97, 100–101
system theory
   dispute on   85
   paradigm shift of the   5
system–environment schema   6, 23, 39

t
teleonomy   17
tradition–attribution scheme   98

u
unique factor   94–95

v
value   66
vital stability   2
voluntary failure   170
volunteer   169–170
volunteerism, will to   188

z
zation-phenomenon   84

CPSIA information can be obtained
at www.ICGtesting.com
Printed in the USA
LVHW10*1145220818
587754LV00011B/75/P